Critical Muslim 23

Bangladesh

Critical Muslim is published quarterly by C. Hurst & Co. (Publishers) Ltd. on behalf of and in conjunction with Critical Muslim Ltd. and the Muslim Institute, London. *Critical Muslim* acknowledges the support of the Aziz Foundation, London.

All correspondence to Muslim Institute, CAN Mezzanine, 49-51 East Road, London N1 6AH, United Kingdom

e-mail for editorial: editorial@criticalmuslim.com

The editors do not necessarily agree with the opinions expressed by the contributors. We reserve the right to make such editorial changes as may be necessary to make submissions to *Critical Muslim* suitable for publication.

C. Hurst & Co (Publishers) Ltd.,41 Great Russell Street, London WC1B 3PL

ISBN: 978-1-84904-898-9 ISSN: 2048-8475

To subscribe or place an order by credit/debit card or cheque (pounds sterling only) please contact Kathleen May at the Hurst address above or e-mail kathleen@hurstpub.co.uk

Tel: 020 7255 2201

A one year subscription, inclusive of postage (four issues), costs £50 (UK), £65 (Europe) and £75 (rest of the world).

The right of Ziauddin Sardar and the Contributors to be identified as the authors of this publication is asserted by them in accordance with the Copyright, Designs and Patents Act, 1988.

A Cataloguing-in-Publication data record for this book is available from the British Library

Critical Muslim

Subscribe to Critical Muslim

Now in its sixth year in print, Hurst is pleased to announce that *Critical Muslim* is also available online. Users can access the site for just £3.30 per month – or for those with a print subscription it is included as part of the package. In return, you'll get access to everything in the series (including our entire archive), and a clean, accessible reading experience for desktop computers and handheld devices — entirely free of advertising.

Full subscription

The print edition of *Critical Muslim* is published quarterly in January, April, July and October. As a subscriber to the print edition, you'll receive new issues directly to your door, as well as full access to our digital archive.

United Kingdom £50/year
Europe £65/year
Rest of the World £75/year

Digital Only

Immediate online access to *Critical Muslim*

Browse the full *Critical Muslim* archive

Cancel any time

£3.30 per month

www.criticalmuslim.io

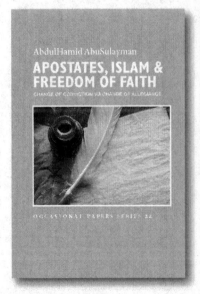

CM23

July–September 2017

CONTENTS

BANGLADESH

BANGLADESH

INTRODUCTION:
PROBING THE PARADOX

Shanon Shah

On a trip to London for a conference, in 2008, I was treated to what the organisers called 'a typically British meal' – chicken tikka masala. They chuckled good-naturedly about it and to me, at the time, this was kind of charming. How encouraging that this former imperial power was able to absorb its multicultural heritage so easily. Later, I learnt that the origins of this dish are contested – did it originate in Punjab or was it 'invented' in Glasgow? I also learnt that up to ninety per cent of Indian eateries in the UK were actually run by Bangladeshis. It simultaneously amused and saddened me that the grub in these restaurants consisted of blandified distortions of the rich cuisine of South Asia. My British Bangladeshi friends elaborated that they had different kinds of food at home. They assured me, a Malaysian who marches on his stomach, that real Bengali cuisine was way more interesting than what could be found in many of these curry houses. To summarise what I learnt – going out for Indian food in Britain meant patronising a vibrant restaurant trade run by Bangladeshis who served stuff they themselves would not normally eat. This was my personal introduction to the Bangladesh Paradox.

The Bangladesh Paradox is an oft-used expression by many analysts to explain how the country has managed to achieve encouraging economic growth despite, to put it politely, its 'governance deficit'. The paradox is even more striking given that this is the same country that was once dismissed as a 'basket case' by US Secretary of State Henry Kissinger. While defining and recognising a paradox requires philosophical and logical rigour, phenomena that initially appear paradoxical can be exciting opportunities to learn. And, as I was discovering, the Bangladesh Paradox could apply to much more besides the country's economy.

And so, I was not disappointed when I asked Saif Osmani, a British Bangladeshi visual artist and designer, if there were any Bangladeshi restaurants in London that he would recommend. Here was a golden opportunity for me to learn about Bangladesh through its food. Of course, he replied. 'Increasingly people are wanting to eat authentic Bangladeshi home food, so there's one I sometimes go to on Brick Lane and a nice biryani place in Whitechapel,' he explained. I said I preferred simpler, smaller outlets. 'You're right,' he said, 'Some of the smaller cafes are better.' I asked Irum Shehreen Ali, a London-based Bangladeshi sociologist and one of the contributors to this issue, if she wanted to join and her email reply crackled with delight. 'I am always up for home food! I swear, it's the thing I miss most after my family – and sometimes probably more! We Bangladeshis are food obsessed, and for me there is nothing that makes me more homesick.'

One weekday evening in mid-March, the three of us sat down to dinner at Kolapata ('Banana Leaf') Restaurant in Whitechapel. From the moment we met and walked from the Tube station, Irum had given me a non-stop tutorial on Bangladeshi food culture, with Saif interjecting occasionally. With home food, she explained, lunch and dinner are different. Usually people don't eat meat during lunch – fish, maybe. Meat is reserved for dinner, especially if it's a special occasion, for example when there are invited guests. According to Irum, when there are guests, Bangladeshis will emphasise the Northern Indian or Mughal influence, serving biryanis and curries that are richer than the usual everyday chow. Although there are now 'biryani houses' and restaurants that specialise in this fare, it was traditionally reserved for weddings and similar occasions because it had to be made in large quantities and was expensive.

At Kolapata, Irum declared that she was abandoning cutlery and eating with her fingers. She said eating like this was de rigueur in Bangladeshi homes. The messy Malaysian in me rejoiced and followed her to the row of washbasins to rinse our hands. Saif quickly followed suit – the peer pressured obviously worked. Then there was a brief period of mutual deflection – they wanted to know what I liked to eat but I asked them to order dishes that they wanted. We struck a happy medium by ordering enough to feed a small army.

We started with *fuchka* – round, crisp, hollow *puri* (small unleavened flatbread) stuffed with chickpea, potato and chopped boiled egg, served with tamarind sauce. Irum said this was actually a popular street food in Bangladesh. 'Part of its charm is that we go out to eat it, rather than have it at home.' It was familiar yet strange, in a delightful way – to me, it was like a cross between fried *popiah* (Chinese Malaysian spring rolls) and *panipuri* (an Indian street snack). But there was no time to explain this to Saif and Irum as the rest of the night's offerings swiftly appeared on our table – beef *bhunna*, *eelish* or *hilsa* fish marinated in salt and turmeric and fried in mustard oil, *bhuna khichuri*, *tarka daal*, *kacchi biryani* and *aloo bhorta*. All of these elicited the same familiar-yet-strange sensations for me. I ordered a drink called *borhani* and Irum and Saif watched my reaction closely. It was like a salty *lassi* – albeit less thick and infused with *jeera* (cumin). It was weird and wonderful. I said I liked it which pleased Saif, who had ordered it too. Irum said it was an acquired taste.

They assured me that most of what we ordered was festive home food. I asked them to rate each item on a scale of one to ten. The fried eelish fish came out tops (a nine from Irum and eight from Saif), followed closely by the bhuna khichuri (an eight from both) and beef bhuna (a seven). The other dishes fared quite well but the tarka daal only mustered a mediocre six (they complained it wasn't properly dressed in toasted mustard seeds or topped with crisp garlic). Although the rating exercise was impromptu, it was serious business. Irum wasn't kidding when she said part of the joy of eating for her was the monitoring and evaluation that came afterwards.

But our conversation did not revolve solely around food. We went back and forth between admiring the food and discussing the Liberation War, Nadiya Hussain (the Great British Bake-Off winner), the politics of language in Bangladesh, radicalisation and terrorism, gender and sexual diversity, and the perils of gentrification (referring specifically to East London). I was struck by how seamlessly Irum and Saif discussed Bangladesh, filling the gaps in each other's narratives or offering differing perspectives on the same issue.

Upon further reflection, their exchange made me think of a project by Katy Gardner and Kanwal Mand, from the University of Sussex, who conducted interviews with British Bangladeshi primary schoolers

in East London. One of the children's explanation of *desh* (home) and
bidesh (foreign places) was particularly instructive:

Q: Where is your *desh*?

Max: I'd say Bangladesh.

Q: What, your *bidesh*?

Max: My home is England ... that's my *bidesh*.

Q: So, your *desh* is Bangladesh?

Max: Yeah.

Q: What does *desh* mean? Is it home?

Max: Yeah.

Q: And what does *bidesh* mean?

Max: *Bidesh* means home and *desh* means away.

Q: Are you sure, I thought it was the other way round... I may be wrong.
I thought that *desh* was your home and *bidesh* was away.

Max: I dunno.

Q: Ok... let's say where is ...home is England?

Max: And away is Bangladesh. I got family in there that I don't really get
to see... Once in a blue moon.

It might be tempting to take this as a 'kids say the darndest things'
moment and laugh. But perhaps Max (a pseudonym) has articulated
something deeply profound – in a globalised world, is it possible to
distinguish between 'home' and 'away' so easily? According to the
researchers, Ted (another pseudonym), put it more simply: 'My "away" is
here.' It is thus possible – and not paradoxical – to have a relationship with
two countries that are both 'home' and 'away'. This makes sense because,
to me, the bits and pieces that Irum and Saif shared were part of one
larger, integrated picture of Bangladesh and its diaspora.

This edition of *Critical Muslim* focuses on Bangladesh while bearing
these nuances in mind. But before exploring these subtleties, some basic
background is necessary. Bangladesh declared independence from
Pakistan on 26 March 1971. Immediately, the Pakistani army launched
Operation Searchlight – a sustained military effort in what it still
considered East Pakistan. The army detained Sheikh Mujibur Rahman, the

leader of the Awami League who proclaimed Bangladesh's independence and, with the help of militias, it killed Bengali students, intellectuals, politicians, civil servants and military defectors during a war that lasted nine months. As Qayyum Khan puts it in his essay, 'on 16 December 1971, Bangladesh emerged on the global stage of independent states with an empty treasury, a destroyed infrastructure and a traumatised population who had suffered inhuman tragedy at the hands of the Pakistan Army.' And then in 1974, the fledgling nation-state was ravaged by a famine that claimed thousands of lives.

Pundits predicted that Bangladesh would not make it. But, as Khan maintains, these 'doomsday soothsayers' were wrong. The country has not only survived, it has prospered – especially when compared to its South Asian neighbours. However, Khan emphatically resists descending into smugness. Instead, he probes the governance issues that gave rise to (and sustain) the Bangladesh Paradox. He offers a sobering assessment of the failures of democratic administration – executive, legislative and judicial – and the toxic structure of party politics. He goes to some very disturbing places, saying that true darkness set in early for the young country, when Mujib and his family were assassinated in 1975. The nation was plunged into constitutional chaos, paving the way for a series of brutal military dictatorships, corruption and the politicised manipulation of Islam. Even the restoration of democracy in the 1990s is now under threat again, this time from a civilian administration. Still, Khan gives us a glimmer of hope at the end – namely, the activism of younger, more conscientised Bangladeshis – but argues that this too can be snuffed if we ignore the heart of the problem:

> Bangladeshis never had a national debate on what kind of a nation state they want. The vote for [Awami League] in the first national elections of Pakistan in 1970 was for provincial autonomy to end the discrimination Bengalis faced in Pakistan, not for independence or secession. When the Pakistan army unleashed terror on East Pakistan (now Bangladesh), the people took up arms and with help from India put an end to the Pakistan army's murderous occupation and liberated their land. But they never had a national discourse on how their country would be different from Pakistan.

For Khan, the lofty ideals in the country's Declaration of Independence – that elected representatives are honour-bound 'to ensure for the people of Bangladesh equality, human dignity and social justice' – have yet to be delivered.

Perhaps the challenge that is most visible to the rest of the world is the rise of religious extremism and violence. In recent years, secular bloggers, sexual minority activists, foreigners, Hindus, Buddhists and Bauls – a local community of musical mystics – have been murdered, many of them hacked to death. In July 2016, the gruesome terror attack on Holey Artisan Bakery in an affluent part of Dhaka stunned the country and sent shockwaves elsewhere in the international community. It heightened the already considerable climate of fear within Bangladesh, even amongst folks who initially thought they were immune. As Sadaf Saaz, one of the founders of the Dhaka Literary Festival, puts it:

> For days afterwards, we were silently making sure we knew our *suras* (when the rumour went around that those had been spared knew their *suras* [Qur'anic passages]). Would I have given in and put a headscarf on, to save my life, to pacify them, these young Turks? Would I start to dress differently now?

It is thus tempting to use Bangladesh as yet another example of how the scourge of terrorism is taking over the entire Muslim world. Yet even in this heinous development, it helps to recall the Bangladesh Paradox. Compare, for example, the brutal murders of the lesbian, gay, bisexual and transgender (LGBT) rights activists Xulhaz Mannan and Mahbub Rabbi Tonoy in 2016 and the historical tolerance towards *hijras* (often glossed as 'third gender') in Bengal.

Hijras are not unique to Bangladesh – hijrahood is an institutionalised subculture throughout South Asia. Over the last ten years, hijra activism has gradually resulted in improved legal status in India, Pakistan and Bangladesh. In 2009, the Chief Justice of Pakistan ordered that the hijras' distinct identity be recognised in national identity cards – a decision hailed by activists. In 2014, the Supreme Court of India recognised the 'third gender' and upheld their rights to education and employment. In Bangladesh, the official recognition of hijra rights came through a cabinet decision in 2014. Yet Pakistan and Bangladesh have also seen increasing hostility towards LGBT activism. In India, the historic decision by the

Delhi High Court in 2009 to read down anti-sodomy legislation – much hailed by local and international LGBT activists – was subsequently reversed. Bangladesh is thus not alone in displaying this apparent paradox between pro-hijra and anti-LGBT attitudes.

There are, however, unique manifestations of hijrahood in Bangladesh that make it a valuable case study in its own right. Across South Asia, hijras can be generally understood as, in the words of anthropologist Adnan Hossain, 'feminine-identified male-bodied people who desire "macho" men and who sacrifice their male genitals to a goddess in return for spiritual prowess'. The region-wide hijra subcultures draw upon both Hindu and Muslim (specifically Sufi) mysticism and asceticism. But they also emphasise different storylines and symbols depending on their location and surrounding demographic. Hijras in India, for example, usually justify their practices through the 'Hindu veneration of androgyny'. The connection between hijrahood and Muslim cultures in India has also taken a particular direction, given the increasing stigmatisation of Islam by Hindutva nationalists. Hindu-born hijras who identify with Islam might be indirectly or subconsciously doing this to symbolise solidarity with a misunderstood minority.

In Bangladesh, however, the reverse does not happen. According to anthropologist Adnan Hossain:

> Muslim-born hijra in Bangladesh do not identify themselves as Hindus based on their ritualistic observance of Hindu-marked practices and beliefs.... Similarly, although there are also Hindu-born hijra in Bangladesh, they generally adhere to and identify with their religion of birth and there is no communitarian pressure on the Hindu-born hijra, or *chaiton* as the hijra call them, to become *surki*, the hijra term for Muslims.

Hossain argues further that many Bangladeshi hijras often accompany other Muslims on *chilla* (proselytising trips). The ones who can afford it go to Makkah to perform the haj. Some communities are even on 'very good terms with the [local] imam'. Hossain observed a *milad* (religious festival), led by an imam who made *du'a* (supplications) that specifically included the hijra attendees.

If the picture is so rosy, then why the hostility towards other sexual minorities? This is why it is important not to romanticise the status of hijras. Despite achieving legal recognition, Bangladeshi hijras still face discrimination and prejudice when trying to utilise various public services. And because of their hybrid and mystical religious practices, hijras are also vulnerable to attacks by radical Islamists who want to stamp out what they see as deviations within the religion.

It is a question of fact and degree, however. For wider Bangladeshi society, hijras are a more familiar sight and part of the traditional social fabric in a way that newer forms of LGBT activist groups are not. Anato Chowdhury thus characterises the position of the government and wider society towards hijras as 'arm's length acceptance'. Yet even the wider reactions towards LGBT activists and communities have not always been overtly hostile. As Chowdhury points out, from the 1990s onwards, the government has either tacitly supported HIV-centred work by the Bandhu Social Welfare Society, a non-governmental organisation (NGO) or displayed indifference towards Boys of Bangladesh (BoB). Things changed, however, when Roopbaan — a newer organisation that published a magazine of the same name — entered the scene. Roopbaan was far more visible and generated greater media interest than Bandhu or BoB, which irked several Muslim organisations, including the National Tafsir Committee and the Awami Olama League, which is affiliated to the ruling Awami League.

In February 2016, the murder of the secularist blogger Avijit Roy — who happened to be a supporter of sexual minority rights — was something of a catalyst. It was quickly followed by the murders of other bloggers and eventually also of Roopbaan activists Mannan and Tonoy. Yet, as Chowdhury points out, the reactions to the murders were more unsettling. On one hand, mainstream human rights organisations, including the National Human Rights Commission, were reticent about condemning the murders too publicly. The government also refused to condemn the murders outright, and instead chastised those who had offended people's religious 'sensibilities'. This was amid the government's own increasing vulnerability to Islamist retaliation due to its efforts to bring war criminals — many of whom allegedly have Islamist connections — to justice.

The Bangladesh government thus asserts it is against Islamist violence, yet it often capitulates to the sentiments it claims to abhor. To be fair, Bangladesh does not have a monopoly on this particular dilemma. Numerous Muslim-majority states are faced with the same situation, from

Morocco to Malaysia. Thus, what initially appears to be a pro-hijra/anti-LGBT paradox is perfectly understandable, given the specific intersections of culture, politics, gender, class and religion.

For Zeeshan Khan, the Islamist-secularist binary has to be tackled head on. Like Qayyum Khan, Zeeshan acknowledges that Bangladesh never developed a clear narrative about itself upon independence. In particular, Zeeshan argues, 'Bangladesh never quite made peace with the strains of Islamism that were injected into its political corpus during the 1971 war of liberation.' Instead, the war's trajectory created a storyline that 'placed Pakistan on the side of Islam and Bangladesh on the side of forces hostile to Islam'. Although this narrative appeared to lay dormant for a couple of decades after independence, it was incubated by developments in national politics and transnational Islamist activity. Beginning from the 1990s, however, a resurgence of Islamism – constantly edging closer towards violent jihadism – began 'pushing at the gates' of the state.

Zeeshan contends that the best antidote to toxic ideological wars is greater awareness of history. The Sultanate of Bengal, established in 1352, maintained a political distance from the Delhi Sultanate for more than two centuries and developed its own brand of multiculturalism. For example, before the arrival of the Muslims in Bengal, Buddhists were persecuted in the court of the Brahmins, which the Bengal Sultans stopped. According to Zeeshan:

> The Sultans were generally appreciative of both Hinduism and Buddhism, culturally at least, and eventually absorbed much of their art and mysticism, grafting chunks of the older culture onto their own. This is the syncretism that has characterised Bengal's politics as well as its theology ever since, a theology that was developed, in no small part, by conversations between Muslim Sufis and Hindu Sadhus.

The Chishti order of Sufism was nourished by vibrant exchange with surrounding Hindu-Buddhist cultures. Muslim Sultans even commissioned Bengali translations of the *Ramayana*, which mortified the Hindu aristocracy. The politics of the British Raj, however, planted the seeds of division between Bengali Hindus and non-Hindus, which then fed into the movement for Partition. Urdu was to become the language of Muslim Pakistan because Bengali was perceived as too 'Hindu'. This, in turn, catalysed the Language Movement in East Pakistan that galvanised the movement for independence. Yet the idea that Bengali is not 'Islamic' enough still informs the sentiments of Islamists within Bangladesh who continue calling for it to be de-Sanskritised.

Again, it is counter-productive to idealise history. Zeeshan clarifies that the Sultanate of Bengal also exhibited periods when Islam was regulated and expressed in punitive and exclusionary ways. It is therefore just as possible to reclaim a Bengali past that celebrated Muslim pluralism as it is to highlight historical precedents for home-grown extremism. The point, however, is that we can draw upon the multi-layered history of the Bengali Sultanate to give contemporary debates 'political depth'. Most importantly, in the war of ideas, this awareness of history can 'defeat the Islamist assertion that Bangladesh is a post-colonial and therefore "Western" creation, divorced from its original orientation as an Islamic kingdom'. It is high time to distinguish between being an Islamic as opposed to Islamist state.

Where do we start, though? The nation-state, after all, cannot be transformed through intellectual debate alone. Entrenched agencies and institutions – many of which are colonial legacies – can block or quash well-intentioned attempts to empower citizens that upset the status quo. This is clearly the case with the historical rivalry between the Awami League (AL) and the Bangladesh Nationalist Party (BNP). Which incidentally brings us to yet another paradox – that of duelling female leadership (or the Battle of the Begums, if you like) which has not necessarily translated into gender equality on the ground and, worse, has exacerbated patriarchy and authoritarian rule.

Bangladesh is not alone in having been governed by female leaders who inherited their authority from towering male figures. Just look at its South Asian neighbours. Bangladesh is unique, though, in that from 1991 to 2008, it had a two-party system dominated by *two* women – AL's Sheikh Hasina and BNP's Khaleda Zia. Power was transferred via elections that were largely free and fair, marred by a failed and rescheduled election in 1996 and a military coup in 2006-7. According to Irum Shehreen Ali, however, since the AL's landslide victory in 2008, 'BNP has been all but decimated as a political force'. BNP boycotted the 2013 elections, accusing them of being rigged. AL took power again and since then, Sheikh Hasina has ruled with an iron fist.

According to Ali, the presence of Sheikh Hasina and Khaleda Zia as prime ministers and party leaders has enormous symbolic power, but their track record on improving women's participation in politics has been disappointing:

> Neither of them challenged the patriarchal and dynastic bases of political power, given that their claim to leadership and legitimacy is via male relatives. For both AL and BNP, the presence of women who reminded voters of strong, beloved leaders such as Sheikh Mujib [Hasina's father] and Ziaur Rahman [Khaleda's father] proved to be effective branding. They represent continuity in a nation defined by familial identities, hierarchal relationships and authoritarian leadership. Their alleviation to power depended on the male party membership and in exchange for loyalty, neither Sheikh Hasina nor Khaleda Zia has rocked the patriarchal boat. For reasons of political expediency, they rewarded the men around them, many of whom are seasoned political operators, with resources, institutional control and policy-making influence. They acquiesced to male dominance in the political space and their attempts to change gendered political power structures for women were tokenistic.

The duopolistic nature of politics makes things worse. Political victors use their advantage of incumbency to dominate all manner of political, legislative and bureaucratic resources and crush the opposition. Ali elaborates: 'they reward loyalty by giving supporters access to resources. They often *ensure* loyalty through violent intimidation and vote buying.' Thus, even with laws and policies ostensibly meant to improve women's political participation, the odds are stacked against them. Yet, despite the herculean effort, numerous Bangladeshi women are passionate about making a difference from the grassroots.

Furthermore, from a grassroots perspective, women often negotiate politics in unexpected ways. Here's another paradox – the appeal of 'covering' amongst Muslim women despite the objections of several secular-liberal feminists. Many established feminist activists still cast radical Islam or Islamism as the prime danger to women. According to Dina Siddiqi, their analysis rings hollow when the purportedly secular state pursues neo-liberal policies that are equally damaging to women, especially those from working class backgrounds. Of course, not all feminists follow the conventional secular-liberal script that portrays religion as 'always already regressive, patriarchal, and by definition against women's interests'. Rather, people like Seuty Sabur, anthropologist at BRAC University, Dhaka, and labour leaders such as Nazma Akter insist that working class women's experiences of religion must be taken seriously. For example, instead of fearing madrassahs as potential hotbeds of misogyny, many working-class women find them appealing because they offer workable day-care options, which employers (and the state) neglect to provide.

For Siddiqi, the politics of gender and Islam cannot be separated from an analysis of class and the economy, specifically the government's neo-liberal development policies starting from the 1980s. This is when Bangladesh entered the global garment industry as an outcome of 'externally imposed structural adjustment'. (Recall that barely a decade previously, this was a country reeling from devastating war and famine and was an infamous 'bottomless basket'.) However, the garment industry needed cheap and preferably female labour. Middle and upper class women already had professional jobs while rural women – middle class as well as poor – worked in domestic settings. Yet the labour market did get filled with millions of women and girls who migrated from rural areas to Dhaka and Chittagong. Suddenly, they were highly visible in public and many became the breadwinners in their families. Men back home started to resent them even though their working lives were hardly paradise – conditions were often exploitative and unsafe. Still, this combination of their newfound mobility, public visibility and paid employment made many of them targets of scrutiny. Were they getting uppity or succumbing to immorality? For many, the solution was a balancing act. They needed to work, but they also needed to be regarded as 'good' women – many thus chose to cover. Amid all of this, the lack of legal safeguards meant that the women remained vulnerable to harassment and appalling working conditions. At the same time, however, the changing religious landscape meant that particular expressions of Islam were becoming dominant – particularly Salafi or Wahhabi-inspired interpretations.

Siddiqi therefore does not argue that garment workers will be treated any better if political Islamists come to power. Rather, she stresses that any analysis of the 'dangers' of Islamism must also be accompanied by an equally hard-hitting critique of the secular state's violation of women's rights. And understanding the appeal of certain expressions of Islam among working and middle-class women entails recognising the gaps left open by the state. One hand cannot clap.

By focusing on women's experiences, the pieces by Ali and Siddiqi demonstrate that the state is not merely a juridical construct (an observation that applies not only to Bangladesh). It can also be seen as a network of relationships – formal and informal – with their own power struggles to determine who gets to impose order (or disorder) on society. In other words, what we call 'the state' is not just made up of formal laws, bureaucratic agencies and political power – it is also built from lived realities that vary from person to person and group to group. In Bangladesh, some of these lived realities are informed by incredibly traumatic experiences which have a ripple effect on other people. For Onjali Raúf, a British Bangladeshi Muslim woman, the discovery of the Birangona – or 'women heroes' of the liberation war – was life changing.

During the war of independence, an estimated 200,000 to 400,000 women and girls – some as young as seven years old – were systematically raped, tortured or murdered by the Pakistani army and its Bengali collaborators. For Raúf, the tragedy was also that, as a British Bangladeshi, she only learnt about the Birangona as an adult after watching a play in London in 2014. This is what unleashed a fresh hunger to find out about this dimension of her personal story, which was never discussed within her own family. As a Muslim woman, Raúf was stunned by the atrocities perpetrated by the Islamic Republic of Pakistan's military and its collaborators:

> From the foot-soldiers who carried out the crimes to the leaders of Islamist parties who condoned them, that any man claiming to believe in God could not only commit or condone a rape but perpetrate it in the belief that Bengali women were '*gonimoter maal*' (war booty) – especially those belonging to the minority Hindu population – remains beyond my imagining or understanding.

Raúf's indignation is understandable but, as a non-Bangladeshi, I was surprised when, during our dinner at Kolapata, Irum Ali said she had always known about the Birangona. Growing up in Bangladesh, she was saturated with stories about the martyrs for independence – men and women. Saif Osmani added that his own father was so wedded to his perspective of the 1971 liberation war that questioning it was tantamount to blasphemy. For Osmani, the focus of the story now is about he can allow his own identity as a *British* Bengali Muslim to flourish.

This issue of *Critical Muslim* cannot pretend to be exhaustive. But it can give a taste for how many ways the story of Bangladesh can be told, depending on the individual's perspective. For a non-Bangladeshi, even the country's brief history can be overwhelming. Hassan Mahamdallie recounts his own journey of discovery in his ode to Dhaka. Mahamdallie meets an impressive range of socially engaged Dhakaites, including a human rights-focused photographer, an architect committed to a just approach to urban slums, a teacher, a maverick left-wing politician, progressive student activists and academics. Every single one of them is concerned about the state of the country's politics and every single one bursts with passion to build a better Bangladesh.

Mahamdallie finds several pockets of hope, but his wonderment is taken to another level when he goes to Kushtia, a town located a hundred miles west of Dhaka and around fifty miles from the West Bengal border. Nearby is a shrine to Lalon Shah, the nineteenth century mystic and social reformer who was a seminal influence on Bengali thought and culture. Mahamdallie's companions urge him to follow and catch the Dol Purnima (Moonlight Festival), celebrated by mystics and Lalon's followers. It is here that Mahamdallie has what he describes as a most fascinating encounter with Farhad Mazhar, a seventy-year-old 'leading member of the '68 generation of revolutionaries; schooled in Marxism, but of the New (anti-Stalinist) Left'.

Mazhar is one of those rare figures whose commitment to leftist principles has remained steadfast through the decades – 'I don't give a damn about Bengali nationalism,' he tells Mahamdallie – but has never entailed demonising religion. At the same time, he has not endeared himself either to the AL or BNP. And there he is, at the Dol Purnima, celebrating the legacy of Lalon. For Mazhar, this is not a dose of opiate for the masses. No, he jokes with Mahamdallie – he is not about to go to New York and 'start Hare Krishna'. Instead, he sees in Lalon's legacy a political movement which was also a spiritual movement. This is Mazhar's way of contributing to a leftist discourse that critiques injustice by drawing upon people's local traditions and spirituality, instead of focusing on Eurocentric Enlightenment ideals. He tells Mahamdallie:

> I understand that in the West the Enlightenment wanted to break the power of the Christian Church, because it was an oppressive force. But that is particular to Europe. Our thinking, culture and practices are very different.... Progressives, in trying to reject [the reactionary face of religion] have also thrown away its core...In the battle against imperialism, we need to rediscover that which is our own asset, the core of our being.

This is why he engages with and writes about Islam but without being an apologist for Islamism, even when he is among Muslim leaders:

> They think I'm not a good Muslim: I don't follow shariah, I don't go to prayers very often – but I do fast very well. I tell the muftis that Bangladesh is a brutal state run by killers and robbers – what's the point of demanding shariah law on the top of a state that is getting more and more fascist?

Mazhar is living proof that one man's paradox is another man's paradigm shift. But not all of Mahamdallie's encounters were this hopeful. There remains the question of how Bangladesh is going to manage its minority populations – especially when some minorities pose more problems to national identity than others. Mahamdallie highlights the plight of the Biharis, an Urdu-speaking population of around 300,000 that originally moved into East Pakistan after the partition of India.

The Biharis were considered a fifth column during the war of independence because of their collaboration with the Pakistani army and anti-liberation paramilitary groups. During and after the end of the war, they were subjected to collective punishment – violent reprisals, arrests, mob attacks, dispossession and mass killings. These were significantly at the hands of the Mukti Bahini (MB, Freedom Fighters or Liberation Forces), formally organised by the Mujibnagar government in July 1971. This guerrilla force was made up of Bengali troops within the Pakistan army who revolted and joined the Liberation Movement as well as civilian fighters. But the minefield of national and political loyalties make it difficult to assess the full extent of the Mukti Bahini's role. Were they simply indefatigable war heroes? Or might some of their actions also count as war crimes? Were they perhaps anti-Pakistan proxies of India? This is where the wounds of Bangladesh's war of independence remain open for a vast number of people – some more visibly than others. In this climate, questioning the established view of the country's genesis can be akin to sacrilege.

What we do know is that many Biharis ended up stranded in refugee camps and became stateless. Even as they were exposed to retaliation within Bangladesh, successive Pakistani administrations were also reluctant to repatriate them. In 2008, 150,000 Biharis who were minors in 1971 or born afterwards were finally granted citizenship and voting rights. Yet many Biharis who grew up in the refugee camps remain socially isolated, under-educated and live in sub-standard conditions. In Dhaka, they remain vulnerable to mob violence and forced eviction from their settlements. The Biharis represent yet another difficult intersection in the development of Bangladesh's national narrative – how to balance justice and reconciliation.

The challenge presented by the presence of the Bihari population is also being played out in the bitter debates about justice for war criminals. Some of this can be seen in responses to those who question the official version of the 1971 war. In 2011, the academic Sarmila Bose – a Bengali and granddaughter of Indian independence hero Subhas Chandra Bose – ignited controversy with her book, *Dead Reckoning*, which she described as 'myth-busting'. 'I am only trying to question the existing narratives of the 1971 war in view of data I have gathered while working for the book,' said Bose at the US launch. One of her claims was that there are 'obvious exaggerations' about the number of people killed or women raped by the Pakistan army. Bengali activists and intellectuals in India and Bangladesh accused Bose of distorting the facts and being an apologist for the Pakistan military. Three years later, the British journalist David Bergman was found guilty of contempt by a Bangladesh court for questioning the 1971 death toll.

And then there is the question of what to do with convicted war criminals. In 2013, Abdul Quader Mollah, secretary-general of Bangladesh's Jamaat-e-Islami party, was found guilty of beheading a poet, raping an eleven-year-old girl and shooting 344 people during the 1971 war. Yet when he emerged from the court, he flashed his supporters the victory sign – because he was only sentenced to life imprisonment, not death. A protest movement swiftly grew around Shahbag, in the heart of

Dhaka, with crowds chanting '*Fashi chai!*' – 'Let him hang!' So here is yet another paradox – how could a movement standing for a progressive, secular Bangladesh so unequivocally call for the death penalty?

These painful debates might seem like more than enough to burden a young country, but Bangladesh also faces a more fundamental threat – the catastrophic impacts of anthropogenic climate change. Because of demography and geography, the country's population is particularly vulnerable to the effects of sea-level rise and extreme weather events. Bangladesh lost 5.9 per cent of its GDP to storms between 1998 and 2009. By 2050, it is projected that 27 million people will be at risk due to rising sea levels. (Bangladesh has a current total population of 161 million, which is projected to rise to 202 million in 2050.) Increased flooding will threaten rice production and exacerbate illnesses from dengue to diarrhoea.

On an encouraging note, the government of Bangladesh knows that the picture is dire and is doing something about it. It has passed appropriate policies and set up the required agencies to help the country mitigate and adapt to the impacts of climate change. The 2015 Paris Agreement is also meant to spur developed countries to provide the resources – financial and beyond – that are desperately needed by more vulnerable countries like Bangladesh. However, the distribution of these resources from the global North to the South is currently blocked by bureaucratic inertia and power imbalances between rich and poor nations. It is indeed alarming that even an issue as urgent as climate change seems to be fraught with neo-colonial nonsense. What is even more disturbing for people in Bangladesh is that the efforts to respond to climate change are also being stymied by domestic governance failures. If nothing changes soon, we might be discussing not the Bangladesh Paradox but an impending Bangladesh Apocalypse.

What needs to happen, then? For Sharbari Ahmed, one of the writers of the US television series *Quantico*, much responsibility rests with writers and artists like her. A first-generation immigrant to the US from a Bangladeshi Muslim family, Ahmed's voice could be marginalised on many different levels. According to her, as a migrant, Muslim woman, her biggest existential threat is her own president, Donald Trump – who incidentally is also a climate change denier. Yes, she considers herself and her friends 'woke' – 'conscious of the inequities and double standards of race and class relations in this country'. But the challenge is how to stay woke and turn consciousness into effective action. For Ahmed, this means being even more committed to writing fearlessly, even at the cost of cosy acceptance in Hollywood. People like her must challenge American imperialism, right-wing nationalism and Islamic extremism and probe the unholy alliances that have sometimes materialised between all three:

> To deny that America's links with Wahhabism and Zionism are not fuelling much of the instability in the region would be as myopic and foolish as to think that having a black president for eight years would somehow destroy the racial divide. I know that America worked with the Taliban to fight Soviet control of Afghanistan and created a monster there. I know that by supporting the Saudi regime America is essentially supporting Islamic extremism to the detriment of Muslims the world over, including me. I also know this is by specific design. I must explore these disconcerting things in my creative work so I can make sense of the world I am now living in but also because there must be a variety of nuanced voices bearing witness to this latest dark night of the American soul.

Ahmed's sentiments also capture what each contributor brings to this issue. They comprise a 'variety of nuanced voices' who explore 'disconcerting things' in each of their pieces. They each caution against the cost of doing business as usual in Bangladesh and among its diaspora. And, to me at least, they each reconcile the Bangladesh Paradox in their own way.

I have realised, however, that the Bangladesh Paradox is a bit of a red herring. See, my initial craving for Bengali home food did not come out of nowhere. It started when I visited a close friend, Shoab, up north in Manchester. One afternoon, on a whim, we stopped over at his family home. Unfortunately, the entire household was out at a wedding, but there were four different curries on the kitchen stove. As a gluttonous Malaysian, I'm intimately familiar with food being constantly available at home. But *four* curries on the go? Shoab chuckled and said this was normal with Bengali families. He explained that each curry was probably prepared on a different day – so these were different curry generations co-existing. When one pot finished, it would be replenished with a fresh batch, and so on. And each dish was made by a different family member – sisters, sisters-in-law or aunts. It truly was a celebration of the family's collective palate.

'Would you like to try some?' said Shoab. 'Is the Pope Catholic?' I replied. We sat down to what was, to this day, the most memorable impromptu lunch I've ever had. I was particularly surprised by a dry-ish fish curry, with its layers of delicate yet spicy flavours. Shoab told me the name of the fish, which I promptly forgot. It reminded me of whitebait or anchovy. 'Why have I never had anything like this before?' I asked. He said these were tiny, bony fish, meant to be eaten at home with your family. They weren't fancy enough for guests or restaurants. I said, quite emphatically, that I'd certainly order this in a restaurant.

This is why, when I went to dinner with Saif and Irum, I was forthcoming about my desire for fish. And they happily obliged by ordering fried hilsa. As much as I enjoyed it, though, this wasn't exactly what I had in mind – hilsa is a species in the herring family and what I ate at Shoab's was definitely not herring. Furthermore, my enjoyment of the fried hilsa has since been tempered by my discovery that this is a species under severe threat of depletion. This and the sobering reality of climate change mean that, in good conscience, I don't think I can ever have hilsa again – or, at least, not for a very long time. I found out later from Shoab that the fish we had at his family home was keski, or Ganges river sprat. I was hoping that by some miracle, unlike hilsa, it could still be found in abundance. Sadly, this is highly unlikely – overfishing is endemic everywhere, not just in Bangladesh.

I wish there was some nifty and inoffensive metaphor in these little food vignettes for the bigger story of Bangladesh. But the only parallel I can think of is fairly obvious. The only way to ensure people can keep enjoying hilsa, keski and all other kinds of fish is to consume less – far less – than we currently do. Individuals need to make more ethical choices while the entire fishing industry also needs to change, urgently. Perhaps it's similar with Bangladesh. It's a complex, exciting country. And even at their most critical, so many of our contributors are fervently proud of their culture and heritage. We can also marvel at how Bangladesh has developed so impressively despite its governance failures. There are certainly good reasons to be hopeful, given the tenacity and creativity of so many Bangladeshis across the *desh* and *bidesh*. Yet the Bangladesh Paradox is comforting only up to a point – how long can the country develop sustainably in the face of environmental degradation, authoritarianism and religious militancy?

DHAKA

Hassan Mahamdallie

Every city moves to its own beat. Although I am a city dweller through and through, it took me some days into my visit to Dhaka before I could sense its unique rhythm. It was only when my friend Mahmudul Hasan took me one evening through the narrow streets of the Old City, down to the Buriganga River boat terminal at Sadarghat, that I felt the Dhakan bassline in my belly for the first time.

As our rickshaw approached the Buriganga that defines the southern edge of the city, the full moon lit up a portside vista – a rank of passenger ferries waiting to cast off, boarded by the streams of people making their way down the gangplanks carrying bundles of possessions and goods to sell, families, many with small children, and elderly people in tow. The low long boom of the ferry horns cut across the incessant treble 'beep, beep, beep' of cars and auto-rickshaws trying to gain an inch advantage through the traffic-jam streets.

Men with nothing else to do leant silently against the riverside wall, smoking cigarettes and watching the flow and ebb. A stall with heaps of toothbrushes was doing good business, making money a few Bangladesh Taka at a time selling to those who had forgotten to pack the essential item for an overnight trip. On a warehouse overlooking the wharf hung a huge banner by the ruling Awami Party, with a picture of its leader Sheikh Hasina's hand raised as if imperiously waving off the masses. The slogan read: 'The Principal of Sheikh Hasina is the Development of Democracy'.

The Sadarghat ferry terminal is one of the largest in the world, with around 200 passenger vessels carrying 30,000 people in and out of the city every day. Mahmudul explains that there are four classes of tickets, the cheapest will buy you a bit of floor down below, while the well-off squat above, coddled in their own cabins and luxurious saloons with TVs and attendants on hand. The ferries are a cheap way for the poor migrant

Sadarghat ferry terminal, Buriganga River, Dhaka

workers who hail from the southern divisions (provinces) of Khulna and
Barisal to get home and back. If the Buriganga River is the aorta of the city,
channelling the rural poor into the heart of Dhaka, then Sadarghat terminal
is the valve that regulates its beat.

Significant human settlement in what is now Dhaka probably goes back
to the Mauryan Empire (324–185 BC) founded by Chandragupta Maurya
and expanded by his son Bindusara and grandson Ashoka. There is evidence
that Bikrampur ('City of Courage'), originally located in what is now the
Munshiganj neighbourhood of Dhaka, was a regional capital during the Sen
dynasty, founded in 1097 AD. The first Mughal Subahdar of Bengal, Islam
Khan Chisti (1570–1613), subjugated the province and established Dhaka
as its fortified capital in 1608. He named it Jahangir Nagar (the City of
Jahangir) in praise of his emperor. Under the Mughals, for the next 140 or
so years, the Queen of the Cities of the East expanded and its trade and
industry boomed. It was the centre of the world's muslin and cotton
industry, employing an estimated 80,000 skilled weavers and turning it
into a cosmopolitan world city. And then after the Battle of Plassey in 1757
the British East India Company took control, ushering in a brutal chapter
in the life of the city and its inhabitants.

That vision thing

On the first morning of my visit I sit in the Dhaka headquarters of Drik, the world-famous photographic agency founded in 1989 by Shahidul Alam, a tireless and fearless social activist. He set up Drik to wrest back ownership of the image from the Western gaze and to empower photographers from what he calls 'the majority world'. Every two years Drik (Sanskrit for 'vision') mounts Chobi Mela, an international festival of photography, the biggest of its kind in Asia. Shahidul also established Pathshala, the South Asian Institute of Photography, to tutor the next generation of homegrown socially conscious photo and film journalists. He set up the Bangladesh Human Rights Network (banglarights.net): 'an independent platform for media professionals and activists… to champion principles of democracy, give voice to people at grassroots levels and address social inequalities and domination at national and international levels'.

Shahidul rarely stands still. The week before my visit to Dhaka I bumped into him on a Tube escalator in central London, and just as I arrived in his city he was jetting off somewhere else. But I am graciously hosted at Drik's headquarters by its CEO Saiful Islam. After sketching the history of Drik, Saiful moves on to a recent multi-faceted project that is clearly dear to his heart – re-establishing the importance of muslin in Bangladeshi culture. This is a delicate cotton fabric described as 'woven air', produced from a strain of the cotton plant that once grew in abundance along the banks of the Meghna and Brahmaputra Rivers.

Saiful explains to me that 'our heritage has been usurped by others. The only book on muslin prior to our project was by the Victoria and Albert Museum, but it hardly mentions it as a product from a plant that grew along our river banks. It was manufactured here, from here it went global. It travelled all the way to Ancient Rome – the Romans had to put in an order three years in advance, it was in demand in Indonesia, where they had to wait two-and-a-half years. We had traders from twenty nationalities based here in Dhaka in the fifteenth and sixteenth centuries, Afghans, Turks, Italians, the Dutch.'

What put an end to the Bangladeshi muslin trade? The British East India Company of course. 'As the East India Company got in on the act and looted India, they destroyed the muslin industry,' says Saiful. By 1800,

Saiful Islam, CEO of Drik

restrictions on trade, taxation and astronomical tariffs designed to protect the Lancashire cotton industry had cut trade in the city by a full half in the space of 40 years. Destitution, followed by a famine (1769-73) cruelly presided over by the British, emptied the city and wiped out half the population of wider Bengal. In recent years, there has been a revival in a particular type of traditional and uniquely patterned fine muslin known as Jamdani, or by its original name Dhakai, but the cloth is still virtually unknown in its purest hand-woven form. Saiful shows me a photo of a nineteenth century piece of the finest muslin in his possession, purchased at a price he would not disclose to me from a private collector.

For Saiful, muslin is 'a question of identity. We are identified as a nation that produces ready-made garments and for the terrible factory fires that kill hundreds of workers, but we do have a richer heritage. We want to offer the nation another identity that we can be proud of.' I am suddenly aware that in preparation for my trip to Dhaka I had picked up some T-shirts in my local Primark for £3 each: 'Made in Bangladesh'. Another major aim of Saiful's project, very much in the Drik ethos, has been to elevate the contribution of those 'nameless and faceless' weavers whose undervalued skills have been handed down through generations. 'I want to talk of the land and the people from where muslin has sprung and how this glory was achieved.' He wants to give power back to the small producers. On my arrival at Drik's HQ I had briefly met Al Amin, one of the master weavers involved in the project. In the literature accompanying the Muslin exhibition, Al Amin has his say:

> We have worked to revive the muslin that we have heard of from our ancestors. I am not literate. I have heard from my ancestors that muslin was so fine and thin it could be kept inside a matchbox. We have never seen it. We have now proven

that we are able to revive our age-old tradition. But the task was not easy! We need a certain cool temperature to do this. Mostly at dawn and after sunset.

The project is ongoing, with Saiful now working with plant geneticists on samples from botanical institutions such as Kew Gardens to trace the evolution of various strains of the muslin cotton plant and see if he can track them back to Bengal.

He also talks to me about early plans Drik has to work with imams and mosques, perhaps mounting exhibitions for prayer-goers to look at. 'Our point is, there is no need to alienate these guys – there is a danger in that. My dream would be a mosque that every week has exhibitions, activities and discussions. But to do that you have to be trusted and accepted. To me part of the identity of this country is Muslim, not secular, but it is not monochrome. My mother prays five times a day and is also at the head of one of the largest women's organisations, dealing in legal affairs. There is no contradiction.'

Then, like many of the conversations I have in Dhaka, Saiful moves on to the political evolution of the country and the present situation. I ask Saiful to describe to me the psyche of present-day Bangladesh. He points out the small flag hanging on the wall behind me. A yellow map of Bangladesh nestles inside a red circle against a black background. He explains that it is handwoven, and was originally tied to the barrel of a freedom fighter's rifle during the 1971 War of Liberation. The map of Bangladesh was later dropped, leaving the red circle against a green background. 'We had a separation from Pakistan and a very violent war,' he begins. 'We have normally been quick to rebel against external authority. I don't think we much believe in the Ghandian ideal of non-violence, which in my opinion just allowed the British to stay longer. We had Sarat Chandra Bose, a brilliant charismatic leader.'

But then he pulls back to explain what he sees as the root of the country's historic identity: 'Bangladesh means "the country of Bangla".' As Saiful puts it, the country is small (equivalent to half the size of Texas) but the language is big, reckoned to be the seventh or eighth most used language globally, with 210 million speakers. It was student-led resistance against the Pakistan government's attempt in the early 1960s to downgrade the Bengali language and ban Bengali literature and culture, including the works of Tagore, from schools and colleges that fed into the desire for independence.

Rickshaw art

Next is Bangladesh's pan-Indian cultural identity:

> A lot of our rituals and culture has a Bangla-Indian flavour. So the way we celebrate our weddings is not 'strictly Muslim'. I don't think we even care or understand what 'strictly Muslim' is. We have a rich cultural heritage of song, of Tagore, of festivals.

Then there is the rural life of Bangladesh and its elemental relationship with water, particularly the country's rivers. Bangladesh has the highest population density in the world, with two thirds of its people living in the rural areas. The land itself is a product of its 700 rivers and the fertile silt-rich soil that lies in between them. It was anger at the Pakistani authorities' lacklustre response to the devastation and deaths that a terrifying cyclone wrought in November 1970 that finally tipped Bangladeshis into insurrection.

Our conversation returns to 1971 and the political forces that emerged from that period – the parties, big business and military interests and how the ongoing significant economic, social and political interventions of non-governmental organisations (NGOs) and donor organisations has sought to influence the direction of the country's development. And then there are the regional politics and geo-politics, including Bangladesh's relations with India, China, and US foreign policy.

What of the country's psyche? 'It is young at heart, because it is not fully formed.' Bangladesh has a young demographic who only know of the war through the interpretation of politicians and historians. Saiful tells me that nearly half of the population is under 25 years old, 'desperately trying to establish themselves, getting a degree and the hope of a job'.

Bangladeshi politics revolves around the struggle over the interpretation of the 1971 War of Independence. Also known as 'liberation war', it has a vice-like mythic hold on the politics and people of the country. The Awami League today lays claim to its inheritance through the dynastic figure of prime minister Sheikh Hasina, whose socialist-leaning father Sheikh Mujibur Rahman is regarded as the nation's founding figure. Saiful tells me that the Awami League has driven its identification with 1971 to such a point that the party, not the people, have come to be seen (at least in the League and its supporters' eyes) as the historic agent of the country's liberation. 'It was a people-led movement, dominated by a party at whose helm was a unique individual – no doubt – but today it's as if the party brought the victory about,' – similar, in a way, to the African National Congress's present claims for its role in ending apartheid in South Africa.

Awami League posters

The Awami League has used its 1971 hegemony to pound and crush its political opposition. The Bangladesh Nationalist Party (BNP) has been labelled extremist sympathisers, mainly through its past electoral alliances with the religious party Jamaat-e-Islami, whose leaders militarily sided with Pakistan during the War of Liberation and formed death squads to carry out mass executions of pro-independence activists and intellectuals.

While I am in town, the Dhaka *Tribune* reports a rally speech by Sheikh Hasina in which she promises further economic development: '*Insha Allah* we'll do that...in the spirit of the Liberation War...If necessary, I'll sacrifice my life like my father to free this country from poverty,' before reportedly coming down hard on BNP, saying 'whenever BNP comes to power they give rise to militancy, carry out killings and indulge in corruption and looting'.

Many people I talked to during my visit to Dhaka, whatever their political allegiances, were clearly worried by the way in which the increasing domination of one party has acted to erode democracy and the essential element that keeps it alive – dissent. For Drik this politically engendered silence has struck very close to home. In 2010, Shahidul Alam's visual exhibition 'Crossfire', (the term used by the government's notorious Rapid Action Battalion to explain away extrajudicial killings of those they deem troublemakers, terrorists or 'criminal elements'), was shut down by the Dhaka police. It was only reopened after Drik's lawyers went to court. Saiful feels that what has been a traditionally vibrant, participatory political culture is becoming 'uniquely dissent-less'. He detects an increasingly general reluctance to speak out, whether it be against widespread corruption, the hundreds of 'disappearances' of opposition activists, Islamists, as well as environmental issues such as the hot-button topic of the building of an India-backed coal-fired power plant in the protected forests of the Sunderbans, the treatment of workers and the poor, or the neo-liberal economics feverishly pursued by successive governments. Those in power have relied on year-on-year economic growth and praise from the World Bank on poverty reduction measures to bolster their base, attract foreign investment and reap the rewards. The political class is intrinsically knitted into the business class, with the armed forces increasingly allowed to move into the economic sphere (presumably as a way of keeping them onside).

Saiful says the triumph of quantitative measures of growth over qualitative measures of the health of civil society has come at a cost. 'The material growth is there, but we need to have a far bigger say in terms of what alternatives we can pursue. There is a lot of activism on the social and cultural side, but not enough on the political. Even on the youth side, politics has become how to profit from the system.'

But Saiful is not at all pessimistic. 'In the future, we want Drik's work to be more strategic. To bring topics to the table to people who would normally shy away. We will continue to highlight stories that matter. At the beginning of every journey, there is an individual, and at end there is a story, and beyond that there is an idea. That is what we do.'

The city and the slums

Dhaka is one of the world's most densely populated cities, growing by four per cent a year. No-one knows the actual number of people living in this 'megacity', but it is somewhere around 17 million. It continues to pull in migrants from the rural areas in the south, where poverty is at is severest. A 2014 census estimated that there were 1.6 million people living in slums in the Dhaka division, reflecting an increase across the country of 60 per cent over the last seventeen years.

I visited the studio of architect Nazmus Saquib Chowdhury, located in the Mohammadpur region of the city. For many years, he has been researching and advocating the needs of the built environment in urban slum areas and those in rural areas affected by cyclones, floods and soil erosion. The basic principle of his work is that 'every person has the right to live and work in a physical environment that takes care of their dignity, privacy, health, comfort and well-being, light

Architect Nazmus Chowdhury

Dhaka the 'megacity'

and clean air; the elements that nature provides being an integral part of it'. While studying in London he became the founding director of PARAA, a social enterprise formed to push forward this agenda.

Nazmus's argument is that the built environment has been largely been neglected by NGOs. 'I got to realise that this particular side of development was being left out. The people I met in NGOs were mostly from a social science background. They were focusing on the environment and disaster management, not on the technical or infrastructural perspective. The areas they work in are absolutely essential to save lives, but in terms of long-term rehabilitation, the funding is less and so the work in that area is minimal.'

When he came back in 2012 from studying for his MA at London Metropolitan University, Nazmus realised that there were scarce funds for the work he saw that was needed, and so he sought out consultancy work where, in his words, 'there was some glimpse of a built environment'. He describes how at an urban level the government is concentrating on mass infrastructure projects – the big picture if you like – but the detail, for people who live in the slums for example, is largely missing. Nazmus becomes animated when he talks about the 'problem' of Dhaka's slums. 'How many generations are there going to be living in the slum areas if we cannot address these issues?'

'When you think about slum areas, you think of a population living in a place that does not belong to them. A place where the poorest of the poor live, who do not have any kind of fixed assets.' But for Nazmus a slum is neither essentially about ownership nor possessions – it is rather 'a condition where people are living without the chance of a better environment with light, air, ventilation and sanitation'. For Nazmus, this is not a 'problem' for slum-dwellers that the rest of us can afford to turn away from – it impacts on wider society and the wider environment.

The solution can only be a holistic one, he says. He takes the example of sanitation to illustrate this: 'When there are health issues such as diarrhoea and malaria, the NGOs tell us that the solution is to provide safe drinking water. So they explore the cheapest way of filtering the water. But will the cause of malaria be gone? I don't think so – it arises from a lack of sanitation or drainage during the rains, or the non-disposal of garbage.' In other words it is the symptoms, not the root cause, that are the focus. 'But if you don't tackle the causes, the problem will persist. You can find funds for clean drinking water, but you might not be able to get funding to change the whole water system.' To back Nazmus up, the 2014 census report found that four out of ten slum dwellers use what are termed 'unhygienic toilets'.

The figures also showed that the vast majority of them find a living in the service industries, including garment manufacture, general trading (for example street vending and shop work), rickshaw-pulling, and domestic service. Nazmus argues 'the authorities must realise that there are needs for this group of people – they serve the city. They need to be officially legitimised'. The slum dwellers have a precarious existence without legal rights, yet many live on government-owned land, and pay 'rent' to unofficial landlords, including corrupt local officials. (The census says 65 per cent of them pay rent, with only seven per cent living 'rent-free'). They go to work in the city, and their children go to school.

These communities have invented ingenious ways in which to protect themselves. Nazmus discovered that 'they have a unique way of dealing with fire, thieves and attacks (with arson becoming more frequent as thugs, hired by powerful interests, try and force slum dwellers off)'. He continues:

> They have a series of whistles in each house and the tone of the whistle alerts people as to whether they are being threatened with fire, or someone is going into houses stealing. When I went into a particular slum area for the first time, my presence immediately went out to some big guys that there is a stranger around. It was not until later that I got to know about it. One guy told me, 'We knew when you were here and we were observing you. This is our secret security mechanism.' I took it as very positive; that they were protecting their homes.

Nazmus believes that rather than denigrating slum dwellers, their contribution to the city should be recognised, their existence validated and their children given a chance to realise their potential. Five years ago, he conducted a feasibility study for a community learning centre at the nearby Mohammadpur Geneva Camp, where a community of Biharis live in poverty and degradation. The report was titled 'Unlimited Dreams in Limited Spaces' and started with this case study:

> Junayed, a fifteen-year-old boy and a student of class 9 dreams of becoming a chartered accountant one day. Living and studying in the dark and filthy 8.69m² room with stained walls does inhibit such a dream. He knows that he will have to be well established in his life to take care of his aged parents and his only younger brother who suffers from serious head injuries. Ignoring the buzzing sounds coming from the camp street and the loud noise from the neighbour's television, he sits in the dark room, trying his best to study. He wishes to be in a place devoid of bad odours, loud noise and poor lighting, a place where he will be able to concentrate on his studies so his dream can come true.

I ask Nazmus whether the political classes and policymakers are sympathetic to what he wants to achieve. This is what his architectural practice should be doing all the time, I say. He tells me he has had some tough arguments. Part of the problem is that NGOs, national and city politicians are all looking for short-term results that they can take credit for. But he is ready any time to lend his vision, insight and skills.

Kushtia: Mystics and Marx

Mahmudul Hasan tells me he has organised a trip out of Dhaka. He and a couple of friends are taking the coach to the town of Kushtia, a hundred miles west of Dhaka and around fifty miles from the border with West Bengal. Just out of the town lies the village of Cheuria, the site of Lalon Akhra, the shrine of Lalon Shah, the nineteenth century Baul mystic and social reformer whose philosophy has had a seminal impact on Bengali thought and culture. He tells me that thousands of people, including the most famous Baul singers and fakirs who follow in Lalon Shah's footsteps, are now making their way to the shrine complex to take part in the Dol Purnima (Moonlit Night) festival. The four of us will meet at the coach

Lalon Shah's shrine

station and travel that afternoon. Even though it is only 100 miles away Mahmudul warns me it will take us maybe eight hours or more to get through the clogged roads. I pack my toothbrush and we are on our way.

At the coach station, we meet up with our travelling companions. Jannati Hossain is a young woman who is building a small business selling traditionally made earthenware that she adapts into household decorative items. Rupom hails from Chittagong and is studying at Drik's Pathshala institute. We get the cheapest class of ticket and board our coach, windows open to create some air-conditioning. The coach has to fight its way out of Dhaka along the western corridor and eventually the cityscape gives way to countryside. We cross the Bangabandhu Bridge, the eleventh longest bridge in the world that spans to the Jamuna River and then later on pass over another river crossing and into Kushtia. As night falls Rupom turns to me and says, 'This is the real Bangladesh – everything looks beautiful in the dark.'

We arrive in town around midnight, have a quick meal and then book into our cheap hotel. At 5am I am woken by a mosquito buzzing in my ear and the sound of people breaking into song in the street below my window. Soon we are riding a CNG (auto-rickshaw) along the rain-sodden route, across a railway line and down a village path to the Lalon Shah complex. The festival is already up and running, thronged with festival-goers moving past the stalls towards Lalon Shah's mausoleum, where devotees are queuing up to honour him. I read a short biography of Lalon Shah set into a plaque:

Lalon Shah – The Humanist (1774-1890)
Lalon Shah was the host of many identities – a mystic devotee of the
Baul discipline, a humanist, a social reformer, a philosopher,
a composer, lyricist and a great singer.

The text recounts the story of how teenage Lalon, while on pilgrimage, contracted smallpox and was left on a Cheuria riverbank to die. He was found by a local farmer and nursed back to health by his wife. This allowed Lalon Shah to be reborn into anonymity – he deliberately drew a veil over his past and what community he was raised in, allowing him to construct a syncretic egalitarian philosophy unhampered by defined religious affiliation, ethnicity, caste or class.

Mahmudul has someone important he wants me to meet. We make our way into a large compound, where a stage has been erected, upon which are seated leading devotees, fakirs and a band of Baul musicians, attended by a large audience of around 300 people. A morning ceremony is underway – songs, poems and speeches. Mahmudul explains that they are performing a recitation named 'The Shepherd's Song'. Then an older man, draped in white, with thinning long white hair and black spectacles takes the microphone. For maybe three quarters of an hour he talks to the crowd, his lecture interspersed with music and chants. I watch him, and although I can't understand Bengali, I know a political orator when I see one. I ask Mahmudul who he is and what he is saying. 'This is the man I want you to talk with, his name is Farhad Mazhar, a very important figure on the Left. He's talking about Lalon Shah and what he stood for.'

After the recitation, I am invited by Roshan Fakir to join him and maybe forty of his followers for breakfast. Roshan Fakir is one of the present-day leading disciples of Lalon Shah, and with his wife leads an ascetic existence in a small settlement in Kushtia. I am seated on his left and he turns to smile at me in welcome. On his other side is Farhad Mazhar, who leans across to talk me through the mealtime ritual. First, everyone seated on the floor in rows gets as earthenware bowl. This is filled with water so we can wash our hands. Then a helper comes around with a pail and empties the water out. Then we get rice, vegetables and sauce put in our bowl. We wait. The guru is given his portion by his wife who prostrates in front of him and gives thanks. When she finishes this short ritual, we are allowed to eat. Mazhar explains that everyone in the community eats, they eat together and at the same time. Thus, no-one goes without.

Afterwards I sit down for a wide-ranging conversation with Mazhar. Now seventy years old, he is what I would describe as a leading member of the '68 generation of revolutionaries; schooled in Marxism, but of the New (anti-Stalinist) Left. He studied pharmacy at university before being forced out of Bangladesh in 1972 in the aftermath of the violent political fallout from the division between those in the Awami League who believed national liberation to be the end goal, and the leftists who believed it only to be the beginning. As Mazhar put it to me, 'National liberation was important to support because it was an act of the oppressed. To fight back against oppression, they needed an identity to unite the people. But I don't give a damn about Bengali nationalism. Nationalism is another form of racism, and nationalism also produces fascism.' In Mazhar's view this nationalistic end game is now coming to pass in his country.

He has had an extraordinarily prolific, influential and activist political career. According to filmmaker and author Naeem Mohaiemen, in the

1970s Mazhar was aligned with the Sharbahara Party, that trod the same path as the armed struggle of the Indian Maoist Naxalite movement. He ended up in New York, where he worked as a pharmacist, studied economics and mixed in radical circles. In 1984, he set up a counter-NGO known as UBINIG (Policy Research on Alternatives to Development). Mohaiemen describes UBINIG's many projects as encompassing 'environmental activism, alternative to traditional farming methods, opposition to Bangladeshis being used as guinea pigs for abortion pill RU 486, criticising American media focus on child labour as an excuse for UN protectionism' and the establishment of a feminist bookshop in Dhaka. Mazhar has always been outspoken and sometimes been made to pay the price. In 1995, he was arrested by the BNP-led Bangladesh government and detained without trial under the Special Powers Act after he wrote an article denouncing the bloody suppression of the Ansar Rebellion of soldiers demanding better working conditions. There was a storm of protest inside Bangladesh at his jailing and internationally. Nadine

Remembering Lalon Shah

Gordimer, Jacques Derrida and Mahasweta Devi wrote a letter to the *New York Times* demanding he be released.

So why Lalon Shah? I ask. 'I want to ground the Left's thinking in those traditional discourses that have been all but eliminated by modernity,' Mazhar tells me. 'Modernity claims that only the Enlightenment counts in civilisational terms, and that we are all uncivilised, have nothing to offer; we cannot create or originate anything. So, I want to identify trends in Bengal that have a global significance and which are based on community building against the centralised modern state which is very repressive, to find ways of avoiding the conflictual model that still exists in my society, and finally, as a Bengali, to critique from my own traditions.'

'Here today, we are celebrating Lalon Shah. Why? Because he started a political movement that was also a spiritual movement. He didn't believe in caste or class, and so he started an anti-caste movement. He attempted to persuade through love and not force and through "theatre" [such as the meal ritual]. He also argued for a [human] food system that would also maintain all other life systems.'

Mazhar explains that it has been a long path to Kushtia. 'I went on this journey where I came to the realisation that Marxism is essentially an extension of the European Enlightenment – which is fine – but I found that what has been developed from the teachings of Marxism is not going to work in a society like Bangladesh. I find it has a serious flaw in denying the role of subjectivity, or the role of the spirit.' That doesn't mean that he has abandoned Marxism, or is about to go to New York 'and start Hare Krishna' as he put it. Neither will he criminalise people fighting back against 'this ugly system' and the 'war on terror', including Islamists targeted by the Bangladeshi state for summary execution, even though he doesn't necessarily agree with what they stand for.

Unlike many on the Left internationally, Mazhar is not an enemy of religion. He opposed the Awami League and Sheikh Mujibur Rahman's 1972 declaration that the new Bangladesh should be a secular state. 'It simply meant you want to eliminate Islam from Bengal. I understand that in the West the Enlightenment wanted to break the power of the Christian Church, because it was an oppressive force. But that is particular to Europe. Our thinking, culture and practices are very different.' He is a celebrated poet, and has recently taken to writing within an Islamic poetic

Ayesha Khatun the schoolteacher

framework because, in his words, 'progressives, in trying to reject [the reactionary face of religion] have also thrown away its core...In the battle against imperialism, we need to rediscover that which is our own asset, the core of our being.'

'I go to all the madrasahs where I have good relations,' he tells me. He adds, 'Many don't like me, which is fine, no problem. They think I'm not a good Muslim: I don't follow shariah, I don't go to prayers very often – but I do fast very well. I tell the muftis that Bangladesh is a brutal state run by killers and robbers – what's the point of demanding shariah law on the top of a state that is getting more and more fascist?' He concludes by arguing that the modern centralised nation state is parasitical upon the mass of the population, and runs counter to the development of communities. 'The Left globally has to redefine revolutionary subjectivity for 2017 – how to organise, how to connect with popular movements that are fighting back.' It's been a fascinating but exhausting conversation for both of us. I will meet him again when I am asked to partake in the communal lunch. Mazhar is an extraordinary, intellectually imaginative figure, and I am thankful that I have met and talked with him.

I retreat to the back of a wooden tea shop to hang out with Mahmudul's student friends from the University of Dhaka where he studies. I talk with an amiable middle-aged lady who sat beside me. She tells me that her name is Ayesha Khatun and she is a local primary-school teacher. She earns the equivalent of £350 a year, teaching her class of 80 children. She would like a wage raise – maybe another £100 a year – to help her make ends meet.

We leave the festival site and take a ten-minute walk back through the village streets and down to the bank of the Kaliganga river, which is a tributary of the Ganges. It is a peaceful idyllic scene – kids mucking about on small boats, nets hanging to dry, and locals and Lalon Shah devotees washing themselves and their garments in the river.

We walk back to the festival, where, unfortunately, due to my foreign appearance and height, I am spotted by the local police officer in charge of security. He engages me in polite, formal conversation before nodding towards his numerous underlings who are lounging about bored, weapons on their shoulders and at their hips, marooned amongst the peace-loving crowds. He calls out and one of his shotgun-toting officers appears at my side. The chief tells me that the

The medicine-man

officer will now be my official police bodyguard for the rest of my time at the festival. I protest feebly that I don't really need an armed escort, but he's not having it. For the next few hours the officer shadows me, as I go to the latrines, trawl the stalls and watch a medicine-man convince onlookers that a painkilling ointment made from the venom of small black scorpions (one of which he dangles by its tail) is worth buying, and the efficacy of the fattest leeches I have ever seen. I am now attracting a lot of attention as people wonder who the armed officer is protecting (and why). I retreat to back of the tea-hut where Mahmudul's student friends gently rib the officer sat next to me, which makes me a little nervous.

And then we suddenly realise we are late and must rush for the coach back to Dhaka. I discharge my protector, we jump on a cart and then into a CNG back to town and onto the coach for the bumpiest, bone-crunching, head-ache-inducing, traffic-clogged ten-miles-an-hour journey I have ever, ever experienced.

Those who 'do politics'

The lives of Dhaka's Bihari population remain perilous, ever since they were rendered stateless at the birth of the state of Bangladesh. Originally migrants who moved into East Pakistan following the partition of India, this Urdu-speaking population were regarded as a fifth column during the War for Independence because of their collaboration with the Pakistani armed forces and anti-liberation paramilitary death squads.

The community were dealt a collective punishment during and after the war, including violent reprisals, arrests, mob attacks, dispossession and mass killings. A Bangladeshi journalist who works in international media told me that this communal dimension of the 1971 war has in his opinion yet to be fully confronted by Bangladeshis in that, in his words, 'their plight was never documented'. He has been convinced by eyewitness accounts that at least some of the killings were orchestrated by pro-independence forces and 'the perfect narrative' of the war of liberation has acted to suppress this bloody episode. Unfortunately, the Biharis have recently been caught up in an unhelpful intervention by some Pakistani commentators and writers whom Bangladeshis accuse of cynically highlighting the atrocities against Biharis as a way of attempting to underplay or cloud the genocidal campaign by the Pakistani forces.

Many of those Biharis who survived ended up in refugee camps, some ad hoc and some established by the Red Cross. Successive Pakistani administrations have proved reluctant to repatriate the majority of the Bihari population. Generations of Biharis have now grown up inside the camps – young people who bear no relation to the events of 1971. Although in the intervening years some Biharis managed to find housing outside the camps and claimed citizenship and thus the chance to assimilate into Bangladeshi society (even if it meant abandoning their Bihari-Urdu identity), those inside the camps remained denuded of their rights.

Almost 300,000 still live in 116 'Urdu-speaking settlements', including the Geneva camp in Mohammadpur, with 25,000 people squeezed into its narrow confines. In 2001, a youth group inside the Geneva camp brought a petition to the High Court demanding voting rights. They won their case and opened the door to a wider court ruling and in 2008 the High Court restored the birth-right of young Biharis as Bangladesh citizens. Despite that victory, as Nazmus Saquib Chowdhury notes, 'many who grew up in the camps remain socially isolated, under-educated, and are employed mainly in the "informal" sector, still living in substandard conditions without much hope for the future.'

The journalist I spoke to told me that the majority of Biharis just want to 'restart', and are reluctant to open 'old wounds'. However, those Biharis living in Dhaka face a new threat — being forced out of their camps because of the astronomical leap in land prices in the city. In June of last year, a mob attacked the Bihari camp in Kalshi, in the north of the city, setting fire to houses and killing nine members of one family — women and children who were burnt alive after their door was barricaded from the outside. Local Biharis accused the police of helping the attackers, who were drawn from local slum areas, and of shooting dead a 35-year-old Bihari man during the disturbance. Although the pretext for the assault was a confrontation between Bihari and local youth, Abdur Jabbar Khan, chief of Stranded Pakistanis General Repatriation Committee (SPGRC), told newspapers that the attack had been pre-planned to drive the Biharis away. 'This incident is not new for us. Following the construction of Kalshi Road, the price of land has shot up. A vested quarter has been trying to grab the camp's land...Those who do politics and have anti-social elements, goons and arms, planned this all. This is not the result of a Bihari-Bengali feud.' Arson attacks are not confined to the Bihari camps, they are an increasingly common tactic used by politicians and connected business interests to clear people off valuable land.

Those 'who do politics' seem to have the upper hand when it comes to controlling the flow of media stories to the Bangladeshi people, and how events, historical and contemporary, are reported and interpreted. The Bangladeshi journalist (who did not want me to give his name) told me that he was alarmed by the way in which the press had been bought off by political and commercial interests. This is of course the situation the world over, but perhaps it has a greater impact on what is a young nation, trying to come to terms both with its past and a true picture of where exactly it is going. The journalist sketched out to me how the juggernaut of economic growth often turns those who find themselves in its path into enemies of national progress, whether that be people highlighting environmental issues, labour activists, the Biharis clinging onto their slum dwellings or

Zonayed Saki

those highlighting corruption and human rights abuses. The journalist told me that a colleague of his, working for a Bangladeshi newspaper, had boasted to him of his cosy relationship with the powers-that-be and then flashed him the Rolex watch gifted to him by a government official. He also pointed out how one of Bangladeshi's biggest newspapers, the *Daily Star*, had signed a deal with the powerful lobby group, the Bangladesh Garment Manufacturers and Exporters Association (BGMEA), to promote its activities. In January 2016, the *Daily Star* signed a Memorandum of Understanding with the BGMEA at the paper's Dhaka headquarters — an event reported by the newspaper under the headline 'BGMEA signs deal with *Daily Star* to devise ways to boost exports'. The article suggested that the Bangladeshi garment industry wanted to rival the Chinese market by reaching a $50-billion export target by 2021. The editor and publisher of the *Daily Star* Mahfuz Anam was quoted in his own newspaper urging 'media outlets to extensively cover garment-related issues so that the barriers to business are removed. The entrepreneurs in the garment sector have been playing a leadership role and other sectors are following them. The engine of economic growth is the private sector. This is why The *Daily Star* has come forward to cooperate with the sector.' One might ask how this fits with the *Star's* published values: 'The uniqueness of *Daily Star* lies in its non-partisan position, in the freedom it enjoys from any influence of political parties or vested groups. Its strength is in taking position of neutrality in conflicts between good and evil, justice and injustice, right and wrong, regardless of positions held by any group or alliance'?

So what of the opposition in Dhaka to this kind of cosy relationship and the wider political cityscape? I went to talk with Zonayed Saki, the high-profile left-wing politician who had run for mayor of Dhaka North in 2015. His office is located inside a commercial building in the centre of

Dhaka, and when I arrive I am ushered into his small workplace, and sit at a desk piled high with papers. Saki is very busy and clearly tired, but polite and engaging. He has a youthful look about him, although the former student leader's hair is now flecked with grey. Saki first rose to prominence as an activist at a time when Bangladesh was under the military rule of General Hussain Muhammad Ershad. He became president of the Bangladesh Students Federation in 1989 and was in the leadership of the movement that toppled Ershad the following year. He tells me, 'I was 17 at the time. It was a very popular movement, the biggest since 1971, and it was a democratic movement against the military regime. Ershad was ousted through a people's uprising, mainly based in the city areas. It started when police killed a student activist, Naziruddin Jehad. Under the pressure of the students' movement the political forces aligned against the regime.'

Although the 1990 uprising was Saki's political baptism, he tells me that it was during the aftermath that his political consciousness developed. Although no two historical events are the same, as in 1971, he realised that the Left had led the struggle, only to find their democratic demands pushed aside as the political establishment grabbed the reins of power. As he put it to me, 'we discovered that the system as a whole that Ershad had been sitting on was still intact.' The 'plunderers' were still in place, and continued to use the state machine to extract vast wealth. The basic demands for the separation of powers between the legislature and the judiciary were not carried through. He also points out to me that the constitution does not even allow for parliamentary dissent – so if for example an MP, wishing to represent his constituency over a particular issue, wants to vote against a government bill he has to resign not just the party whip, but his parliamentary seat. 'You can't even raise your hand against the prime minister,' he says. 'If you go against her, you are expelled.' The scrutiny committees in the parliament, such as the ones dealing with corruption and human rights abuses, are under the control of Sheikh Hasina's ruling Awami Party. 'This is one-person politics,' Saki says. He also tells me that the Awami League has used the War Crimes Tribunal to prosecute those who ordered or carried out atrocities on behalf of the Pakistani forces, for party political purposes. As he put it, 'Sheikh Hasina has used history in the [most] maximum way ever.'

In April 2015 Saki ran for the position of mayor of Dhaka North under the banner of his party Ganasanghati Andolan (People's Solidarity

Movement), of which he is chief coordinator. But he tells me that the election was stolen – the ballot boxes had been stuffed with votes and sealed before election day, and by 11am on the day itself the polling stations had been 'captured' by Awami League activists and shut down. At that point, Saki called on his supporters to boycott the poll, so as not to legitimise what he saw as a crooked result.

So for Saki and Ganasanghati Andolan the first struggle is for fundamental democratic rights, both in terms of the constitution and the right of people to protest and strike (*hartal*). 'We have to establish citizens' dignity,' he says. 'At the moment, they have no dignity – they are always being harassed by the state or by corporations. I stood for mayor saying that Dhaka has to be a city that its citizens can participate in, and build its future. I talked about development and planning issues, transportation and public health. We stand for the rights of women, the disabled and gender rights, including transgender. We want cultural and religious freedom – in the spirit of the Liberation War.'

He tells me that ordinary people are scared to protest: 'They are afraid that if they get on the street they may be shot dead. There is a huge fear, and a frustration that nothing is happening.'

Food adulteration protest at Dhaka University

At Dhaka University

A few days later, I go with Mahmudul to spend a day at the University of Dhaka. As I enter the university grounds I spot a small demonstration making its way across the road. It assembles in thirty seconds, the banners go up and the chants start, and thirty seconds later it begins to move. A minute later it is surrounded by police, some with weapons, and a minute later the event is over. I rush across the road just as the marchers are dispersing and ask them what they were protesting over. They seem glad to see someone taking notice and explain they are highlighting the adulteration of food with toxic chemicals. I manage to get them back together for a couple of seconds for a photo before they break up.

Mahmudul walks me around the grounds of the university, pointing out the different faculties, including the science faculty housed in redbrick Curzon Hall, a mishmash of arts and craft and Orientalist design, built at the turn of the last century and named after the then Viceroy of India. We watch the end of a student cricket match (the underdogs were victorious), pass by groups of students chatting under the shade, others cycling between faculties. Everywhere there are visual references to 1971.

It seems all very relaxed. We pick up some of Mahmudul's friends on the way through. One young men tells me he is very interested in drama, but with what seemed some regret was studying fisheries administration because he was worried about getting a job after graduating. Another is a talented photographer, but studies engineering. Every young person I talked to during my visit, student or otherwise, told me the most pressing issue facing them was finding a job. 'This is our greatest crisis' was the phrase I heard most often. Lecturers unsurprisingly report high levels of stress and depression in the student population.

Nearly half of all graduates in Bangladesh are unemployed. According to the World Bank, about 41 per cent of Bangladeshi youth are considered NEET (not in employment, education or training). More than 95 per cent of employed youth are reportedly working in the informal sector, 30 per cent are said to be self-employed and 11 per cent are in unpaid family work. The gender balance is stark, with young women being the majority of NEETs, and 90 per cent of women workers being concentrated in vulnerable employment sectors. A 2013 World Bank report found that 'eighty per cent of young women are at home and not in the labour force. Two thirds of young women are not in employment education or training (NEET), and two-thirds of school drop outs are women.'

Anti-Terrorism Raju Memorial Sculpture, at TSC, Dhaka University Campus

One of my group of students, a young man named Sahad, tells me that there is great competition to get a place at the University of Dhaka and that undergraduates were fortunate that their higher education was largely paid for by the state. What is the state of campus politics, I ask Sahad, considering there are plenty of issues for students to get organising over, and given that the university's students had played such an important role in the democratic revolts of 1971 and 1990? Sahad himself came from a progressive family background; his late father was a community activist and campaigner. To answer my question, he walks me to a hall used by student union activists. Just as we approach it, we are forced to stand back as a contingent of male students march past us, double-step, in formation, as if they were on an army parade ground. I found the spectacle to be quite menacing. Sahad explains to me that they are from a particular hall of residence and have allegiance to the Bangladesh Chhatra League, the

Students at Dhaka University show inter-religious solidarity by celebrating the
Hindi Holi festival

student wing of the ruling party. They have heard that their leader has called
a meeting and they are on their way to see him. We get to the building and
have a look in on the gathering, some standing around the leadership,
others seated in rows, male students in front, female students behind.

It is not just the Awami League that has sought to control student politics
through the promise of political, financial and career rewards. All the main
parties have in effect militarised their student organisations. An Associated
France Press report from 2010, headlined 'Violent student politics wreck
Bangladesh campus life', reported that 'all three of Bangladesh's main
political parties have strong student wings, which they fund and allegedly
arm with swords and even old guns.' The article quoted a professor emeritus
at the University of Dhaka: 'There is no idealism, this is about greed.
Student political leaders make money from extortion, from selling tenders,
they control the student accommodation, the canteen.' He went on to say,
'In return for providing a ready reserve of young rioters when needed, the
political parties allow their respective student wings to make money from
their control of the university education system.' The article said that

student body regarded Chhatra League leaders as 'gangsters' and quoted one student who said 'we must pick sides in order to access basic services'. The student said he only got accommodation when he agreed to join JCD, the student wing of the BNP, but then had to switch to the Chhatra League when it took control of the campus. Battles between rival groups have resulted in many students being murdered on campus, including at the University of Dhaka alone, along with hundreds seriously injured.

It's difficult to comprehend, particularly since all of the students I have met during my visit have been so open-minded, warm and intelligent; but that is naïve. I realise it's not about the students themselves, or Bangladeshi young people in general, the vast majority of whom I assume want a peaceful life. It's a reflection of a wider malaise spread by those in power, or competing for power, who have made violence the way of doing business, and as that violence has permeated through society it has taken on a murderous life of its own. In student life, this violence erupts in the space between the dire situation facing most youth and the potential rewards for those few who are prepared to literally fight their way into the political and economic nexus. Now I begin to understand what Saiful Islam was referring to when he talked of 'how even on the youth side, politics has become how to profit from the system'.

I sit down for coffee with a female lecturer who wished to remain anonymous. She tells me that in her view the government is involved in 'a sort of terrorism against us', in the name of development. 'They are completely besieging us.' She mentions flyovers in Dhaka under construction by companies attached to politicians collapsing and killing workers, the network of profiteering leading back to the prime minister's family, arson attacks on slum dwellers, throwing rural communities off government-owned land where they have been cultivating staple foods and the setting up of unregulated Special Economic Zones invested in by multinationals. 'The ruling party are so powerful now, they just don't care,' she says.

I ask her about the legacy of 1971. She sighs. 'I am pro-1971. That is a very touchy subject for me. The war was won by common people, men and women. That fight had to be won, but it doesn't make all the other fights irrelevant.'

REAL BENGALI MUSLIMS?

Zeeshan Khan

The presence of violent religious extremism is as old in Bangladesh as it is globally. The first attack of this nature in the country took place in 1999 on a cultural troupe, not long after the first Al-Qaeda strikes on US embassies in East Africa in 1998. Several attacks have followed since then in fairly consistent succession, on writers, on Bengali New Year celebrations, on artists, on minorities, on mystics, on shrines, on women's education and more than one serious attempt has been fielded to replace the People's Republic with an 'Islamic' one. The 2016 attack at Holey Artisan Bakery and Cafe, the country's deadliest terrorist attack, claimed by Daesh, is a clear indication of how Islamists everywhere are keeping up with an evolving ideology. And though the Republic of Bangladesh has thus far succeeded in thwarting larger scale attempts by local and international outfits, contentions that the Bangladeshi state is an aberration until it conforms to a particularly unique take on shariah make this an issue that cannot be taken lightly.

But these are not new circumstances. Bangladesh never quite made peace with the strains of Islamism that were injected into its political corpus during the 1971 war of liberation. The term 'Islamism' was not used in those days, of course, and is controversial in any case because of the aspersions it casts upon the word 'Islam'. Still, in lieu of a satisfactory substitute it serves to describe an ideology which, though basing itself on Islam, is often thought to have departed considerably from the religion's spirit.

So why did tensions arise between Bangladesh and Pakistan in the first place? After all, East Pakistan, as Bangladesh was then known, belonged to a political arrangement that placed Islam, and by extension political Islam, at its centre. And although the conflict had nearly nothing to do with ideology, the underpinnings were apparent from an early stage, which were given voice in convenient arguments made by the religious right, manifested at the time as the Jamaat-e-Islami. These arguments placed Pakistan on the side of Islam and Bangladesh on the side of forces hostile to Islam.

This narrative was never completely defeated and has resurfaced, bolstered by global, militant Islamism that positions itself as a moral alternative to the international status quo. Beginning in the late 1990s and carrying on through the first and second decade of the twenty-first century, a rising tide of the Salafist interpretation of Islam is pushing at the gates of the Bengali state, placing demands that are often at significant odds with its social and legal orthodoxy. To understand these contrasting perspectives on statehood, we need to spend some time examining the historical orientation of Bengali Muslim society and the subsequent kingdom it established in the fourteenth, fifteenth and sixteenth centuries. This will show the direction it took, and perhaps still takes, in its aspirations to a polity that preserves its distinctive national character.

Genesis

The *Sultanatiya-i-Bangala*, the Sultanate of Bengal, began in 1352 as a sovereign Muslim kingdom a little over a hundred years after an Islamicate Delhi took the throne of Bengal from the Hindu Sens – a hundred years during which numerous attempts at independence were made by a string of Delhi's governors. Shamsuddin Iliyas Shah, who ruled the kingdom of Shatgaon from 1352 to 1358, annexed the two short-lived Muslim kingdoms of medieval Bengal – Lakhnauti and Shonargaon – after all three parts of the partitioned province declared independence from Delhi. The enlarged kingdom, now called Bangala, stood as an independent country in the medieval era for some 230 years. Much of what Bangladeshis can identify as their cultural and political heritage is rooted in this period. Beginning with things as basic as its name (Bangala, now Bangla), currency (Tanka, now Taka) and state language (Bengali), to more personal elements like literature, music, folk culture and spiritual traditions, Muslim Bengal's socio-political identity stems, in significant amounts, from the Sultanate of Bengal.

When Muslim forces arrived on the Bengal delta, Hindus and Buddhists had already been engaged in a centuries' old struggle for dominance, with the Buddhists all but defeated following the fall of the Pala Empire.

According to the *Shunya Purana* by the tenth century poet Ramai Pandit, Buddhist persecution at the hands of a resurgent Brahmanism in Bengal was halted by the arrival of the Muslims, portrayed as the revival of Dharma:

> In Jajapur and Maldah, sixteen hundred families of Vedic Brahmins mustered strong. Being assembled in groups of ten or twelve they killed the Sat-Dharmis (Buddhists) who would not pay the religious fees, by uttering incantations and curses. They uttered mantras from the Vedas and fire came out of their mouths as they did. The followers of Sat Dharma trembled with fear at the sight thereof and prayed to Dharma; for who else could help them in that crisis? The Brahmins began to destroy the creation in the above manner and acts of great violence were perpetrated on the earth. Dharma who resided in Baikuntha was grieved to see this. He came to the world as a Mohammedan. In his head he wore a black cap and in hand he held a cross-bow. He mounted a horse and was called Khoda. Niranjana incarnated himself in Behest (Heaven). All the gods being of one mind wore trousers.

Muslims were expected to weigh in on the side of the Buddhists and, though they didn't exactly do that, their arrival shifted the balance of power decisively away from Brahmanism. It gave Buddhism in Bengal a renewed lease on life and 200 years after they conquered the country, Bengali Sultans were sending Buddhist monks to China to propagate the religion on the Chinese Emperor's request. The Sultans were generally appreciative of both Hinduism and Buddhism, culturally at least, and eventually absorbed much of their art and mysticism, grafting chunks of the older culture onto their own. This is the syncretism that has characterised Bengal's politics as well as its theology ever since, a theology that was developed, in no small part, by conversations between Muslim Sufis and Hindu Sadhus.

Syncretism

Mutual curiosity between different religious orders existed in Bengal since the twelfth century, when *Amritakunda (The Pool of Life)*, a Sanskrit manual on tantric yoga, was translated into Persian and Arabic and circulated as far away as Kashmir. While the Sufis of the time sought to incorporate the esoteric philosophies and practices of local yogis into their own religious lives, the Hindu mystics began redefining their devotion according to Sufi doctrines of divine love. Sri Chaitanya Mahaprabhu, the enigmatic fifteenth century Hindu reformer, was influenced by the Sufi love of music, and adapted his own mystical practices to include the use of *kirtans* – musical tributes to God. Sri Chaitanya's reforms led to what has become known as Gour Vaishnavism, a Monist tradition, which also contributes to the existence of *Bauliyana*, Bengal's entirely indigenous mystical order. Bauls draw from both Islamic and Hindu but also from Buddhist mystic references that are found in the Charyapadas (a collection of mystical poems in the Vajrayana tradition), and their music has historically been among the most relevant vehicles for spiritual enrichment on the Bengal delta.

Of the Sufis, the Chishti order did particularly well. In fact, it is probably safe to say that Bengal's majority Muslim population is a direct result of the mass appeal Chishti mystics had in the area. Although Muslim settlers and preachers arrived on the delta as early as the tenth century (if not earlier) it wasn't until the thirteenth century that an established order began weaving itself into the spiritual fabric of the culture. Akhi Sirajuddin Usman, a disciple of Nizamuddin Auliya and a contemporary of Amir Khosrau (1253-1325), went from Gour to Delhi to study with the great Sufi and on his return, established the Chishti *khanqah* (building for the order) in the Sultanate of Bangala. The *silsila* (spiritual genealogy) was quickly endorsed by the people as well as the rulers of the Sultanate and many of the better known Bengali Sufis belonged to the order, with the notable exception of Shah Jalal of Sylhet, who predates Akhi Siraj by over a century. As the late Peter Custers noted in a lecture at Leiden University:

> The Chishtis' openness is reflected in several striking practices. Among the different Sufi brotherhoods that spread their influence in India from the thirteenth and fourteenth century onwards, the Chishtis appear to have stood out as especially eager to communicate with Indian yogis. At Chishti *khanqahs* 'in each and every city' where these were established, yogis were welcome guests. Again, historians recount that the Chishtis encouraged the reciting of Vaishnav poetry at *sama* gatherings held at the hospices — surely yet one more proof, if needed, of their spirit of liberalism...

Akhi Siraj was succeeded by Alaul Haq, who was a wealthy member of the ruling elite, and his spiritual transformation from nobleman to mystic strengthened ties between the Sultanate's throne and the Chishti *khanqah*.

The close personal relationship between the Sultans and the Sufis had an impact on the kingdom's character, reflected in a variety of ways – one of which was an appreciation of plurality.

When the second Sultan, Sultan Sikander Shah (r.1358-1390), undertook to build the largest mosque in South Asia at the time, the Adina Mosque at Pandua, he used a blended style of Pala, Sena, Islamic and pre-Islamic Persian influences. The mosque was intended as a statement of power and prosperity, and also to distinguish them from their co-religionists in Delhi. It was a decisive split from the North Indian Islamic fold, done by incorporating both Islam and multiculturalism or, more specifically, Bengali multiculturalism into their architecture. It was also a ploy for support; by showing deference to the Pala and Sena dynasties, they were carving a place for themselves in the natural progression of Bengali politics. In his phenomenal book, *The Rise of Islam and the Bengal Frontier*, Richard Eaton writes:

> Stylistic motifs in the mosque's prayer niches reveal the builders' successful adaptation, and even appreciation, of late Pala-Sena art. The imposing monument is also likely to have been a statement directed at Sikandar's more distant Muslim audience, his former overlords in Delhi, now bitter rivals. Having successfully defended his kingdom from Sultan Firuz's armies, Sikandar projected his claims of power and independence by erecting a monument greater in size than any edifice built by his North Indian rivals..., these kings yielded so much to Bengali conceptions of form and medium that, as the art historian Percy Brown observes, 'the country, originally possessed by the invaders, now possessed them'.

From the very beginning of the Sultanate's existence, Hindu-Buddhist motifs and architecture influenced Sultanate structures, while pre-Islamic articulations of political authority were readily adopted by Muslim kings. The titles *Raja* and *Ishwara* were liberally used instead of *Sultan*, and Muslim Bengali kings were, as late as the sixteenth century, sending for water from the River Ganges to be used during their coronation rituals – a distinctly Hindu practice. The fifteenth century Hindu poet Vijay Gupta was full of praise for Sultan Allauddin Hossain Shah (d.1519), among the more enlightened of the Bengali Sultans:

Sultan Hossain Raja, nurturer of the world:
In war he is invincible; for his opponents he is Yama [god of death].
In his charity he is like Kalpataru [a fabled wish-yielding tree].
In his beauty he is like Kama [god of love].
His subjects enjoy happiness under his rule.

Hossain Shah was also well known for his patronage of literature. A couple of translations of the *Mahabharata*, along with a number of *Vaishnava padas* and a few works on *Manasa* the snake-goddess, were published during his reign. But he wasn't the first to support Bengali and Hindu writing. His forebear Ruknuddin Barbak (r. 1459–1474) patronised both Hindu and Muslim writing in Bangla, and before that, in the 1300s, Bengal's most flamboyant Sultan, Ghiyasuddin Azam Shah (r. 1390-1411) supported the poet Krittivas Ojha's publication of the *Ramayana* in Bengali. As mentioned earlier, Azam Shah also famously sent Buddhist Monks to China to propagate the religion. All this suggests that Muslim Sultans were not encumbered by the communal prejudices that dominate religious discourse today.

It would also be wrong to suggest that the Bengali Sultans were not aware of themselves as Muslims or that they were not aware of Bangala as a Muslim Sultanate. They affiliated themselves with the larger Islamic realm, paying homage to the Caliph in Cairo, and donating money for the building of mosques and madrasahs in Mecca. When the Hindu landlord Raja Ganesh overthrew the founding dynasty of the realm in the early 1400s, the leading Chishti saint of his day, Nur Qutb-e-Alam (Alaul Haq's son and sheikh to Jalaluddin Shah, the first ethnically Bengali Sultan) threatened to facilitate an invasion from neighbouring, and allied, Muslim Jaunpur if the throne of a Muslim kingdom was not returned to a Muslim ruler.

In spite of this, such was the decidedly multi-religious nature of that early Bengali state that when Sri Chaitanya ran into trouble with the Hindu orthodoxy for his unconventional ways, it was the venerable Raja Hossain Shah who protected him and ordered his court to provide the preacher with assistance in propagating his Bhakti creed anywhere he wished. Two of Hossain's Hindu cabinet Ministers were even celebrated gurus of the Bhakti movement. The influence of Chishti Sufis on the Sultanate's rulers and consequently its social climate cannot be overstated. They were instrumental in forging a polity that was representative of the various traditions which existed on the delta at the time, and in encouraging a society that was based on an appreciation of differences. One of the areas where this is evident is in the transition from solely Persian to both Bengali and Persian as official languages of the realm. Nur Qutb-e-Alam is credited with beginning this trend by introducing the *Rekhta* style in Bengali, where half a composition was rendered in Farsi while the rest was written in Bengali. Nur Qutb was Sultan Ghiyasuddin's friend, the pair having been students of Alaul Haq's, and this connection served to propel Bengali into the Sultanate courts and ultimately into official usage. Jalaluddin Shah furthered state patronage of Bengali so that by the 1500s edicts of Sultan Hossain Shah were being issued in Bengali and the Chishti Sufis had adopted Bengali as their own first language.

By contrast, the Sen dynasty that preceded the Sultanate displayed a positive revulsion for the language and refused to allow literature, especially religious literature, to be translated from Sanskrit into Bengali. Rulings forbidding the use of Bengali were issued, resulting in Hindu scripture being out of reach for most of the population. When Muslim Sultans commissioned Bengali translations of the *Ramayana*, Krittivas Ojha's famous work, the surviving Hindu aristocracy went into fits, issuing warnings in Sanskrit of the impending doom that would await Bengali Hindus, now that a sacred text had been uttered in their profane tongue. One wonders if their real fears might have been the loss of their monopoly on religious dogma, which had now finally been made accessible to Hindus, in a Muslim Kingdom. Dinesh Chandra Sen, a scholar from the early 1900s writes:

> This elevation of Bengali to a literary status was brought about by several influences, of which the Mohammedan's conquest was undoubtedly one of the foremost. If the Hindu kings had continued to enjoy independence, Bengali would scarcely have got an opportunity to find its way to the courts of kings.

This connection between Bengali and Muslim rule becomes relevant when one considers how the Bengali language was regarded as too 'Hindu' for Pakistan almost immediately after Partition. Classifying people as either Bengali or Muslim began some time before that, with Hindu Bengalis lumping their Muslim co-linguists together with the population of non-Bengali speaking Muslims who promoted Urdu as their national language. But Muslim North India's disdain for Bengali only became clear after Partition, when Jinnah announced, rather ignorantly, that 'Urdu, and only Urdu' represented the spirit of Muslim nations in South Asia. The awkwardly fashioned two-nation theory even inspired attempts at 'purifying' Bengali by suggesting its script be changed from Brahmi to Nastaleeq (the Persian script used for Urdu) or by purging it of its Sanskritic vocabulary. Poetically, it was an Islamic organisation, the Tamaddun Majlish, which first took up the cause of defending Bengali in East Pakistan and pioneered the Language Movement which became a full-blown revolution by 1952. But those communal notions haven't entirely gone away. As recently as 2014, an Islamic talk show on Bangladeshi television considered whether some words in the Bangla language – like '*lokhkhi*', a term of endearment – should be replaced because of their connections to 'un-Islamic' elements – in this case the goddess Lakshmi's name.

Islamist pedants bemoan what they perceive as the Kolkata-centric 'Sanskritisation' of Bengali, preferring to use Arabic, Farsi or even Urdu alternatives wherever possible. And the fact that such conversations are had in a nation that places a premium on its linguistic heritage speaks volumes about the power of the Islamist narrative. Reaching into literature, Bangladeshi society's respect for the likes of Jibonanondo Das and Rabindranath Thakur, whose own faith was syncretic through and through, has been objected to, and the fact that Kazi Nazrul Islam is Bangladesh's national poet makes some people uncomfortable because he wrote tributes to Shiva and Krishna.

Secularism

These throwbacks to an idealised Islamic Republic have drawn strength from the steady Islamisation of Pakistan, and are also getting support from global and proximate chapters of aspirational caliphates like Daesh. But Bangladesh and Pakistan were meant to have different trajectories. Pakistan was never intended as a religiously heterodox place, despite secular utterances by the country's founder Muhammad Ali Jinnah. Even as East Pakistan came into existence, a significant portion of East Bengali society was never completely comfortable with Pakistan's national lashings, which were inconsistent with Bengal's own interpretations of religion and culture. There was always an insistence that Muslims are one nation and Hindus another, regardless of the fact that there are many Muslim nations and many Hindu nations, and many unique ways of being both Hindu and Muslim. This reductionism created for Pakistan, especially in its relationship with East Pakistan, an identity crisis regarding its roots and orientation, the tensions of which were felt from the start. So much so that a united, independent and necessarily multi-religious Bengali state – separate from India or Pakistan – was drafted and proposed as an alternative to East Bengal joining Pakistan as late as May 1947, three months before Partition.

Since breaking from Pakistan, Bangladesh has consciously tried to steer in an opposite direction, away from the communal maladies of 1947. And so, it should be somewhat more difficult to peddle Salafism in a country that is not officially Islamic, as opposed to one which is.

Much of Bangladesh's political DNA is also inherited from its deeper past. The Sultanate administration was a relatively non-communal apparatus, and from Jalaluddin Shah's reign onwards, had numerous Hindu ministers, officials, administrators and judges in positions of power and influence. The commander of Jalaluddin's army was Hindu. Successive Sultans continued to appoint people to high positions based on merit rather than religious orientation. The *jizya* tax on non-Muslims was also lifted. The *umara,* or nobility, consisted of Hindus and Muslims as well as of Bengalis and non-Bengalis. That is not to say there weren't periods of religious bigotry, as in the case of Raja Ganesh, who after capturing the throne was particularly intolerant of both Muslims and Buddhists, or during the reign of Sultan Shamsuddin Yusuf, who enacted strict *hudud* laws. But these were exceptions rather than the norm and ran contrary to the political maturity upon which the kingdom was built.

This maturity seems to have also allowed attributes of a modern state, like institutions and budget lines, to develop, creating an apparatus rather more based on intellect than sentiment, which perhaps further blunted the possibility of theocratic turbulence. Religious jurists, too, seem to have preferred pragmatism to passion, as was demonstrated in the city of Shonargaon where, during the late 1300s, madrasah students brought a case against the use of oyster shells in the production of slaked lime, claiming that it was against the shariah. The leading mufti of the city issued a fatwa allowing the use of oyster shells on the basis that it was integral to the production of lime and that lime was a necessary product. The Sultanate's policies were anomalous enough in the medieval age of empires to prompt Babur the Mughal (1483–1530) to remark about it in his *Baburnama*:

> There is an amazing custom in Bengal: rule is seldom achieved by hereditary succession. Instead, there is a specific royal throne, and each of the *amirs*, viziers or officer holders has an established place. It is the throne that is of importance for the people of Bengal... The people of Bengal say, 'we are the legal property of the throne, and we obey anyone who is on it.'... Whoever becomes king, must accumulate a new treasury, which is a source of pride for the people. In addition, the salaries and stipends of all the institutions of the rulers, treasury, military and civilian are absolutely fixed from long ago and cannot be spent anywhere else.

In effect, Bengali society – multi-faith and multi-ethnic in its composition – fused into a nation sometime in the thirteenth century and into a state sometime in the fourteenth century. As Richard Eaton notes:

> in reality, the emergence of the independent Ilyas Shahi dynasty represented the political expression of a long-present cultural autonomy. In the late thirteenth century, Marco Polo made mention of 'Bangala', a place he had apparently heard of from his Muslim informants, and which he understood as being a region distinct from India....

> [Balancing] the Persian symbols that pervaded their private audiences, the later sultans observed explicitly Indian rites during their coronations, events that were very public and symbolically charged. Contemporary poetic references to these kings as raja or isvara should not, then, be dismissed as mere hyperbole. They had become Bengali kings.

But all of that is in the past. In the present age, as a reaction to political disenfranchisement, modernist concepts like religious nationalism (in some ways a legacy of European colonialism) essentially brought communal politics into the picture by the late eighteenth century. A resurgent Hindu nationalism beginning with the rise of the Marathas and morphing into 'Hindutva' by the early 1900s, along with global Islamic revivalist movements, like the Wahabbi-inspired Faraizi movement, attacked the very syncretism that had made the Sultanate successful. By the eighteenth century, the Faraizi founder Haji Shariatullah (1781-1840) was attempting to undo history and purge Bengali Muslims of their 'Hindu' influences. Similarly, Hindu Bengali society began distancing itself from its Muslim compatriots, claiming Indian civilisation as its own exclusive – and superior – domain.

However, in the final analysis, Hindus and Muslims in Bengal didn't end up at each other's throats because they belonged to different faiths but because they belonged to different social and economic strata, and because colonial machinations, both Mughal and British, pronounced their differences in an elaborate attempt at social engineering. By originally patronising Hindus in order to contain a Muslim imperial presence in India, the British had created cultural and educational tiers, with Muslims largely left out of the European colonial project. And Muslims, remaining nostalgic about glories past, held on to Urdu and Farsi, refusing to absorb English influences. A Hindu gentry developed in Kolkata, Bengal, at the expense of the previously Muslim and Murshidabad-centric elite.

But shaken by the 1857 Anglo-Indian War and the second Anglo-Afghan War, the British, in the form of Lord Curzon, became eager to appease Muslims and economically develop Muslim-majority areas for fear of an attack by disadvantaged and marginalised Muslims. This thinking directly informed the creation of Aligarh Muslim University and the first partitioning of Bengal in 1905. Dhaka was made a capital and developed politically, with the creation of administrative and judicial structures and the establishment of Dhaka University, running contrary to previously Hindu-leaning polices of governmental and academic patronage. These reversals caused ruptures that led to Bengal being divided again.

So, it was really fear, contempt and resentment – encouraged by colonial divide-and-rule tactics and exasperated by racial prejudice – that created tensions between the different communities in Bengal. Religion had very little to do with it, and it might be prudent to examine if similar patterns exist in the communalisation of today's international political order. Narrowly focused identities are replacing pluralist notions like multiculturalism and supranationality as the Brexiteers, Trumps, Modis and Daeshes of the world seem well on their way to setting the agenda. But as was the case in colonial India, this could have less to do with nationalism, religion or ethnicity than is instantly apparent.

Proto-Islamism

It would be hubris to believe that Bengal's political DNA doesn't also contain indigenous and entrenched Islamist elements. After all, Bengal was the scene of the very first communal riots in undivided India following the 1946 Direct Action Movement, which unleashed terror and violence across India – and was instigated by Bengali Muslims. East Bengal also overwhelmingly supported the Pakistan Movement more so than most of what was then West Pakistan – the Muslim League was created in Dhaka – meaning Bengali Muslims were among the people most eager to live in an Islamic polity. As mentioned earlier, Bengal was one of the few places in the world that took up Wahhabi founder Muhammad Ibn Abdul Wahhab's call for a puritanical purging of culture and hosted the Faraizi Movement which sought to rid Bengali Islam of 'pollutants' that had entered its body through Hindus and Europeans. Several governments of Bangladesh have flirted with Islamism as well, for example by supporting the persecution of Ahmadiyyas or by inserting an official religion clause into the Constitution of the country. And so, Islamists can also find, if they were intent on looking for it, an historical legitimacy to their aspirations. The area that now constitutes Bangladesh, more than most other parts of South Asia, has entertained these competing notions of statehood in an almost schizophrenic manner, each in turn determining its political orientation. However, it is the non-Islamist version that gained ascendency after 1971, and is, for all intents and purposes, the foundation of the Bangladeshi Republic.

For Bangladesh, contending with these forces of division means being able to assert, however shakily, an inclusive cultural and political space. The insistence by Islamists on a Salafist Islamic atmosphere weighs heavily on the society and a Faraizi-style purging of Bangladeshi Islam continues to this day. Sufi *mazaars* (shrines) have been attacked, Sufi thought dismissed as heretical and Sufis themselves attacked and killed. Customs like marriage rituals and mourning ceremonies have been subject to intense criticism for their inclusion of practices that are either pre-Islamic or contain elements of Islamic flourish, such as *milads* — South Asian ceremonies to mark auspicious moments. These are pejoratively called *bida* (innovation) by Islamist puritans while pre-Islamic traditions are deemed *jahil* (ignorant). Both of these terms, along with *shirk* (polytheism) are routinely used to discredit anything at all that goes against stringent, Salafist notions of orthodoxy. Minorities are increasingly being attacked, with a clear intention to eliminate their religions and lifestyles, and a rising intolerance is setting the country up for an existential battle of epic proportions.

Indeed, for much of 2016 and 2017, Dhaka has felt more dangerous than a war zone. Academics, activists, bloggers, atheists, gays, Hindus, even Italian priests have been targeted by Islamic militants. Both the diversity of killings and the authorities' response have been quite astonishing. When an innocent Hindu man, Nikhil Joarder, was hacked to death, the police suggested he may have made blasphemous comments against Prophet Muhammad. In February 2015, when US citizen and science writer Abhijit Roy was murdered at a book fair, the Prime Minister's son went on record in the international press to say that the government could not strongly condemn the attack, because it would make them look like they support atheism and that this would be used against them by their political opponents. But one wonders what the government intended to gain from this sort of posturing. If it expected to be able to win over the religious right by appearing to share their indignation and their values it is mistaken, because the Islamist endgame has no room for democratic traditions, secular institutions or legislative bodies — it certainly has no room for a female head of state. There is nothing the governing Awami League can do, short of declaring itself an Islamist party, to appear legitimate enough for the likes of Daesh. Ironically, Jamaat-i-Islami might have been more amiable, but they have been all but chased into the arms of a more uncompromising brand of political Islam.

On the other hand, the execution of several convicted war criminals, many of whom resisted the creation of Bangladesh out of a sense of religious loyalty to Pakistan, and some of whom are also regarded as religious figures today, has antagonised Islamists. Leaving out the controversy on due process that has besmirched the War Crimes Tribunal, the fact that several senior members of the Jamaat-e-Islami have been among those found guilty has convinced religious hardliners that the state is waging a war of attrition against political Islam, if not against Islam itself. Other controversies have also dogged the War Crimes Tribunal, such as the support it enjoys from the Bangladesh Online Activists Network or BOAN, which has atheist members whose writings have been used to confound the public about the nature of the trials, further polarising the state and the religious right. Several of these bloggers have subsequently been murdered by Islamists and a massive rally of 500,000 people, led by a group called Hefazat-e-Islam, came out in support of an Islamic State in 2013, pushing Bangladesh closer towards the precipice.

There are several other issues that Islamists have taken exception to, which have allowed them to convince themselves, and their sympathisers, that Bangladesh is inherently anti-Islamic. The appointing of the country's first Hindu Chief Justice is one of these issues and the debate about whether the *bismala* (literally, 'in the name of Allah') along with the provision for a state religion should be left out of the Constitution, is another. Other issues, like the women's empowerment policy and the government's refusal to enact blasphemy laws also cause Islamists a great deal of discomfort. The country's close ties to India are seen as a betrayal of the Islamist ideal, and though that relationship does carry complications regarding asymmetries of power, attempts at addressing these give the Islamist narrative an unintended and essentially imaginary sort of leverage, making it difficult to separate standard international relations from emotionally charged subversion.

Various Bangladeshi governments have at varying times tried to find common ground with proponents of political Islam. At other times, the government has taken hard lines against Islamists like recently, with an extremely problematic spate of extra-judicial killings targeting suspected militants. The use of fatal excessive force was also alleged following the Hefazat-e-Islam rally in 2013, but this was never verified, mostly because the government did not allow an independent inquiry into the matter. These pendulum swings have caused damage to the position of the Republic by leaving gaps that can be exploited, so much so that it has now become important to draw clear distinctions between the state and the government. While Bangladeshi governments have found it politically expedient to oscillate between accommodating and opposing Islamist demands, there should be no ambiguity about what the state of Bangladesh stands for. In other words, sets of values must be identified that can go well beyond *raison d'état* and firmly into *raison d'être*.

By drawing on the example of the Bengal Sultanate and by positioning itself as an heir to it, Muslim Bengali society may be able to find the political depth it needs to make these judgements. In doing so, care must be taken to ensure that no room is left for the Islamists to deride the state as immoral, something that is easy to do in an atmosphere of bad governance and corruption. And though it will not matter much to people who are convinced that an Islamic state is morally superior, it will go a long way towards denying them legitimacy in the public eye. It will also defeat the Islamist assertion that Bangladesh is a post-colonial and therefore 'Western' creation, divorced from its original orientation as an Islamic kingdom. By associating Bangladesh with Bangala, Bengali Muslims will be able to show just how well their state is aligned with their origins, which is indeed in an Islamic country – just not an Islamist one.

THE FRAUDULENT CIRCLE

A Qayyum Khan

Bangladesh emerged as an independent state on 16 December 1971 with an empty treasury, a destroyed infrastructure and a traumatised population who had suffered inhuman tragedy at the hands of the Pakistan Army. A large part of the population was displaced by the war, homes were destroyed, the principal breadwinner of many families killed, and innumerable women raped. In 1974, the country faced yet another human tragedy in the form of a famine where thousands perished. At that time, various pundits stated that Bangladesh would not survive as an independent nation. Some even called the new country a 'bottomless basket'.

While the predictions of collapse have proved wrong, the country has had a turbulent history. Two presidents were assassinated and national leaders have been shot and killed inside the Dhaka Central Jail. Today, inter-party and intra-party political assassinations take place with terrifying frequency. In the past forty-six years, Bangladesh was under military rule on three occasions and each rule lasted several years. The last time the military took over it was practically invited by politicians to do so because the leading political parties could not agree on how the caretaker government or the election commission should be composed. The nation is divided between the two main political parties – the Awami League (AL) and the Bangladesh Nationalist Party (BNP). Professional associations are also divided along the same line, no longer pursuing the goals for which they were created – to benefit the profession. Instead, lawyers, engineers, doctors and other professionals pursue narrow political interests often driven by corrupt motives. Consequently, university teachers look after neither the interests of the university nor that of its students. The leaders of student political parties are in their forties and are not students. Many are associated with the underworld. Bangladeshis cannot expect any government service due to them without greasing the palms of officials who provide the service. The same is true if one is aggrieved and seeks justice in the courts.

Bangladeshis never had a national debate on what kind of a nation state they wanted. The vote for AL in the first national elections of Pakistan in 1970 was for provincial autonomy to end the discrimination Bengalis faced in Pakistan, not for independence or secession. When the Pakistan army unleashed terror on East Pakistan (now Bangladesh), the people took up arms and with help from India put an end to the Pakistan army's murderous occupation and liberated their land. But they never had a national discourse on how their country would be different from Pakistan. All Bengali aspirations seemed to have been weaved in a single phrase, Sonar Bangla - the 'Golden Bengal' of Rabindranath Tagore. Nevertheless, the provisional government during the liberation war captured the national mood in its Declaration of Independence on 10 April 1971, which stated: 'We the elected representatives of Bangladesh, as honour bound by the mandate given to us by the people of Bangladesh whose will is supreme duly constituted ourselves into a Constituent Assembly and having held mutual consultations, and in order to ensure for the people of Bangladesh equality, human dignity and social justice declare and constitute Bangladesh to be sovereign and thereby confirm the declaration of independence already made by Bangabondhu Sheikh Mujibur Rahman'. Bangabondhu means 'Friend of Bengal' – a title conferred on Mujib in a public meeting in 1969.

The objectives of the declaration of independence are as true today as they were in 1971 because Bangladesh has yet to deliver on them for all its citizens. The leaders of Bangladesh have made errors that have manifested in various ailments in the instruments of the modern state and in the branches of the government.

Democracy

The AL was created in 1948 by the Bengali leaders of the Muslim League – which negotiated with the British for the creation of Pakistan –when their voices within the League were stifled. Between 1948 and 1966, the AL had four different presidents. In Lahore in 1966, the Six Points were announced as AL's manifesto. They laid down the constitutional framework of Pakistan as a Confederation where only defence and foreign policy would be under the control of the Central Government – all other government matters would be dealt with provincially. But Abdur Rashid Tarkabagish, AL President in 1966, was not in favour of Six Points, opposing Mujib's announcement without party authorisation. Yet the AL did not break up and political difference between the two was resolved in a party council in which Mujib was elected president. He succeeded in convincing his peers to accept the Six Points because the party practiced pluralism and its procedures allowed debate and contest of ideas.

This is a far cry from the state of affairs today. In the last two AL Councils, the party adopted resolutions that the party chief's decision was also the party's decision, without any discussion. The BNP too passed similar resolutions in successive councils. Hence, it seems the two leading political parties of Bangladesh are shy to practice democracy internally. Any dissent with the party chief is sufficient reason for expulsion, even when the leader makes an error. The hopes and aspirations of ordinary citizens are never considered important enough for any deliberation.

The Mujibnagar Government was the first government of Bangladesh. It assumed office in trying times with no advance preparation for leading the liberation war and achieving independence. During the war, there was considerable divergence of views within AL and even within the cabinet. There was a strong challenge to Prime Minister Tajuddin Ahmad by Mujib's relatives, namely, Sheikh Fazlul Haq Moni and Abdur Rob Seraniabat. Faruk Aziz Khan, Tajuddin's Private Secretary, reports that Moni even sent an assassin to kill the PM. These anti-Tajuddin elements attempted to table no-confidence motions in both of the AL party councils held during the liberation war. As PM, Tajuddin did not try to silence his opponents but debated them in the first council in Siliguri and obtained a strong mandate from his peers. Thus, even in trying times where the tendency for many would be to deviate from democratic norms, Tajuddin depended on pluralism and democratic practices to strengthen his own position as well as that of the provisional government.

After the war and Bangabondhu's return to Bangladesh from imprisonment in (then) West Pakistan, those who had opposed Tajuddin during the liberation war drove a wedge between the two leaders by poisoning Mujib's ears. Mujib never found out from Tajuddin how the provisional government organised the liberation war and achieved independence. The rift became so difficult that Tajuddin resigned in 1974. Slowly, AL moved away from democratic norms; pluralism was no longer encouraged in party meetings. Then the Fourth Amendment to the constitution was passed by the parliament in January 1975 extinguishing multi-party democracy in Bangladesh and removing the Supreme Court's jurisdiction over the protection and enforcement of fundamental rights.

The assassination of Bangabondhu and his family on 15 August 1975 was probably the biggest setback to constitutional rule in Bangladesh. Rationally, one would expect that at a time of national crisis the national institutions would be sufficiently strong to follow the constitution and a successor would assume office according to the law. But that did not happen for two reasons.

First, the political apparatus that took over after Bangabondhu's death was led by Khandakar Mushtaque Ahmed, a senior leader of AL and a member of Mujib's cabinet. The politicians who supported Mushtaque were also from AL, including some cabinet ministers. This suggests that there was considerable dissatisfaction within the AL with Mujib's rule and those who joined Mushtaque's cabinet did not have problems with Mujib's murder. This automatically raises the question – would Mushtaque have succeeded had the AL practiced democracy within the party?

The second reason was that after the gruesome killings of Mujib and his family, the three defence service chiefs – hand-picked by Mujib – pledged support to Mushtaque without any consideration of their oath of office and constitutional obligations.

Bangabondhu's assassination triggered other events that seemed like a series of implosions of pent up frustrations after the trauma of the war and famine. In order to get some semblance of legitimacy for his rule, Mushtaque played the Islam card that had been successfully used by the British and the Pakistanis to divide and rule. But Mushtaque did not even last three months and was overthrown by a coup on 3 November, led by Khaled Musharaf. Before leaving office, Mushtaque ordered the assassination of the four leaders of the Mujibnagar Government in Dhaka Central Jail in order to eliminate any future political challenge for himself and his extra-constitutional actions. A mutiny in Dhaka, initiated by the Jatiyo Samajtantrik Dal (JSD) – a socialist political party created in 1972 by disaffected AL youth – ended Khaled Musharaf's reign on 7 November, accompanied by a frenzy of killings in Dhaka Cantonment. Khaled Musharaf was killed by mutinous soldiers and Ziaur Rahman took control of the army, quickly distancing himself from JSD. Politics in Bangladesh had become deadly.

Zia's reign was marked by more than twenty mutinies, some quite bloody. One could argue that the mutinies helped Zia consolidate his position as he was the only person who could stand before the mutineers and convince them to give up their rebellion. But the situation eventually became unmanageable for Zia. He hanged Col. Abu Taher, a war hero and a leader of JSD, who led the 7 November 1975 mutiny that brought Zia to power. The evidence against Taher was mostly concocted and his trial by a special martial law tribunal was held inside the jail in camera without any observers. Eventually, Zia's regime executed more than a thousand soldiers. The defendants were tried in martial law tribunals where each trial lasted about ten minutes and they could not appeal against the capital punishment.

After consolidating his position in the army, Zia assumed the country's presidency in April 1977. To legitimise his rule, he sought a mandate through a referendum in May 1977 that was largely rigged by state agencies. The results showed that Zia had 99 per cent approval which even he found hard to believe. Zia understood that Bangladesh could not be ruled by military power alone and, at some point, he would be challenged politically by AL. Although the party had suffered a terrible setback after the assassination of its principal leaders – some of who were also the nation's founders – it was still the largest political party whose tentacles reached every town and village. Zia prepared himself to meet that challenge under his terms rather than allow his opponents to take the initiative. Using state agencies, he put together a coalition of politicians and political parties that included both the left as well as the ultra-right, and the BNP was born. Many AL members who had joined Mushtaque now joined Zia.

In order to keep street agitation under control, Zia had to allow political activity and eventually a national election. These actions were seen favourably by the media, who gave Zia credit for restoring multi-party democracy. A close examination of BNP's constitution, however, shows that within the party all decision-making powers lay with the party chairman with little scope for collective decision making. Zia only appeared to be benevolent but was actually an autocrat who did not attach much importance to democratic norms. Zia's assassination in 1981 by some military officers was the outcome of the stress between the freedom fighters and repatriated officers in the army which cleared the path for Hussain Muhammad Ershad's military rule.

Ershad's rule was marked by unprecedented corruption, moral turpitude and divisive politics. It was similar to that of the military rulers of Pakistan in that he used Islam for political purposes and made a mockery of all national institutions. As dictator, his style of governance was oligarchic, characterised by cronyism and nepotism. He got away with it for nine years but in the end, even the army abandoned him and he was overthrown after a popular uprising in 1990.

After Ershad's ouster, elections were held under a non-partisan caretaker government and won by the BNP, although not with an absolute majority. After the restoration of parliamentary democracy in 1991, there was a period where activities inside the parliament were marked by lively debates and it appeared that parliamentary democratic practices were once again taking root in Bangladesh. In 1994, the loss of an AL candidate who was expected to win in a by-election in Magura in an AL-held seat brought the issue of fair elections to the forefront. AL wanted national elections under a non-partisan caretaker government and after a period of prolonged strikes and a virtual shut-down of the economy, the Thirteenth Amendment that provided for a non-partisan caretaker government during national elections was adopted in March 1996. AL won the election that followed and was able to form a coalition government that served its full term of office. Thus, between 1991 and 2009, the two major political parties alternated in forming governments when elections were supervised by caretaker regimes. In 2014, the Supreme Court ruled that the caretaker government system was unconstitutional because it was not elected by the people. However, the Court observed that the system could be continued for two more elections but the AL Government scrapped it even before the full written judgment was made available. As a result, the BNP did not participate in the elections of 2014 because they feared rigging – the same fear the AL had in 1996 about participating in elections under BNP rule.

This resulted in an election where more than half the MPs returned to parliament without any electoral contest.

Although the popular uprising in 1990 re-established parliamentary democracy in Bangladesh, the system leaves much to be desired. Apart from inter-party issues, there is also the culture of sycophancy within each party. This problem became quite acute in the second terms of both party chiefs – 2001–6 for the BNP's Khaleda Zia and 2009–14 for the AL's Sheikh Hasina – as their sons entered politics as aspirants to lead their respective parties after their mothers retire. Sycophancy is so deeply entrenched in both political parties that local party members of a constituency have no say on who their party nominee shall be in a local government election. This problem became clear especially during the caretaker government of 2007–9, when several politicians sought reform of the political system with the help of the military. Unable to present and pursue their views on important issues within party forums, these reformers convinced the military to implement the 'minus two' policy that would send the party chiefs into exile and bar them from Bangladesh politics – a bold but unsuccessful move. Thus, democracy in Bangladesh starts and ends with elections.

Elections

On 7 March 1973, two years after Bangabondhu's historic speech at Dhaka's Ramna Race Course, Bangladesh held its first national election under its new constitution. The AL government's performance in the first year of independence left much to be desired and the general expectation was that it would not be able to sweep the elections like it did in 1970. Nevertheless, there was no doubt that the party would win an overwhelming majority because of Mujib's stature and the party's role in the liberation war. Still, pre-election campaigns showed that the National Awami Party (NAP) and JSD were drawing large crowds. Most people felt that there would be a meaningful opposition in the parliament. Vigorous debates in the parliament would in turn reduce the need for street agitation as well as nurture the nascent democracy. Mujib, however, wanted a landslide victory and the AL bigwigs decided to ensure it, fair or foul. When the election results were announced, AL was declared victorious in 291 seats in the 300-seat parliament. In several constituencies, the opposition candidate only lost in the last minute after leading the vote count all night. The results were simply not credible.

Similarly, the referendum, presidential and national elections held during the Zia and Ershad years were all rigged and some results were downright comical. On the other hand, national elections held under caretaker governments between 1991 to 2009 saw incumbent governments unable to return to power. In the opinion of national and international observers, elections conducted under the caretaker governments were fair and acceptable barring a few isolated irregularities. But the national election of 2014 cannot even be accepted as an election since the majority of the MPs came to the parliament without an electoral contest.

Bangladesh implemented the system of caretaker government because of the weaknesses of the Election Commission (EC). Instead of the caretaker government, as a permanent solution to the election crisis, the country should have reformed and strengthened the EC as an independent constitutional body with adequate resources and power backed by strong laws. In fact, in 2017, the issue of EC Act came to the forefront again before the appointment of the incumbent Commission. In the end, the EC took its oath of office without the passage of the law.

Ideally, Election Commissioners should be people of integrity who will not succumb to inducements or threats. At the same time, the EC needs resources in terms of personnel, material and money to perform their task successfully. Effective laws are necessary so that the EC has adequate powers to take action against anyone who violates the election laws and rules. In reality, successive ECs have not been able to meet this standard. A notable exception was the EC headed by Shamsul Huda from 2007 to 2012. They corrected the voters' list and detected almost ten million fake voters. They conducted successful national and local elections. On the recommendation of the Huda Commission, changes were brought in the election rules enhancing the powers of the EC so that it may take action against errant officials as well as others who don't play by the rules, including disqualifying rogue candidates. The subsequent EC, however, proposed to the government to take back some of its powers. This indicated that the EC was still subservient to the executive branch and it lost public confidence.

Logic dictates that if any candidate exceeds the spending limits set by election laws and rules, he or she should be disqualified. And if such a person wins, the result of that constituency should be declared invalid. This standard is never applied in Bangladesh. Using this benchmark, every election victory in Bangladesh could be termed as illegal because spending limits were exceeded by everyone. Yet we know of no case where an election result was nullified by the EC because the victor exceeded spending limits. The importance of setting limits has special significance in former colonies like Bangladesh where the distribution of wealth is skewed and expensive elections are the most effective barrier of entry into politics. Today, a competent and honest candidate with good ideas cannot even participate in elections because he or she is unable to raise the required money.

One can argue that the root of all corruption in Bangladesh is expensive elections. Being elected to office guarantees many benefits including protection from legal proceedings and new money-making opportunities that are not always legal. Consequently, many underworld dons and tax-evading businesspeople buy nominations in national and local body elections. Grapevine reports suggest that the average purchase price for a nomination in the 2014 national election supposedly exceeded fifty million takas (more than £500,000). And this practice of selling nominations exists in all major political parties. In addition to the money used to buy the nomination, millions are spent in buying votes or for bribing local officials to look the other way when the candidate violates electoral rules or commits other irregularities.

Once elected, goodies flow to the MP like an overflowing river, that include licenses for regulated businesses such as banks, insurance companies, finance companies, TV and radio stations, international gateways and other government contracts. As a result, the MP who buys his or her nomination sees the electoral expense as a business investment that yields high returns for the next five years. The elected MP has little interest in matters of national policy or the passage of laws. He or she is completely focused on becoming the effective ruler of his or her area by establishing control through muscle power, if need be. It is not unusual for MPs to demand exorbitant amounts from their constituents for any help they render in resolving problems with government agencies. People who are unable to pay end up selling their homesteads or agricultural lands to the MP at throwaway prices. This explains why, after becoming an MP, an individual also becomes one of the biggest landowners in his or her constituency.

It is therefore important to consider what citizens can do to make elections fair so that money alone shall not decide future outcomes. If the situation has reached the point of no return, then the country's future leaders shall have to consider whether elections need to be publicly funded from the national exchequer, so that wealthy individuals and big corporations do not unfairly influence the vote. Perhaps the use of private money in national and local elections also needs to be banned so that politicians who run for office will have any reason to ask for money or raise it in a non-transparent manner. With unlimited private funds cut off from elections, politicians shall not have the resources to maintain their musclemen who are responsible for most of the election-related violence. But this can only happen when the people of Bangladesh realise that the present system of elections does not serve the interests of ordinary citizens and only benefits a tiny fraction of the population.

The Legislature

Bangladesh's first legislature was the Constituent Assembly of 1972, composed of representatives elected in 1970, before independence. The draft constitution was placed before the Constituent Assembly on 11 October 1972 and the constitution was adopted on 4 November after less than a month of debate, which was insufficient. Notably missing was any public discussion to accompany the parliamentary deliberations. Although the constitution embraced the noblest of ideas, the real question was how these would be upheld in everyday life – which remained undefined because of the lack of debate.

Then, the Second Amendment curbed the fundamental rights of citizens in periods of emergency and the Fourth Amendment ended multi-party democracy and removed the Supreme Court's jurisdiction over the protection of individual rights. Thus, many of the checks and balances between the legislature, executive and judiciary that are essential for the effective functioning of a democracy were lost. The Fifth Amendment gave indemnity to Mujib's assassins. Subsequent amendments gave legal cover to Ershad's various unconstitutional actions. In 2012, the Supreme Court ruled that martial law is unconstitutional and anyone who tries to impose it by ousting a constitutional government is liable to be charged with high treason. Yet, the court did not order that Ershad be tried for the usurpation of a constitutional government and for imposing martial law. Perhaps this was because he was a special envoy and ally of the PM at that time. In 1988, Ershad passed the Eighth Amendment that proclaimed Islam as state religion when this was clearly at variance with one of the pillars of the constitution – secularism. None of these constitutional amendments came about because of public demands but were made to strengthen the ruler's hand.

The Bangladesh legislature never became the Westminster-style parliament after which it was modelled. Vigorous substantive debates in parliament are rare. One can argue that this is because Article 70 of the constitution that prohibits floor-crossing in parliament. Abstention from voting along party lines is also prohibited, even when MPs feel that the government is making an error or when their conscience cannot support a bill because the majority of voters in their constituency are against the government's position or the provisions of the bill are detrimental to their constituents. Some constitutional scholars have argued that Article 39(1) which guarantees the freedom of thought and conscience to every citizen prevents an MP from acting according to his or her conscience in the parliament. The curiosity here is that no MP has ever invoked Article 39(1) to defend his or her disagreement with the party line. But it is ultimately Article 70 that prevents parliament from becoming the national repository of open debate. Experts also argue that this article encourages sycophancy because MPs have no choice but to follow their party's dictates. The best an MP can do in the parliament is to participate in the question-and-answer period and make periodic appeals for development projects in his or her constituency.

The MP is everything to his or her constituents but a parliamentarian. MPs spend all their time and effort in establishing rule in the constituency with little interest in parliamentary matters. This explains why MPs were so vehemently opposed to allow elected Upazilla Parishads (UPs, local government bodies) to function even though the UP elections were held before the national elections in 2009. It took more than a year after the elected government assumed office for the UPs to become operational, and only after the law was changed to make the local MP an advisor in the

UP. No elected government has ever taken any initiative to frame local government laws although Articles 59 and 60 contain provisions for municipal and local governments. It was the caretaker government of 2007–9 that held local government elections in the face of MPs who were unwilling to dilute their authority, even in favour of local leaders from the same party.

Many MPs abhor attending parliamentary sessions. There are several instances when the scheduled sessions could not start on time because of a lack of quorum. After the restoration of parliamentary democracy in 1991, there was a brief period when both the treasury bench and the opposition attended parliament sessions and the proceedings were livelier Then the opposition resigned from the parliament to demand fresh elections under the caretaker government. After these elections, when a new government took office and the incumbents became the opposition, they stopped attending parliament sessions.

The Executive

To accomplish their colonial objectives, the British ensured public order at the cost of individual rights – opportunities for Indians were restricted. Arbitrary official decisions and extreme state violence was used whenever the natives attempted to organise to improve their lot. No consideration was given to the plight of the natives as long as profits from colonial rule were remitted to Britain. An exploitative land revenue administration through a system of Zamindars, other landlords, and the colonial bureaucracy who saw themselves as masters of India kept the colonial machinery running. The system largely employed Indians and only a small of number of British people actually lived and worked in the subcontinent. In return, the collaborating Indians were rewarded with money, titles and more money-making opportunities at the expense of ordinary Indians. Even after the first Indian provincial elections under the India Act of 1935, the elected premier of a province was not able to protect the interests of his electorate if it clashed with the interests of the colonial masters. This is what caused the Great Bengal Famine of 1943 which claimed three million lives. The Bengal Premier, A. K. Fazlul Haq, fought tooth and nail with the Governor and Viceroy to stop the Denial and Scorched Earth Policies that removed country boats and excess food stocks from the Bengal countryside, which resulted in the Great Bengal Famine. Haq was forced to resign – the Muslim League and the Governor of Bengal conspired to bring down his ministry so that Denial and Scorched Earth could continue.

After the partition of India and against the expectations of most Pakistanis, the Pakistani regime did not dismantle the colonial administrative and legal systems. Pakistan used the colonial setup to exploit the Bengalis of East Pakistan for twenty-four years after partition. After their independence, Bangladeshis expected the colonial mindset to end and a true republic to take form as articulated in the Mujibnagar Government's declaration of independence. But no government has yet deemed it fit to dismantle the colonial system. As a result, the state has unlimited powers to deal with its citizens arbitrarily and inflicting tremendous violence including incarceration and death on those the government considers as enemies.

Since the birth of Bangladesh, all heads of government were strongmen and women, irrespective of whether it was a presidential or Westminster form of government. Their leadership style was invariably authoritarian. Bangabondhu Sheikh Mujibur Rahman had no peers in his party and his wishes became party dictates. Those who joined the BNP at its birth were either first-time politicians or discredited ones because of their anti-Bangladesh role during the liberation war. They rode on Zia's coattails to win their parliamentary seats. Besides, the BNP constitution vested all powers with the party chairman. The same was true of Ershad, whose power was absolute and could not be questioned in any forum. After the restoration of parliamentary democracy in 1991, the leaders of both major political parties have enjoyed similar levels of absolute power. Even bodies that have a constitutional mandate to act independently, such as the Election Commission, subordinate themselves to the executive branch even though this violates their oath of office.

Within this sycophantic political culture, it is the sycophants who become the leader's gatekeepers and use the leader's office for personal gain through corrupt practices. This explains why the current finance minister of Bangladesh stated in parliament that he is unable to act against those who manipulated the stock market and conned hundreds of thousands of unsuspecting small investors of their life's savings because such individuals are too powerful. All major incidents of fraud, including the cyber heist at the Central Bank where US$100 million were embezzled, are examples of the impunity enjoyed by these gatekeepers. Because of their ability to dish out favours in the form of government contracts at inflated prices, they attract flocks of admirers. Infrastructure projects are plagued with cost overruns. The construction cost of one kilometre of a paved road in Bangladesh is several times higher than that of Western European countries. What is notable is that the scale of corruption with each successive political government exceeds that of its predecessor. The consequence is of course fewer roads, hospitals, schools, and other facilities for ordinary citizens.

The bureaucracy has adapted well to the political culture of winner-takes-all. Bureaucrats oblige their political masters willingly even if doing so violates their sworn professional duty because corruption allows them to prosper. Political masters have no problem in accepting this practice as long as the official concerned shares the spoils with party loyalists. Given that politics is dominated by the two major political parties and both parties have won elections and formed governments on more than one occasion, the bureaucracy is also split along party lines. It is now standard practice to send hundreds of government officials to oblivion as 'officers on special duty' (OSD) as soon as a new political party forms a government because they were loyal to the other side. Even if an official is not made an OSD, it is not uncommon for those who were favoured or had important assignments in the previous government to be deprived of professional advancement or any meaningful responsibility. Thus, at any given time, hundreds of government officials remain in service with full pay and benefits while they perform no work, year after year, within an environment where the quality and delivery of public service is already poor. Yet, every government in Bangladesh has explained this away as a problem of paucity of personnel while hundreds of civil servants vegetate as OSDs.

This political culture requires a lot of muscle power to crush dissent and silence criticisms. The student wing of whichever political party is in power, backed by law enforcement agencies, provides that muscle. As soon as a new government takes office, its affiliated student party takes control of all public universities and colleges without holding any student union elections although this is contrary to the law. Non-affiliated students are forced to support the government-backed student political party, or else the privileges due to them from the university are withheld. Ruling-party student leaders not only determine which of their peers get to live in residential halls or receive other benefits from the university – they also control the procurement process and even have a say on which new faculty member gets hired. Armed with machetes, iron rods, sticks, and even guns, ruling-party student activists frequently attack their rivals in campuses as a demonstration of their political power. Because of such violence, public universities and colleges are often closed down and campuses emptied to bring the situation under control. Students and even faculty members become victims of violence but the perpetrators never have to face the consequence of their actions. In one public university, a ruling-party student leader celebrated his hundredth rape with a feast! Public university vice chancellors are the principal patrons of government-backed student political parties who often subordinate their judgment to the demands of these students. The student leaders are almost never good students, and seldom have qualities that would endear them to the general students. Furthermore, the government-backed student political parties take control of underworld activities in and around the campus. The problem is not limited to educational institutions only as these regime-propping 'students' have penetrated city neighbourhoods as well as villages.

With the cooperation of bureaucrats, student 'activists' and law enforcement agencies, the political party in power quickly establishes complete control over the country. Even legitimate demands by workers for higher wages or better conditions are met with police violence, including fatal shootings. Custodial deaths due to 'heart attack during interrogation' or 'cross fire' are reported in the media with frightening regularity. Given that businesspeople constitute about half of the ruling-party MPs, the government invariably sides with corporate interests against workers, villagers or any other groups that dare protest for their legitimate rights. According to the media, the underworld drug trade in Bangladesh today is controlled by a syndicate of politicians, policemen and ruling-party activists. The recent shooting and death of four people in Banskhali, Chittagong, who protested against the setting up of a coal-fired private power plant in their area is an illustration of what happens when public interest clashes with big business interests. In Ashulia and Savar

Export Processing Zone (EPZ), law enforcers killed workers who demanded timely disbursement of pay and benefits – using the four-wheel drive vehicles that the Bangladesh Garment Exporters and Manufacturers Association (BGEMA) gave to the newly set up industrial police.

This unholy alliance between big business and the executive may take any action against their opponents including assassinations. In the post-1991 political scenario, many journalists were killed and investigations have not shed any light on the perpetrators. Consider the case of the home minister of a previous government who facilitated, under instructions from the PM's son, the grenade attack on the leader of the opposition and a former PM – with the police helping indirectly. The perpetrators then framed an ordinary poor villager for the attempted assassination. Recently, officials of the Rapid Action Battalion (RAB), an elite law enforcement agency, assassinated seven people in Narayanganj in a private contract killing. The RAB battalion commander behind these murders is the son-in-law of a sitting cabinet minister who was convicted in a corruption case himself that was upheld by the Supreme Court. The minister continues to serve in government with no regard to the verdict. The ward commissioner who contracted the RAB personnel for these murders is a follower of a ruling party MP on whose behalf the PM spoke in parliament even before the matter was investigated.

As a result of this environment, ordinary people do not receive the service that they should from the government. Often, loyalty to the ruling political party determines whether or not one is served but, in some cases, even being a party loyalist may not be enough. One has to know the right person in the party hierarchy. Even duly elected local governments UPs cannot function autonomously. While the constitution gives local governments taxation powers, UPs have no independent sources of revenue other than the payments they receive from leasing out markets. Consequently, UPs are in no position to provide much of the services that people need although they are the closest government to the citizens of Bangladesh. All important matters of local significance such as the administration of agricultural programmes or improvement of schools or management of public hospitals are determined by relevant ministries and departments of the national government in Dhaka, resulting in poor service delivery. The field officers of different ministries and departments of the national government have no reporting obligations to the UP.

The number of people a government can serve effectively depends on the size of the population and the nature of services. Municipal services and others, including education, health, public safety and security and regional communication, are best facilitated by local governments. Presently, the UP and the newly created Zilla Parishad (elected indirectly from UP members) are the only local government bodies. They are hamstrung by a multitude of problems. There is no instance in the world where a single government has been able to serve 160 million people satisfactorily. Most countries have several tiers of local government, each providing a limited number of services. If Bangladesh were to upgrade its current administrative divisions into provinces with their own government, legislature, and high court, each province would have an average population of 20 million, bigger than the population of many countries. If this were the case, many of the functions of ministries today could be transferred to the provinces, thereby improving the quality and delivery of public services. Although the two major political parties have no interest in such matters, it could benefit them as well. If a major political party is unable to form a national government, it could still form one or more of the provincial governments. And as long as a political party has one or more provinces where it is in power, it shall not be tempted to undertake insane political programmes such as attacking public buses with Molotov cocktails.

The Judiciary

Articles 95, 96 and 97 of the 1972 constitution envisaged an independent judiciary. It was expected that in the years to come the safeguards for judicial independence would be strengthened and consolidated but that did not happen. Subsequent constitutional amendments diluted the courts' independence. While the constitution clearly stated that judges shall be independent, the lower courts and the magistracy remained under the executive for a long time and are now under the Ministry of Law and Parliamentary Affairs. The first law commission headed by Justice Kamaluddin Ahmed, formed in 1976, suggested a three-point implementation process so that, step by step, the judiciary would become fully independent. The government did not implement the Ahmed Commission's recommendations. Since 1991, both major political parties included separation of the judiciary and repeal of black laws (or provisions that infringe on a citizen's fundamental rights) in their election manifestos, but never actually restored the courts' independence when they were in government.

Separation of the judiciary does not technically require any constitutional amendment or passage of any new laws because the 1972 constitution empowered the president of the republic to formulate rules for the judiciary. But the president, elected by the parliament, has no independent powers to act without the advice of the PM. This effectively limits the president's ability to formulate rules on the judiciary unless the PM desires it. The caretaker government of 2001 drafted the necessary rules for separating the judiciary but did not act upon it because, after winning the election, the BNP vowed to implement it. Then the BNP broke this promise – nothing new. In 1999, the Appellate Division of the Supreme Court, in a case ruling, instructed the government to frame the rules for the separation of the judiciary. The government of the day dragged its feet. The law minister at that time, a senior lawyer of the Supreme Court, stated to the press that the ruling would take six to seven years to implement. In February 2006, the Appellate Division rejected the government's petition for an extension after allowing 26 adjournments over a period of seven years. Finally, in February 2007, the caretaker government amended relevant sections of the Criminal Procedure Code (CPC) and formulated the necessary rules to grant limited independence to the judiciary.

Meanwhile, the present structure of the judiciary cannot effectively deliver justice to the population if not for any other reason other than the number of pending cases that far exceeds what the courts can handle. Even if the number of courts and benches are doubled, the backlog would not be cleared within a reasonable time. And court procedures contribute to this delay significantly. Nowhere are the vestiges of colonialism more visible in Bangladesh than the lower and magistracy courts. Invariably, the physical facilities are inadequate for the number of people who have to go to court for justice or have to work there. Many of the cases filed before the courts are trivial and should be dismissed after a review of the plaint or the charge but, in reality, that does not happen. The colonial era laws and procedures make arrest and detention relatively easy for the state. Bail is not only a tradable commodity for the lawyers but also for court officials and costs can be quite substantial for the average person. Those who are unable to pay languish in jail.

Several surveys have shown that the people of Bangladesh rank the judiciary at the same level as the police when it comes to corruption. In criminal cases, the most compelling evidence against a defendant in Bangladesh is the confession made by the defendant while in remand – usually after torture by investigators. Although such confessions are not valid in a proper court and should be thrown out in a trial, in many cases they remain as evidence even when there is no corroboration. This is especially true for poor defendants. Public defence lawyers are ineffective in defending the poor because their continuation of service eventually depends on the state.

Protest

Bangladesh cannot be governed by laws that only benefit the ruler at the cost of the masses – a legacy of colonial rule. Concurrently, the country's biggest problem is endemic corruption. The caretaker government of 2007–9 tried to tackle this in an isolated manner and failed. Given that the root of all corruption is in the manner in which elections are financed, the easiest way to deal with this problem would be to adopt a system of publicly-funded elections.

At the same time, repressive laws that limit citizens' fundamental rights have no place in an independent country. In the past, Bangladeshi leaders have tried to deal with national problems by limiting the fundamental rights of citizens but experience shows such methods do not work. They make the government more tyrannical, leading to its downfall and replacement by an equally autocratic opposition.

Periodic cycles of political violence are a trait of contemporary Bangladesh. Invariably, the government of the day sees such problems through the prism of law and order. Consequently, the resulting measures may diffuse the tension temporarily but do not resolve the underlying problem. Real solutions require addressing the underlying social and economic inequities that caused the unrest in the first place. Or the problem manifests in many forms at different times, just as it did when the country was part of Pakistan. The Pakistan government did not address the underlying causes of the Bengalis' dissatisfaction. Instead, it unleashed its army on the Bengali population, leading to the breakup of Pakistan.

Yet there are reasons to be optimistic about the future. The economy is growing and the majority of Bangladeshis are young. They want and deserve a better future than their parents. If one considers the voting patterns in the 1991–2009 period, when elections were held under the caretaker government, neither of the two major political parties were able to win consecutive elections. This suggests that both political parties need the votes of non-partisan citizens and swing voters to win elections. But once a party wins an election and forms a government, it seems to forget about the aspirations and demands of the swing voters. This causes the swing voters to choose the opposition in the next election, suggesting that the ruling party is unable to convert them into party loyalists.

Non-partisan citizens are not as helpless as one may think – their views may even be more important than party loyalists for winning elections. The Bangladesh electoral pie may be sliced into three parts, with the two main political parties taking a slice each. The third slice is made up of swing voters. Hitherto, they have not demanded specific reforms from the major political parties. But they have the potential to change the situation dramatically if they can organise themselves and collectively negotiate the terms for their support with one of the major parties. Unlike political parties, however, non-partisan citizens do not have the institutional and financial resources to organise events. However, in the digital age, these shortcomings are not as debilitating as they once were, given that Bangladesh now has more than 131 million mobile phone users. Mass protests mobilised through social media are not only possible but inevitable.

In any case, the country cannot continue on its well-trodden path of polarised political confrontation. Bangladeshis must find a way to live in peace with each other rather than living with a system marked by violence, widespread corruption and lack of the rule of law.

GARMENT WORKERS

Dina M Siddiqi

On 5 May 2013 leaders of the Hefazat-i-Islam ('Guardians of Islam'), an obscure coalition of Islamist groups, marched into the commercial centre of Dhaka city for an indefinite sit-in. It was their second such attempt in a month. Over the course of the day, the crowd swelled to an estimated half a million men and young boys, some barely out of adolescence. The occupation of Shapla Chattar, a plaza facing the headquarters of Bangladesh Bank, by several hundred thousand bearded, white-capped males waving sticks and/or Bangladeshi flags, was at once political theatre and a calculated show of force. This nationally televised performance sought to dramatise Hefazat-i-Islam's (HI) position as a powerful counterweight to the secular-nationalist protests unfolding just kilometres away at Shahbagh. The core demand of Shahbagh protestors was capital punishment for individuals found guilty of war crimes in the 1971 Liberation War. To its detractors, Shahbagh stood for atheists and bloggers intent on defaming Islam.

In its previous 'siege' of Dhaka, HI leaders presented the government with a 13-point charter, the contents of which reflected the group's objections to the Shahbagh movement as well as long-standing preoccupations with gender, morality and public space. Thus, along with demands to introduce an anti-blasphemy law and the death penalty for 'atheist bloggers', the 13-point charter called on the government to put a stop to 'free mixing' in public, using language that cast feminists as promiscuous bearers of alien values and immoral practices. HI also demanded cancellation of the National Women's Development Policy, an issue that had first brought it to the national spotlight in 2010. Notably, the charter incorporated some subjects typically raised by the women's movement – steps to prevent sexual harassment and violence against women and the elimination of dowry demands.

The sit-in ended anti-climactically, after state forces plunged the area into darkness, stopped live transmission and cleared the crowd overnight. Prime Minister Sheikh Hasina's government, it appeared, was willing to indulge groups like HI but only up to a point. It took this opportunity to shut down the two major Islamist-owned television stations. Regardless, the unprecedented number of supporters that HI had mobilised, drawn from a network of 25,000 *qawmi* or private madrasahs, unsettled liberal audiences. The spectacle of primarily working class male bodies – explicitly marked 'radical' Muslim – occupying the secular space of commerce would probably trigger liberal panic in most contexts today. For historical reasons, to many Bangladeshis this display of 'fundamentalist' Muslim masculinity carried an extra charge; it went against the very grain of national ontology.

In response, a coalition of women's groups organised a counter demonstration. Most speakers at the much smaller 11 May Women's Grand Rally hewed close to a conventional secular-liberal script: they condemned 'medieval mullahs', called for gender equality and the protection of working women's rights, and generally extolled the virtues of Bengali nationalism (in opposition to the religious nationalism of HI). Concern over the future of female garment workers, should Islamists come to power, formed a powerful subtext. For, if 'public mixing' were to be banned, what would happen to the garment industry in which women were compelled to work alongside male colleagues, supervisors and managers?

The singular focus the rally's organisers brought to bear on radical Islam/HI as the danger to women rang oddly hollow in some quarters. The rally took place just three weeks after the Rana Plaza collapse in which over 1,100 garment workers were killed, untold others had gone missing and many more were permanently maimed. Numerous families had already lost their main or only breadwinner. Few survivors had the means to gain access to treatment for physical injuries or mental trauma. In the midst of mourning, family members found themselves navigating intractable bureaucracies designed to stymie claims for compensation, which were minimal in any case. State indifference or complicity, along with transnational and local capital's relentless desire for profit were ultimately responsible for what transpired. The failure of the state's inspection apparatus allowed the owners of Rana Plaza to construct a nine-story building despite an inadequate foundation, flouting all existing safety regulations. On the fateful morning of the collapse, in the face of obvious cracks in the structure, banks and other commercial establishments housed in the building closed down operations. Only the five garment factories insisted workers come in or risk losing their wages.

Under the circumstances, it is not unreasonable to assume that most garment workers would not consider the HI to be their immediate or even primary adversary. In a sharply critical op-ed, longtime feminist activist Seuty Sabur observed that the women's counter rally felt more like a ritualistic affirmation of class solidarity than an active call to action. Sabur recalled that labour leader Nazma Akter had expressed a qualitatively different relationship to religion than her middle-class counterparts. Indeed, in her comments, Akter sought to complicate feminist politics premised on liberal notions of religion as always already regressive, patriarchal, and by definition against women's interests. By highlighting the class-specific concerns of poor factory workers, Akter foregrounded the differential interests hidden in the ostensibly unitary category of 'woman'. She reminded the audience that for many garment workers, madrasas were hardly objects of fear; indeed, the lack of day care options made them especially appealing. The latter provided shelter and food and, most significantly, guaranteed safety unlike the slums in which most workers were forced to live. Akhter's comments went unremarked for the most part, perhaps because they brought into sharp relief unstated tensions between class and gender and unsettled the standard liberal feminist script.

I have narrated this episode in some detail because it illuminates the many fissures around class embedded in Bangladeshi liberal politics. It is also telling of the way that historical concerns over religion and nation are transposed unproblematically onto other times and spaces. Older nationalist preoccupations set the terms of public debate so that the political imagination itself is narrowed. Thus, some readings of the relationship between women's interests and religion are amplified while others are minimised or erased.

Veiling as nationalist anxiety

Religion, or rather Islam, and dominant strands of nationalism sit awkwardly together in Bangladesh. Independence in 1971 came after the (West) Pakistani state launched a brutal war against its Bengali speaking citizens in East Pakistan (now Bangladesh), ostensibly to 'save' Islam. In the liberal-nationalist imaginary, then, religious forces are always already anti-liberation. Contemporary manifestations of Islam in the public sphere tend to be read back through this lens. Thus, the HI march constituted a serious threat to (an already fragile) secular sovereignty, the sign of a menacing future based on a past not quite vanquished. At the same time, the liberalist impulse embedded in nationalist politics means that Islam in particular comes to be represented as the shadowy other of democracy, freedom and women's rights. The language of 'medieval' mullahs with 'feudal' mindsets is illuminating in this respect. It evicts certain kinds of Muslims from secular time, relegating them to a space that is by definition backward and atavistic. The war on/of terror and its associated discourses that turn Islam itself into a 'security threat' – the 'securitisation' of Islam – have only intensified this ostensible clash between secularism (assumed to be good for women) and Islam (read backward, confining and oppressive for women).

Bengali ethno-nationalism has been challenged on multiple fronts since independence. Among other things, the contested and unsettled relationship between the nation-state and religion in majority Muslim Bangladesh has undergone considerable transformation. If, at an earlier moment, the question was whether Islam has a place in the nation, today it is not whether but which form of Islam is most appropriate. The effect is to symbolically excise religious minorities from the body politic. Islam was declared the state religion in 1981. The representational practices and political vocabulary of the state and most political parties are explicitly Muslim. In addition, the emergence of Islamic print media and TV stations, the proliferation of madrasas, including a large number for girls, and a dramatic rise in women's veiling since the 1990s attest to an overtly Muslim public culture. The rising popularity of Islamic reading/discussion groups – *talim* and *tafsir* – across the class spectrum corresponds to a certain 'democratisation' of religious authority. Most visible in matters of dress, understandings of religious 'authenticity' increasingly tilt toward a standardised, textualised and 'Wahhabi' version of Islam. Other ways of being Muslim – such as visiting shrines or celebrating the Prophet's birthday – are under strain or discredited.

Middle Eastern money, and the forces of globalisation – especially migration and access to electronic media – are often cited as the main factors behind this turn to 'orthodoxy.' It should be noted, however, that globalisation in the form of neoliberal capitalism has also produced extraordinary wealth for a few. Women who belong to this tiny cosmopolitan world form part of a larger transnational class. Their structural location affords them privacy and protection from the public gaze. Some are veiled (there are several high-end hijab stores in affluent sections of Dhaka city) but most are not. Women in form-fitting jeans and skimpy tops are common enough but they tend to be invisible as they travel from home to work to clubs and dinners in their SUVs and luxury sedans. The sexualisation and commodification of bodies such as these rarely generates liberal apprehension. In contrast, in its early years the new veiling produced profound unease along with a sense of puzzlement. Liberal women's groups were unable to comprehend why any woman, especially someone educated, would willingly take on a practice that to the former represented the antithesis of modernity and emancipation.

An anecdote to illustrate my point. Several years ago, when women's veiling first became a public issue, a rumour began to circulate: the Jamaat-i-Islami (JI) – a political party directly involved in collaborating with the Pakistani army in 1971 – now offered monthly stipends to students at a public university on condition they wear burqas. Here the veracity of the story is not as significant as the narrative logic behind it. The story is structured to make liberal sense of a practice that otherwise appears counterintuitive. The narrative rests on the assumption that donning a burqa is by definition against women's self-interest and no rational woman would do so in the absence of material incentives or strategic considerations. As the anthropologist Maimuna Huq puts it, in this discursive world, signs of religiosity can only be a 'disguise for secular concerns'. This reading precludes the idea that individuals can be moved to action through a genuine desire for piety. Further, since JI was involved, here veiling could also be construed as a sign of coming fundamentalism. Invoking a host of historically mediated fears, veiling as a visible sign of

Islamist forces not adequately dealt with in the past folds neatly into global discourses of Islamophobia.

Here it is worth recalling that during the struggle for independence, women's bodies had been central to securing the liberal state's secular credentials. The figure of the middle-class sari-clad woman critically differentiated secular Bengali ethno-nationalism from Pakistan's explicitly religious nationalism. Just as the former came to represent secular modernity and its promises, Bengali women in strikingly foreign styles of covering stand for the 'Arabisation' of national space and culture. Commerce and culture go hand in hand, of course. The streets of old Dhaka are dotted with stores selling burqas by national origin, presumably catering to the newly formed tastes of migrants returning from various Middle East countries. This dramatically different visual landscape cannot but jar secular sensibilities.

Today, covered women and girls are a common sight in urban and rural spaces. Burqas, hijabs and even the niqab are visible everywhere from doctor's offices to private universities and public recreational spaces. Secular-liberal women's groups have therefore been forced to grapple with the various practices of covering around them. Curiously, the country's largest and avowedly secular women's organisation, Bangladesh Mahila Parishad, now endorses World Hijab Day. This could read either as a reluctant admission of acceptance or the outcome of donor pressure to be 'inclusive'. (Both readings are speculation on my part).

Where do garment workers fit into the increasingly fraught performance of public piety, and overall increase in religiosity? Like all poor women, garment workers have long been the object of social disciplining. Anyone who lives in a slum is familiar with the ubiquitous 'NGO *apa*' (older sister, a term of respect for women). These agents of the developmental state and its non-governmental allies offer a range of pedagogical activities and programmes – from hygiene practices to the dangers of underage marriage – along with services such as legal aid and the extension of credit. The production of 'proper' neoliberal citizen-subjects is the ultimate objective of such attempts to re-engineer 'backward' social practices and cultural norms. More recently, a religious version of the NGO *apa* – the '*Talim apa*' – has also entered the scene. Female leaders of Talim or Tafsir reading groups, they too seek to re-shape subaltern subjectivities, in this case into 'proper' Muslim ones.

How garment workers negotiate these two poles – somewhat blurred with the advent of faith-based NGOs – in their daily lives is deeply inflected by the cultural and economic conditions under which the first generation of workers entered the industry. It is worth exploring the early days of the industry with conditions today.

'Matter out of place'?

Bangladesh's entry into the global garment industry in the early 1980s was the outcome of domestic policy shifts initiated by externally imposed conditions of structural adjustment. At this time, global financial restructuring and shifts in international trade agreements led to the relocation of manufacturing units from Euro-America to countries of the South. The appeal of places like Bangladesh as destinations for global capital lay in the assumed availability of 'low-cost' labour, preferably female. As it happened, Bangladesh did not have a reserve army of women waiting to be absorbed into industrial wage labour. On the contrary, unless they were desperate, 'respectable' women rarely worked for wages in the public domain. Middle and upper class urban women, often employed in professional services, lived rarefied lives not legible in everyday public spaces. Poor and middle class rural women engaged in economic activities located primarily in the domestic sphere.

Thus, for Bangladesh to compete globally, a reserve labour force had to be produced, economically and culturally. Remarkably enough, within a decade, around two million women and girls, primarily rural migrants, took up work in factories scattered across Dhaka and Chittagong. The negative connotations of factory work barely staunched the flow of women and young girls from rural areas. In the first place, uneven development, immiseration and dispossession in the countryside had already created the economic conditions for a mass exodus. The profile of the first generation of factory workers makes this evident. Defying expectations, it was not only the poorest who came to the city in search of work. Many were women from once affluent backgrounds, now forced to recalibrate their sense of self and their gendered obligations. Furthermore, factory owners actively enabled the process. They often turned to their village of origin to recruit a reliable (and pliable) labour force. As locally known figures, budding entrepreneurs provided cultural assurance to families concerned with the security and reputation of potential factory workers.

The relative ease with which this labour force was mobilised complicates debates on the (presumed inverse) relationship between practices of seclusion and poverty. Among other things, this speaks to the plasticity of cultural formations such *parda* (literally curtain; which can encompass a range of practices, from total physical seclusion to covering the head with a scarf or *orna*) and their imbrication in political economy. It also points to the limited analytical utility of the religion/secularism binary. In the context of rural Bangladesh, the political scientist Elora Shehabuddin observes in relation to her female interlocutors that contrary 'both to the charges of Islamists and the wishful expectations of secularists, such women do not see themselves as either rejecting religion or embracing a secular modernity'.

The first generation of factory workers had to negotiate multiple social and cultural complexities. Not only workers themselves but those around them had to be convinced of the legitimacy of the former's presence inside factories and in the spaces of the city. That is, both 'community' and 'self' needed to be recast. Until then, the streets had been the domain of men – of all classes – and very poor women, often sex workers. The presence of female workers commuting to work, hyper-visible in their density, disrupted conventional meanings and uses of urban public space. At the same time, women workers' earnings, in contrast to their unemployed male relatives, upset traditional conceptions of the *bhatar* (literally 'he who provides rice/food') or male breadwinner.

This emergent working-class initially encountered tremendous social stigma and hostility – from neighbours, strangers, religious authorities and even male colleagues. On the shop floor and on the streets, their presence signified the failure of their male relatives to live up to their role as breadwinners. Along with the male hostility this generated, workers had to contend with discourses of morality and sexuality inflected by class. Their presence on the streets after hours, in the dark, jeopardised their reputations as respectable women. The conditions of their work exposed women to verbal, physical and sexual harassment on the shop-floor and in other spaces. While the government and secular feminists lauded them as bearers of developmental modernity, both middle class society and religious leaders discursively constructed these women as immoral and dangerous. Although *waz mahfils* (religious lectures, often circulated as cassette and other recordings) condemning 'garment girls' circulated widely, for the most part, the social language of disapproval was not explicitly religious. The policing of women's bodies in public spaces was carried out not by religious authorities but by neighbourhood thugs, policemen and male passers-by with a strong sense of patriarchal entitlement.

In short, at this juncture, garment workers were, in the words of anthropologist Mary Douglas, 'matter out of place', the equivalent of 'cultural' dirt. Finding themselves under cultural assault, charged with being *bewarish* (literally, 'without a male guardian'), workers sought to remake a proper place for themselves. One way to navigate these conditions was through the discursive reworking of *parda*. Garment workers had no choice but to walk through public spaces coded male and dangerous. They did so with heads covered, gazes lowered, insistent on their 'good woman' status. In an effort to reclaim their purity, they shifted focus from spatiality to embodiment (self-disciplining marked on the body through a set of habits and dispositions). I have argued elsewhere that such aspirational identities were intimately bound up with 'secular' notions of sexual respectability. This of course cannot be easily disentangled from religious sentiment or religion as 'belief'. I should add that some workers resisted the entire endeavour, refusing to conform to what they considered bourgeois hypocrisy.

Workers' use of *parda* was not instrumental in the liberal-rational sense. The young girls and women I knew were profoundly hurt by the attacks on their morality. They had a deep investment in familiar ways of being in the world and experienced the hostility toward them as a form of violence. Rethinking the meanings of *parda* was a means of coming to terms with the moral injury to which they were now exposed. In any case, *parda* – like any other cultural/religious formation – is not a fixed thing or object, the form of which individuals change at will to accommodate new conditions of labour. Women workers were not free floating agents who could simply declare and so determine what counts as modesty or *parda* socially. This is a dialectical process, profoundly suffused with power, and the outcome of long-standing but contested discursive traditions.

Renegotiated modes of *parda* allowed workers to present themselves as self-regulating subjects, thereby muting some of the disapproval to which they were subjected. At the same time workers played up disciplinary regimes within factories to shore up their respectability. Put differently, workers reconstituted moral codes and social regulations in conjunction with specific forms of capitalist discipline that focused on the control of space, body and morality. These women exercised what I call 'reluctant' agency through the surveillance of their own bodies and those of other women.

Much has changed in the three decades since the first garment factories were set up. The sector has made spectacular gains; today, next to China, Bangladesh is the largest exporter in the world of low cost apparel. Valued at around US$27 billion, the industry brings in the lion's share of foreign exchange. It is also the single largest industrial employer in Bangladesh. Of an estimated four and half million garment workers, between seventy and eighty percent are female. Social stigma around 'garments girls' has abated considerably. The sight of young women commuting to and from work is no longer noteworthy; on the contrary, their presence has been incorporated into the visual landscape of the city and its environs. Garment workers are central to the national imagination, signifying progress and secular modernity.

The Islamisation of public culture referred to earlier does not appear to have affected women's decision to work in factories. Counter to liberal assumptions, *talim* and *tafsir* sessions evidently do not present work outside the home as barriers to being good Muslim women. Even so, the rise in public religiosity might lead one to expect increasing numbers of women in hijabs or burqas. The use of these forms of covering seem to be quite limited although some workers do use a small skull cap like piece of cloth beneath their *ornas* which, among other things, can help protect the hair from fabric dust. Why these forms of dressing remain limited in popularity remains an open question.

With some exceptions, studies of women and Islamisation in Bangladesh turn on the question of whether practices of covering liberate or oppress women. This, I suggest, is an unproductive and reductive line of inquiry. By its very structure, it gives religion an all-encompassing deterministic role. As a result, contemporary research on *parda* tends to be ahistorical and context-free. Further, *parda* is an important but not exclusive aspect of garment workers' lives and sense of self. As I have argued throughout this essay, 'religion' and 'culture' are enfolded into each other; they are not self-contained or stable categories. Thus, for garment workers, the meanings of *parda*, rooted in materiality, have shifted over time. My ethnographic encounters of twenty years ago offer up narratives that are distinct in critical ways from those found today.

Curiously little research exists on the relationship between the new religiosity and the lives of garment workers. Findings from the only study I could locate suggest garment workers today tend to reject the beliefs and practices of the previous generation, in favour of a textualised, more 'conservative' – and to them more authoritative – version of Islam. This is of a piece with the expansion of madrasas, and various *talim* and *tafsir* sessions geared toward slum populations. Most workers in a study by the anthropologist Samia Huq reported enjoying and feeling more knowledgeable about Islam through these sessions. For them, being a good Muslim entailed cultivating a pure *mon* (mind, heart, mentality), rather than observing the more ritualistic aspects of religious duty. Huq's interlocutors invoked 'religious rulings and social moorings' interchangeably in speaking of *parda*, recalling the folding of culture and religion that workers of an earlier generation had expressed to me. Reference to the 'purdah of the mind and the eyes' echoes the disciplining of the self and body that my own interlocutors called on to remake the contours of *parda*.

Nevertheless, there are some distinct differences on the place of *parda* in the construction of self. Twenty years ago, questions of what constitutes a good Muslim were not relevant; throughout my fieldwork, garment workers aspired to present themselves as good women, in opposition to *noshto* or fallen women. For an earlier generation, self-regulation was associated with the dangers of sexuality; the performance of religious ritual was not explicitly tied to ideas of the good woman. This shift in register reflects broader cultural shifts and the turn to public religiosity. In addition, there are methodological considerations. Religion could be more pronounced in Huq's study simply because that is what she set out to investigate, unlike my research which centred on the general experience of factory work among women who happened to be primarily Muslim.

Notably, not a single of the many high profile female labour leaders and organisers in the industry – among them Nazma Akhter, Kalpana Akhter, Mushrefa Mishu and Lovely Yasmin – cover their heads. This is striking given that most female politicians figures observe some kind of *parda*, if only to cover their heads with the ends of saris, in a nod to the public's apparent Muslim sentiments. I would venture to suggest that garment workers form a cultural exception of sorts. They constitute a potentially disruptive category, one that is useful to think with to complicate what it means to be a (Muslim) woman in Bangladesh today.

A celebratory national discourse obscures the many dark sides to the garment industry. Before turning to the subject of structural violence, it is worth dwelling on subaltern male resentment, which remains stubbornly entrenched. Anthropologist Hasan Ashraf reports that in the course of fieldwork in 2011, he came across a *waz mahfil* organised by male garment workers, in association with the disciples of the powerful and charismatic *pir* of *char monai*. Those who spoke at the *waz* recognised the economic imperatives that compelled women to work in factories. Their message was simple: at work, women should be appropriately covered, or veiled. More revealing however is the men's descriptions of female co-workers. I offer a snippet below. Suffice it to say, no translation can do justice to the original phrase in Bangla:

> *sno-powder-lipstick maikha dang dangiya haate, emon ekta bhab medam office e jaitechen.*

> All made up, powdered and lipsticked, marching ahead, limbs akimbo (that is, walking with no sense of propriety or modesty), as though madam (here a mocking reference to middle professional women) were off to the office.

This vivid description says more about the imagination of the male speaker than the reality of female workers. The statement is suffused with class-inflected male resentment. While there is grudging acceptance of the necessity of factory work, in the speaker's opinion women workers do not know their place in the social order. The implication is that not only do these 'upstart' workers wilfully transform themselves into desirable sexual objects, their confidence in public spaces indicates a misplaced sense of class superiority.

The men who profit, directly or indirectly, from the labour of women workers celebrate the latter unhesitatingly. In contrast, working class men have a more complex and layered relationship to their female co-workers. This is not surprising given that subaltern male social identities have been undermined in critical ways in the last few decades. It is the outcome of a development model that discursively foregrounds women and girls and devalues or marginalises poor men.

Structural violence and the limits of individual agency

Did the individual workers who entered the Rana Plaza complex on the morning of 24 April 2013 have the option of refusal? Well aware of the cracks in the building, they could have stayed home. That is, if they had been willing to lose not just the day's wages but also the three months of arrears they were owed; to risk being thrown out by their landlords for non-payment of rent; to have their store credit for basic supplies cut off, not to mention facing the consequences of unpaid school fees or unforeseen medical emergencies. They could have refused had they been willing to risk arbitrary dismissal and have their names circulated on a blacklist making it impossible to find another factory job in the locality. The stark choice that workers faced – between probable death or probable starvation/destitution – lays bare the myth of free choice empowerment. Focusing on individual consciousness renders invisible the webs of power through which workers make their lives meaningful.

In this backdrop, the sociologist Shelley Feldman, a long-time observer of the industry, remarks, 'women are increasingly viewed as disposable and redundant even as their labour is becoming central to imaginings of family maintenance and sustainability'. Rana Plaza forced the disposability of women workers to the surface of public consciousness.

Recall that Bangladesh's 'comparative advantage' is its cheap(ened) and relatively unskilled female labour force. Paradoxically, what is an advantage for the national economy can actually be fatal for the individual worker and any collective effort to address working conditions. If low labour costs are central to being globally competitive, then labour repression can be justified as a valid 'cost' of maintaining the nation's competitive edge. This line of argument becomes even stronger in a place like Bangladesh, where the economy is inordinately dependent upon the apparel export industry. Labour resistance can, and is, reframed as sedition or action that directly challenges the 'national interest'. Notably, the government reserves the right to prevent any demonstration or strike it deems 'disruptive' to the community or harmful to the 'national interest'. Suffice it to say, what counts as the national interest or as disruption is informed by the logics of power. A 2015 report by the International Labor Rights Forum states that 'workers describe a chilling web of social relations of intimidation and violence that spans factories and apparel companies, workers' communities, government agencies, law enforcement, and even their families. The effect of this web is that workers are silenced.' Blacklisting, physical and verbal intimidation and entanglement in false cases remain routine. In December 2016, sixteen hundred workers were fired and 1,500 workers were incriminated in false cases of vandalism and theft, following a movement for a higher minimum wage (which is currently below a living wage) as well as an end to verbal abuse and arbitrary dismissal.

Beyond sacred and secular violence

Over the past three years, HI has transformed itself into a formidable, if shadowy, force in Bangladeshi politics. It has taken credit for controversial changes in the language of school textbooks, made to reflect an explicitly Islamised national identity. A 2017 legal provision that allows – under extenuating circumstance – for the marriage of girls under 18, is rumoured to have been instigated by HI. Finally, in line with its earlier objection to sculptures in public spaces, the group is currently agitating for the removal of a newly installed figure of the goddess of justice on the Supreme Court premises. HI has petitioned the High Court to demolish the 'idol' which it claimed was part of a conspiracy to undermine Islam in Bangladesh.

Curiously, despite the sanction on 'free mixing', HI has had little to say about garment workers in particular. This is not surprising, given that Islamist parties in general are perfectly comfortable with neoliberal capitalism. They are also acutely aware of the significance of the garment sector to the national economy and are unlikely to actively deter women from factory work.

Does HI have any appeal for garment workers? Women interviewed in 2013 responded pragmatically to HI's charter. 'Who will feed our families if we stay home? Will the mullahs or anyone else who criticises us?' This is a familiar refrain, echoing past responses from poor women castigated for working in NGOs or factories. In a short phone conversation with me in March 2017, this is how Nazma Akter recalled the women's rally: 'Shafi [head of JI]? We're not afraid of people like him. Listen, the entire madrasah sector runs on our money. Our blood and sweat. Those who don't have any place to leave their children turn to madrasahs.' Once more, Akter reverses conventional wisdom, both the widespread assumption that Bangladeshi madrasas run on Middle Eastern money, and that they represent a prime threat for garment workers.

Women garment workers find themselves trapped – caught between the discursive politics of both Islamists and liberal-secular feminists as well as the neoliberal state's vacillating relationship to religion/Islam. The historical burden 'Islam' carries in both liberal-secular and Islamist imaginaries in Bangladesh complicates 'the woman question' for garment workers in contextually specific ways. Islamist groups such as the HI stake a claim on all women's bodies to promote their vision of an appropriate Bangladeshi Muslim nationalism. Liberal secular claims on the nation-state rely on foregrounding the dangers to women from religion tout court, to the exclusion of other factors. The ensuing terms of debate – set through the religion-secularism binary – occludes difference and narrows the political imagination. Consequently, liberal feminist fears for the future of garment workers can often seem misplaced. This is precisely why it is possible to mobilise large numbers of concerned citizens to a demonstration denouncing the government's latest child marriage policy (as mentioned earlier, rumoured to be a sop to the now powerful HI), while a competing rally just kilometres away, demanding the return of bodies of industrial workers killed in an on-site accident, had few takers.

Put differently, if secular logic recognises only 'religious violence' then it is only the secular state that can offer protection. Hence the liberal stress on secularism as a prerequisite for women's rights. This dualistic formulation misrecognises the sites and circuits of power, so that secular violence of the kind most garment workers face on a routine basis is rarely recognised as violence. Further the singular focus on religion as peril – to the exclusion of other factors – erases critical differences among women.

To clarify, my argument is not that if the HI came to power, garment workers will not be affected. They may well be. Rather, the relationship between women's interests and religion/Islam cannot be taken for granted. It is urgent to transcend the nationalist burden that allows some issues to be identified as fundamental feminist battles (child marriage) and others (for example, the persecution of labour activists by the state) as of secondary concern. This calls for dislodging easy oppositions between secular and religious violence. It is equally essential to illuminate the complex historical processes through which religion is secured as a 'social fact' rather than as a deeply politicised and unstable formation, steeped in relations of power.

PATRIARCHY AND PATRONAGE

Irum Shehreen Ali

I met Sultana Begum, a homemaker from a small village in Comilla district, during my research into democratic ideals and the realities of political participation in Bangladesh. During our interview, she unknowingly summarised the essence of women's experience of democratisation in the country. As she pulled her sari's *anchal* tightly over her head and tucked it behind her ear as many women in Bangladesh do, she smiled and gently asked me:

> Why are you talking to me about this? I am a woman, and these are men's matters. We might vote sometimes and have an older sister running things, but she is different. Some of the women have taken part in the local *parishad*, but it's very hard for them. What can they do? They try, but this is how things are for us. We still have to bribe, ask for favours from the big men and just hope we can feed our children.

Over time, Bangladeshi women's representation in politics and elected office has increased manifold. But it has not been transformed into true participation and agency. Their desire to partake in the political process is clear – millions have queued at polling booths for hours in the baking sun and monsoon rain and thousands have surpassed formidable barriers to put their names on ballots and serve their communities. However, though they believe strongly in democratic values, their view of the patriarchal social structure and political system is clear-eyed. While democratisation may allow women to participate in elections as voters and candidates, their ability to exercise political power is tempered by the inaccessibility of education, financial resources and mobility. They are deeply aware of the corruption, weak institutions and the zero-sum game of 'resource capture' played out by the victors after every election. They understand that with the exception of a very small elite, the majority of both female citizens and politicians do not have entry to the types of power networks, decision-making processes and policy implementation that create systemic socio-political change. In a patronage-driven political system predicated on the existence of a few powerful individuals hoarding resources meant for the many ('elite capture') and traditional hierarchies of power, the female political leaders of both main parties and their narrow coteries have no interest in widening women's access to politics. They would rather consolidate their power and perpetuate a duopolistic system that rewards undemocratic behaviour.

The female politician's job is made harder by the flawed, but essential, quota-based system of representation at both parliamentary and local government levels. One major effect is that the system makes it difficult to establish themselves as legitimate political actors. It also burdens them with far larger constituencies than their male colleagues. In a society governed by patriarchal norms, female politicians struggle to be efficacious against constant harassment, social approbation and hostility from male colleagues and local elites. The work is difficult, change is slow, and victories rare. But nevertheless, they persist.

Beyond the Begums

Since Bangladesh's independence from Pakistan in 1971, a cavalcade of military and civilian regimes that run the gamut from pure dictatorship to democratically-elected have governed the country. Sheikh Mujib, the father of the nation, founder of the Awami League (AL) party and the first Prime Minister, ruled until his assassination in a military coup in 1975. Instead of establishing the institutional bases of a democratic state, Mujib oversaw a centralised system dominated by personal alliances. The dictatorships of General Ziaur Rahman and General H. M. Ershad followed. Both regimes championed neo-liberal economic policies and a market-based development model promoted by the Bretton Woods institutions. During Ershad's regime, both the opposition parties, AL (headed by Mujib's daughter Sheikh Hasina) and the Bangladesh Nationalist Party (BNP), which had been established by Zia but was now led by his widow Khaleda Zia, created a broad-based anti-dictatorship movement. With the backing of civil society, media and much of the population, this movement ultimately deposed Ershad in 1990.

The new democratic era saw the establishment of a parliamentary system based on regular elections, conducted by a three-month neutral caretaker government headed by a non-partisan figure. The BNP won the first election in 1991, and alternated in power with AL via mostly free and fair elections. This period was marred by a failed and re-scheduled election in 1996, and a period of military-backed caretaker government in 2006-7. However, since AL's landslide victory in the 2008 general elections where they won 230 seats to BNP's 30, democratic accountability has dramatically declined. BNP has been all but decimated as a political force. AL did away with the caretaker system and replaced it with an ineffectual Election Commission. In 2013, it was the first party to be re-elected to a second term in office, but BNP and its allies did not contest the election, claiming that AL had rigged the process. The 2015 Municipal elections, which were meant to be non-party elections for mayors and ward commissioners, were rife with AL cadres and activists intimidating voters and capturing voting booths. The Islamic party Jamaat-i-Islami Bangladesh (JIB) and General Ershad's Jatiyo Party (JP) have also been major players in governmental alliances with the two main parties, but are much smaller in size.

The establishment of elections and democratically-elected parliamentary and local government members could have been a golden opportunity for democratic consolidation, but this was not to be. The stability of the state is based on an alliance of urban elites – the bureaucracy, military and political leadership – who are reliant on the political support of the rural landowning elite. What exists is an 'illiberal democracy' where the bare minimum of procedural democracy exists within a zero-sum duopolistic system of 'winner-takes- all' when in office. The patronage structures across the country built by the two parties form two confrontational factions competing for power. The ruling party uses their advantage of incumbency to centralise control over the political and legislative agenda, government resources, and bureaucratic and executive institutions of governance. They reward loyalty by giving supporters access to resources. They often ensure loyalty through violent intimidation and vote buying. This system reinforces clientelism – rural patron-client relationships that shape social organisation and people's everyday lives across the country.

When in opposition, parties refuse to take their seats in parliament and use extra-parliamentary strikes, protests and street violence as tools of political protest. But the overwhelming mandate given to AL in 2008 and BNP's absence from the polls in 2013 has led to an autocratic style of governance. Sheikh Hasina rules with an iron fist, and the veneer of procedural democracy wears ever thinner. The lack of inter-party democracy is fuelled by a culture of intra-party feudalism, dynastic power and centralised decision-making. The political climate in Bangladesh is dominated by the personal vendetta between Sheikh Hasina and Khaleda Zia who – with their allies – constantly seek to undermine the other's personal integrity, right to leadership, political capital and place in the national historical narrative.

And what of ordinary women's representation in this tumultuous political history and ever-shifting landscape? Despite the nation's successive female leaders, women's participation at parliamentary and local government levels has been controversially quota-driven and of limited success. In 2011, the Fifteenth Amendment to the Constitution mandated the reservation of 50 seats (out of 300) for women. However, these seats are distributed among political parties based on their representation in parliament. In the 2008 general elections, a total of 18 women were directly elected out of 250 contestable seats. Previously, a 1997 constitutional amendment mandated the reservation of one-third of local government seats by direct election instead of party nomination – this led to an increase of women in politics in rural areas. In elections that year, 44,134 women contested quota seats and 13,437 were successful. However, the 2003 elections saw the number of women candidates decline by almost 5,000. The work of women who do get elected has been marred by discriminatory regulations and negative attitudes from their colleagues and the public. Yet women's legal organisations successfully challenged a circular from the Ministry of Local Government, Rural Development and Cooperatives (MLGRD&C) that would have excluded female ward commissioners from serving in the Law and Order Committee, issuing certificates relating to succession and nationality, and overseeing local infrastructure projects.

Within the context of a deeply patriarchal society, the journey of women in Bangladesh towards greater well-being and control over their lives has been slow but steady. Many suffer from a loss of agency due to traditional early marriage – the mean age of first marriage is 19.4 years – and joint-family living arrangements. The Child Marriage Restraint Act 2017 ostensibly aimed at stamping out the practice, still allowed girls under 18 to be married under 'special circumstances for their best interests'. Human rights and women's groups have argued that in the context of the patriarchal familial structure, this loophole will have the opposite effect. Women already have a subservient position to male household heads – husbands, fathers, brothers and other members of the extended family – and are expected to be compliant, modest and willing to sacrifice their own interests in favour of their families' priorities.

Meanwhile, over the last three decades, government policies such as the Food for Education Programme and free secondary education for women have increased female enrolment and completion at all education levels. These increasing levels of education are linked to declining fertility, later age of marriage and better health. While gender-specific patterns of labour determine women's access to income and work, recent socio-economic changes have meant a growing commercialisation of women's work, the undertaking of home-based income-generation and entrepreneurial activities, joining the industrial and service-based labour force, and participating in public sphere activities. The specific targeting of female clients by development and poverty alleviation programmes of non-governmental organisations (NGOs), specifically microcredit, have increased millions of women's control over income, productive labour and decision-making power within the home and community. However, socio-economic empowerment has not been meaningfully translated into political empowerment. Women's organisations have worked tirelessly to improve constitutionally guaranteed rights and living conditions, highlighting issues like political representation, domestic violence, rights of sex workers and working conditions for women. Their efforts to mobilise women around political issues have often been stymied by a combination of donor reluctance to fund radical mobilisation and a clientelistic socio-political context that does not tolerate alliances among traditionally excluded groups.

Aspirations and realities

In my journeys around Bangladesh, getting to the heart of what many women felt about politics often meant that I had to assure them repeatedly that their opinions mattered, that they were entitled to have them, and that they were capable of engaging intellectually with democratic ideals and performance. Many were aware of democracy as an ideal. However, they were less vocal in their support for democracy than men, and less likely to be able to answer questions regarding its suitability and practice. There was a conceptual disconnect between the idea of supporting democracy as an ideal and the actual performance of current and past governments. When asked about democracy, they understood it as a proxy for governance as an output. They were, in effect, championing delivery-based rather than procedural aspects of democracy. For many, a language of rights, entitlements and well-being emerged as their democratic ideal. Those who favoured procedural aspects, such as the freeness and fairness of elections and the political neutrality of state institutions, were educated and urban – their daily existence was not constantly at the mercy of the powerful. Overall, however, women's experience of dictatorship and patriarchal culture gave them a deep affinity to voting. They appreciated the participative act of expressing choice, but their continued experiences of poor governance made them sceptical regarding its impact.

The women I met across the country strongly expressed that they often felt distant from political power. They thought they knew little about institutions outside their lived experience and said they were desperately underserved by political institutions and politicians alike. Their institutional distrust was grounded in their negative experiences of local governance. At opposite ends of the economic scale, respondents looked down on politicians and political parties for the same reasons – corruption and misuse of power. Their instrumental relationship with the state and its representatives reflected the hierarchal patronage ties that characterised their daily lives and livelihoods. Many of these women pragmatically chose to align with the rural political elites, who can provide social protection and resources, rather than with each other. But women's willingness to positively evaluate politicians' and local government performance depended mostly on their ability to provide for constituents – representation by fellow women still held symbolic power. Keenly aware of the obstacles they face in office, women were sympathetic to their female local government representatives but also honest about their failures.

Virtually all the women I spoke to were aware that they are nurtured as a constituency at election time, to be discarded later. They were aware of their value to politicians and angry at the latter's lack of performance once in office. There was a pervasive idea that politics is a money-making business and that politicians are manipulative and self-serving. However, politicians were seen as capable of benefitting those they serve if the incentives for re-election were strong enough. Even women with poor knowledge of politics castigated the two main parties' inability to cooperate on matters of national interest and their perpetuation of political deadlock to the public's detriment. Many conflated the party with the leaders, having lived with decades of dynastic rule and authoritarian styles of party leadership. They bitterly noted that with this much power, why would the elder sisters (the leaders) not want to help their younger ones (themselves)?

From their experience of democratisation as citizens outside and within political institutions, Bangladeshi women's journey for power, representation and effective participation is a complex one. Women's organisations have continuously fought to increase the number of women directly elected to political office. While well-intentioned, the quotas for women's representation in parliament and local governments were half-hearted attempts to mainstream women into politics while not upsetting the current system. Even though the presence of female national and party leadership and the widening of access to parliamentary and local government representation have given women a larger space within politics, this has not empowered them to create long-term changes within the patriarchal and patronage-driven landscape.

Hollow symbolism

It cannot be denied that Sheikh Hasina and Khaleda Zia's presence as Prime Ministers and party leaders has enormous symbolic power. But their actual impact on increasing the quality and quantity of women's participation in politics is less positive. Neither of them challenged the patriarchal and dynastic bases of political power, given that their claim to leadership and legitimacy is via male relatives. For both AL and BNP, the presence of women who reminded voters of strong, beloved leaders such as Sheikh Mujib and Ziaur Rahman proved to be effective branding. They represent continuity in a nation defined by familial identities, hierarchal relationships and authoritarian leadership. Their alleviation to power depended on the male party membership and in exchange for loyalty, neither Sheikh Hasina or Khaleda Zia has rocked the patriarchal boat. For reasons of political expediency, they rewarded the men around them, many of whom are seasoned political operators, with resources, institutional control and policy-making influence. They acquiesced to male dominance in the political space and their attempts to change gendered political power structures for women were tokenistic.

The amendments to reserve seats for women in parliament has been allowed to lapse three times under both Hasina and Zia's leadership. There are now 50 of these seats, but these are drawn from party membership proportionally based on parliamentary representation. While strengthening their own grip by appeasing traditionally powerful alliances and treating general seats as a power bloc, Hasina and Zia have made other's access to leadership dependent on the goodwill of male party elites. Many women do run and win general seats, but it is extremely difficult for them to contest and win against men without familial connections and other resources in the constituency. Thus, while the majority of women aim for reserved seats, the process of capturing the nominations for these seats is neither meritocratic or transparent. Those who secure nominations seem to fall into one of three categories – those who are close to the current leadership; a wife or daughter of a deceased or incapacitated Member of Parliament; and those who have been politically associated with the party for a long time. As parties do not want to risk nominating ordinary women who do not already have political capital, women's path to political power remains incredibly limited. Increasingly, both parties are 'selling' nominations for parliamentary and local government elections for a hefty fee. The very nature of the limited control of financial resources amongst the majority of women makes this a vastly higher bar to entry. At the local level, nominations to party councils and committees are not decided via elections, but are rather made through selections from on high.

Party elections within both AL and BNP – including for party leader – are conducted behind closed doors and procedurally approved by the party convention. While formal mechanisms exist for the party to elect members of the presidium, executive and advisory/standing committees, in practise these are chosen by the leader, called the president (AL) or chairperson (BNP). The leadership of both parties will likely be passed on to the current leaders' sons, regardless of their political experience. Within the extremely confrontational and centralised framework of Bangladeshi politics, Hasina's and Khaleda's desire to preserve and enhance personal power and control over their party and polity has meant that they have also not worked to enhance democratic practices within or between political parties. The double-bind of female presence in public and political space meant that they were judged by different standards than men, while their actions were seen as representative of all women. The personal vendetta between the two leaders and their unwillingness to behave with civility within the norms of procedural democratic practice – for example, demonising each other and refusing to take their place in parliament when in opposition – meant that they are often seen as unserious, quarrelsome women who do not put the nation first. This is a characterisation that does nothing to help attitudes towards their fellow female political representatives.

The bad behaviour of both women has also resulted in important initiatives and institutions for women's advancement – such as the National Policy for the Advancement of Women (NPAW), the Ministry for Women's and Children's Affairs (MoWCA) and the National Council for Women's Development (NCDW) – to be ignored, underfunded and side-lined. The robust implementation of long-term gender mainstreaming policies and the establishment of pro-women institutions are simply not high enough priorities in a political culture mired in short-term gain and the appeasement of competing power blocs. As the most recent retrograde step towards legalising child marriage in 'special circumstances' such as rape, pregnancy and family interests demonstrates, all-powerful women leaders are more than willing to risk the lives and futures of those women who have none.

Lack of access to power networks and financial resources prevent women from running for and entering political office. The 1997 Second Amendment to the Constitution that reserved three seats out of nine at Union Parishad (UP) level (each *parishad* is made up nine villages) was a landmark in increasing women's participation in local government. In its wake, thousands of women contested elections across the county, seeking to have a voice and determined to serve their communities. However, their experiences in both urban and rural local government has been fraught with structural and social obstacles. Still, female constituents who have finally found a public voice and representation have welcomed their efforts. Many women spoke of the integrity and dedication their representatives brought to the job despite a hostile working environment. Women members' presence on parishads and wards has encouraged their female constituents to raise and to address issues such as domestic violence and property disputes with male relatives. Members have been able to promote greater transparency, a focus on gender-related issues, act as members of the informal village justice system (*shalish*), implement pro-women community and development programmes, and create more participatory styles of governance. Some have even been able to redirect government assistance and safety nets that were being hijacked by local male elites.

In Bangladesh, competitive clientelism is pervasive and for local representatives to be seen as effective, they have to direct resources from party and local elites to their constituents. The lack of operational terms for female members from reserved seats and the institutional attempts to discriminate against them in favour of their male colleagues – such as denying them rights to the same duties and committee positions – often leads to marginalisation by both colleagues and constituents. Given the traditional lack of women in political office, many local government members are unaware of the formal and informal modes of behaviour required within the almost exclusively male patronage system. The fact that female UP members from reserved seats are each responsible for three wards in comparison to the general members (usually male) being responsible for one places an unfair burden on them and fosters unrealistic expectations from those they serve. Local elites and male politicians' reluctance to allow outsiders, in this case women, into the closed circles of power has meant hostility for the female local representatives. They are often left out of meetings or decision-making bodies, harassed and at times publicly smeared by false rumours to discredit them. In extreme cases, they have been physically assaulted when they were seen as disruptive to existing corrupt practices. In a society where a woman's honour is of vital importance to her family, facing these obstacles has no doubt discouraged many from entering political office. But many others persevere, hopeful that their continued presence and persistence will change things. This is despite the reality that women's organisations, especially those working for political mobilisation, are often funded inadequately. This means that they are not as effective as they could be in designing and lobbying for policies that can help women enter, navigate and empower themselves in the political sphere.

Plus ça change ...

Bangladeshi women are mired in a patriarchal authority structure that entrenches the belief that their primary place is within the private sphere and their primary responsibilities to their families. And so, they have traditionally relied on men for economic provision and social protection. But this has limited their agency and mobility in the public sphere. Many women have aspirations towards a democracy that will give them rights, protection and access to livelihoods and well-being. Yet, for many, lack of education makes institutional engagement and participation extremely difficult. And while rising labour force participation, education and involvement in NGO development programmes have increased other women's financial and personal space, they are still at the mercy of male dominance and have poor resource and information access. What this means is that women have to negotiate multiple restrictions as citizens and political actors.

The already-high socio-cultural and resource bar for women's entry into formal political processes is made even higher by a clientelistic political context and institutional barriers. Most importantly, women must have the money to contest political office. This rules out the average woman living within a conservative environment where she may not have control over finances and where familial obligations trump personal ambitions.

If this hurdle is crossed, the next obstacle is the collusion between powerful elites and politicians – many of whom are often one and the same – which bars entry to and engagement with the political apparatus from outsiders. Whether it is nominations for electoral candidacy, positions in the party or local leadership, the most important qualifiers are familial connections, long-term association with party elites and more recently, monetary contributions to the party. In the case of parliamentary representation, it is extremely difficult for non-elite women without long-standing familial roots within the constituency to win general seats against male counterparts. The winner-takes-all corruption that both political parties have engaged in when in power makes the party leadership loathe to risk losing a seat and so they would rarely take a chance on a long-shot female candidate. Thus, women are relegated to the quota of reserved seats for which their party nominates them. Not only does this make them dependent on the patronage of their male colleagues, but also on the cultivation of close ties with the party leadership.

Even if these initial barriers are crossed, the system of reserved seats often denies women legitimacy as authentic political actors. Many representatives have experienced both colleagues who are unwilling to recognise their authority as 'real politicians' and constituents who doubt their ability to access the necessary resources and networks to be efficacious. The MoWCA guidance that sought to deny female local government chairpersons the same rights as their male colleagues elected through general seats is only but one example of the institutional discrimination women face. The quota system also burdens female political representative with larger constituencies than their fellow male politicians, making a difficult job almost impossible. The lack of specificity regarding the tasks, duties and obligations of female local government representatives creates a situation where they are unable to carry out their mandate in a forceful way, often pushed by their colleagues and the needs of their constituents towards 'women's issues'.

And then the patriarchal context makes it extremely difficult for female political actors to express agency. They are harassed and ignored by male colleagues and intimidated and coerced by local elites. It is rare that they are able to work autonomously without capitulating to the patronage system, in which they pay obeisance to party leadership and engage in corruption. They must constantly renew their connections to an often-shifting set of power brokers, depending on who is politically in charge. These negative experiences prevent women effectively serving their constituents and lead to many not wanting to be part of the system anymore.

Finally, despite decades-long efforts, there are yet to be viable networks for women at the grassroots level that provide them with political leverage and power. The Bangladeshi women's movement has been trying to create these through both their mobilisation and policy advocacy efforts. But while many women's organisations have managed to mobilise poor and underprivileged women towards a greater knowledge of their political rights, entitlements and participation, most development efforts have focused on providing access to microcredit, goods and services. Local elites have encouraged the latter and actively fought the former, fearing their loss of power. Women who come against these forces rarely win. In addition, tools for women's empowerment such as the NPAW and MoWCA have been side-lined by successive regimes and rarely given the resources they need to implement strong policies.

For far too long, the political elite has had no real interest in deepening democratisation and building accountable institutions. Their goal is to attain and hold onto power and resources by creating alliances of patronage. The female-led parties themselves have not widened access for those traditionally excluded from politics, especially women. While formal structures of intra-party democracy exist, these are routinely ignored and power lies with the leader and her small band of allies. With the recent electoral boycott of the 2013 elections by opposition parties, the current AL government's eschewal of procedural norms and embrace of authoritarian governance only reinforces structures of exclusion and political retribution. Unless the leadership works towards establishing intra-party and inter-party democratic processes, the prospects for democratisation and women's place in it are bleak. The networks of clientelism need to be broken to extend power beyond rural patrons and their supporters. The women's movement and its component organisations need to somehow reverse their decline and once again build networks of resistance among grassroots women. They need to educate, mobilise and train women to participate both as political citizens as well as political actors. The policy, legislative and institutional tools meant to enlarge women's representation and participation within the political sphere have too long been unused because of a lack of resources and mandate for action. But the tools are there to help in defining women's duties in reserved seats, redressing their constituency demarcations, and encouraging a culture of acceptance and respect among their male colleagues. A wider range of women need far more support and resources from their political parties and social support from their families and communities to stand for general election. This allows them to move beyond quota representation and be seen as legitimate political players who draw their power from election, not selection.

For women who strive to be of service to other citizens through political representation, it is a herculean effort not to be discouraged. And many are not. The path to agency and change is neither linear, smooth, nor timely. But Bangladeshi women are committed to the journey.

AN UNCOMFORTABLE CLOSET

Anato Chowdhury

For a twenty-something Bangladeshi who moved to Britain a few years ago, not much has changed back home. Memories of my childhood – from pollution to political corruption – are rejuvenated every time I return. Yet I must admit some things are different now. Sexual minorities, for example, were never seriously discussed during my college years in Dhaka. With limited access to information and no local resources, I lived out this period of my life hiding my sexuality. Over the last few years, however, it seems that an increasing number of Bangladeshis are speaking about sexual diversity and their own sexuality. Or at least this is what it has seemed like to someone looking in from afar. But there is only so much we can learn from the news and social media, which is why I have been talking to members of sexual minorities who are closely involved with events in Bangladesh.

In 2013, the elopement and consequent arrest of two women – let us call them Sraboni and Oporajita to protect their identities – made the local news to the bemusement of many. Public reactions revealed much about Bangladesh's ignorance of sexuality. Many wondered how two women could sexually satisfy each other, while others condemned same-sex attraction as an illness to be cured. Their story had a dark ending, as the police tracked the couple down at the behest of Sraboni's parents. Oporajita, older at twenty-one, was charged with the abduction of Sraboni, who at sixteen years old was a minor in the eyes of Bangladeshi law. This is the environment within which sexual minorities in Bangladesh live, where we can never be sure if our families, neighbours and government will collude to bring misery to our lives. Gender and sexual diversity in the region of Bengal may predate the creation of modern-day Bangladesh, but the mainstream visibility of our people has so often brought us pain. Our experiences have taught us to be careful around heterosexual members of society, be they family, friend, government, medical professional or religious figurehead. Even here, in an essay on the current state of our lives, I've had to anonymise several names on the grounds of safety, and in many cases, on fear of death.

There has been a quiet movement among sexual minorities in Bangladesh for a long time. The Bandhu Social Welfare Society, a non-governmental organisation (NGO), has existed since 1996, and counts United Nations (UN) bodies, foreign embassies and the Ministry of Health and Family Welfare amongst its sponsors. A large component of Bandhu's work involves a sexual health orientated approach to working with men who have sex with men (MSM), hijras (transgender women who were born male, also referred to as 'third gender') and kothis (effeminate men who are the receptive partners in male same-sex relationships). This perhaps explains Bandhu's palatability to the government, as preventing HIV and providing healthcare is something the government feels it can support – the associated demands for social change are minimal. However, Bandhu's stated goals extend beyond the framework of sexual health and they tackle everything from social stigma to legal equality. Anyone following their activities will realise there is a deliberate cultural dimension to their work. Bandhu organised Bangladesh's first Hijra Pride in November 2014, an event that may not have garnered as much attention as the activities of other organisations but was arguably more extensive. Hijra Pride was supported by the government, indeed with government officials among NGO professionals and foreign diplomats in attendance at some of the associated events. In 2015, Bandhu also rolled out a programme as part of the International Day Against Homophobia, Transphobia and Biphobia (IDAHOT) and organised Reincarnate, a South Asian festival celebrating gender, diversity and the arts in early 2016. Aside from the government's support, they have a number of relationships with mainstream media, including the television channel ATN Bangla and the newspaper *Dhaka Tribune*.

It is interesting to note that unlike some of their contemporaries, reports of Bandhu's work do not generate much controversy. It can be assumed that Bandhu's primary focus on the hijra community grants them a level of relative acceptance in Bangladeshi society. Hijras are people of a third gender who have existed in Bangladesh for hundreds of years, intertwined with local culture. By virtue of this history they enjoy a degree of arm's-length acceptance and limited government recognition. But Bandu is also careful about how it operates - they avoid emphasis on terminology that denotes homosexuality when communicating in Bengali. Bandhu most likely also benefits from a halo effect afforded by government support, whether this is intentional or not. National Islamic groups – and indeed Islamist groups – are less likely to target an organisation with government recognition. This is something that other activists have never benefited from, whether in the realm of sexual minority rights or among the secular and atheist activists who have found themselves to be targets of Islamist fury in recent years.

The ignorance and hostility surrounding sexual diversity in Bangladeshi society often means working for equality in a more nuanced way. According to their current members, this is the strategy Boys of Bangladesh (BoB) have employed for much of the past decade. They trace their roots to the early 2000s, when they started as an online group. Over the years, they have established a physical presence, quietly enabling sexual minority men to form communities. The group's volunteers organise various events for their membership, anything from casual social meetings to large, organised parties. At their peak these parties were hosted at venues like hotels and were attended by up to a hundred mostly male guests. The organisers did not explicitly broach the topic of the attendees' sexuality to venue owners, and they always made sure to follow certain self-imposed rules – they allowed no drugs or alcohol and, as is required by Bangladeshi law for large gatherings, they always notified the local police station of their presence. BoB members believe this is what kept them safe, for instance, when a disapproving member of the public called the police to one of their parties in 2008. It would have been obvious that many of the men were not heterosexual, and there were attendees dressed in drag. But the party had no narcotics and was fully authorised, and the police pressed no charges.

Apart from their community work, BoB also lobbies for equality within Bangladesh's human rights framework. Their members have interfaced with the government alongside other more recognised organisations such as the lawyer and human rights activist Sultana Kamal's Ain O Shalish Kendro. According to BoB, they have never felt any hostility directed towards them from government officials at these meetings. One member even recalls having a meeting solely focussed on sexual minorities organised by the National Human Rights Commission (NHRC) of Bangladesh, where he was told by a senior official that the government was sympathetic to their plight. These words of support came with limits, however, as the official further explained that the government cannot work with sexual minorities publicly due to social taboos. This seems to be the government's guiding principle – avoid anything that could create negative publicity. This became especially apparent when BoB members were privately rebuked by another official in 2013 for contributing to the UN's Universal Periodic Review (UPR) of human rights in Bangladesh, where BoB had described the discrimination felt by sexual minorities in the country. The official went on to question the need to bring international bodies into matters that could be handled at the national level. This was a questionable assertion, given that the government had just declined to accept the UPR recommendation to repeal Section 377 of the Bangladeshi Penal Code, which condemns 'carnal intercourse against the order of nature' and can be used to criminalise same-sex intercourse.

Roopbaan, a newer organisation that published its eponymous print magazine for sexual minorities – Bangladesh's first – has operated differently to the more established organisations. Promoting themselves on Facebook and inviting local and foreign dignitaries to their inaugural event in January 2014, the group was not exactly discreet. However, speak to any of the founding members now, and they will be the first to admit their surprise at the level of interest their magazine generated. After the launch, news of Roopbaan spread quickly thanks to both traditional and social media. Reactions were mixed, with the first issue of the magazine inviting congratulations and condemnations. While the majority of the excitement was contained online, there was some early resistance from Muslim organisations. The chairman of the National Tafsir Committee, Maulana Ahmed Abdul Qayyum, expressed his distress towards the promotion of homosexuality in the country. But brushing aside these and other negative reactions, Roopbaan kept up their momentum, rolling out a suite of activities in Dhaka and establishing a rather public profile. In April 2014, they held their first Rainbow Rally to coincide with the Mongol Shobhojatra that parades through Dhaka every Pahela Boishakh, or Bengali New Year. While Roopbaan officially stated the rally was to celebrate friendship and diversity, people drew their own conclusions from the contingent's use of rainbow colours. Soon the internet, including international media, was awash with news of Bangladesh's first gay Pride parade. This brought in another round of expected backlash. But Roopbaan persevered, bringing out a second issue of the magazine over the summer and hosting Transhion Show, a transgender fashion show, at the Shilpakala Academy.

It is important to pause here and consider how the group were able to continue their work, especially in Bangladesh's typically hostile environment. Transhion included members of the hijra community and gay men under the leadership of hijra activist Jaya Shikdar. Roopbaan members believe hijra presence at Transhion would have helped foster a level of tolerance for the event. Additionally, the national prominence of the venue where Transhion took place would have also granted the group a level of legitimacy. Speaking to Roopbaan members, these stories of tacit support from fellow Bangladeshis are not uncommon – from NGOs who provided assistance with Roopbaan's projects to business owners who provided meeting and rehearsal spaces. In this milieu, Roopbaan slowly grew from a magazine publisher into a platform that campaigned for a person's right to love. The organisation published an anthology of poetry, made plans for a third issue of the magazine, and marched on Pohela Boishakh again in April 2015, seemingly turning their Rainbow Rally into an annual fixture as part of a new, highly visible campaign for acceptance in Bangladesh.

Extremism and murder

For a while, with the existence of multiple organisations and their various approaches to sexual and gender minorities in Bangladesh, the outlook felt positive. There was visibility, there was some limited government interaction, and it seemed societal engagement with the heterosexual majority was imminent. But by 2015, the plethora of work by activists was overtaken by pain and fear.

The murder of Avijit Roy in February that year was a keenly felt blow. Roy was a prominent blogger and founder of Mukto-Mona, a platform for Bengali freethinkers. He was an openly supportive ally of sexual minorities – so much so that he wrote a book in Bengali explaining homosexuality from a logical and scientific perspective. Roy's murder was followed by the murders of other bloggers, and by the end of the year, Islamists had moved on to threaten members of Roopbaan and BoB.

This was a new development – sexual rights activists hadn't previously been prominent enough to draw Islamist ire. People in the community were accustomed to getting anonymous threats online, but these newer threats were different. They were targeted towards specific individuals, delivered to their phones, email addresses or Facebook accounts, and in certain cases they were written in good, grammatically correct English. Organisations did their best to persevere within this environment – BoB launched a campaign centred around their lesbian comic character Dhee in September 2015, which aimed to build awareness about the struggles of being a sexual minority. But they faced more than just anonymous threats, as at the project's inception the Bangladesh Awami Olama League, which claims affiliation with the ruling Awami League, condemned Project Dhee and its supporters, including the British Council and several local NGOs. The Olama League falsely claimed Bangladesh was 98 per cent Muslim, and stated their belief that homosexuality was haram within Islam. They justified this stance by making prejudiced interpretations of the Qur'an, and asked the government to punish homosexuals according to Section 377 of the Bangladeshi Penal Code. In this environment, BoB's more prominent members took greater caution – only leaving home if absolutely necessary and never staying out late. Some told me they believed they were stalked, and by October 2015, the threats had escalated to the point where at least one individual was no longer able to go to work and had to move around to different parts of the country for fear of being targeted for murder.

Certain members of Roopbaan found themselves in similarly dire circumstances. Extremists visited the home of the organisation's secretary, Mahbub Rabbi Tonoy, and delivered multiple death threats to his family in person. Tonoy identified as pansexual, and often varied the way he presented his gender. This was something many around him took in their stride given his immersion in the Bangladeshi theatre scene, but it had obviously attracted the wrong kind of attention. Tonoy's friends claim that given the taboo around sexuality in Bangladesh, his parents never felt able to call on the police for help.

Xulhaz Mannan, Roopbaan's founder, also received his share of threats, though he hid this from others. Xulhaz came from a fairly well-to-do family. His late father was a freedom fighter in the Bangladesh Liberation War of 1971, and his cousin Dipu Moni previously served as Foreign Minister for the current Awami League government. Xulhaz disliked labels, but his friends say he was a gay man. He was open about his sexuality and had long been an advocate for the equal treatment of sexual minorities. Publishing a magazine for the community had long been his dream and it all came together with the formation of Roopbaan. His friends claim that he had kept quiet about the threats made to him to maintain a sense of calm – the community, especially younger members, drew strength from his confidence, and he did not want to jeopardise that. More than one of his friends remembers how being the son of a freedom fighter had shaped his outlook; and how he had shared with them the thought that our rights would never be gained without blood being spilled. He elaborated that while he did not want to die, he felt that it was inevitable that some of us would, and he had already decided to accept his death, if it happened, as something unpredictable – akin to an accident.

Roopbaan's final attempt at organising a Rainbow Rally on 14 April 2016 took place against this backdrop, again to coincide with Bengali New Year. But their efforts were halted by the government, who denied Roopbaan permission to march, and warned Dhaka University and hijra groups not to involve themselves with the rally. The official reason was that threats had been made by Islamists, and the government implemented further measures such as banning masks at the main parade. The move was not entirely surprising – Roopbaan had created a public Facebook event for the rally, and Islamists created their own event in response, where they threatened to physically assault participants of the rally. Even today screenshots of posts by Islamist groups such as Basherkella, encouraging the Bangladeshi public to join the attack on Roopbaan members, can be found online.

The government's ban came at very short notice, leaving the organisers little time to communicate the cancellation. As such, many participants arrived at the venue on the day unaware of the ban and, when informed by Xulhaz, chose to march as part of the main Bengali New Year procession anyway. Their rainbow attire was noticed and they were stopped by the police, who apprehended four activists and took them to the local police station. Xulhaz went with them, eventually securing their release, but the experience left many wondering if the state would now begin to actively persecute sexual minorities. The police compounded this environment of fear over the next few days, adding to the pressure activists had been put under by Islamist threats. The police picked up activists from Bandhu and BoB - officially to question them and protect them from threats, rather than to arrest or charge. According to one person who was taken in for questioning, the police seemed convinced that this sudden surge of activism had support from the de facto opposition party, the Bangladesh Nationalist Party (BNP) – which currently does not hold any seats in Parliament after it boycotted the 2014 elections. This is a somewhat surprising suspicion, given that the BNP is known for its Islamic conservatism and ties to Jamaat e Islami Bangladesh (Jamaat). Widening their net, the police also made calls to prominent members of society supporting sexual minority rights, asking similar questions.

Sadly, the foiled rally was Xulhaz's last act of public campaigning. On 25 April 2016, Islamist extremists linked to Al Qaeda in the Indian Subcontinent (AQIS) broke into Xulhaz's flat and murdered both him and Tonoy. In retrospect, his friends believe that as Roopbaan's founder he was the Islamists' primary target. Xulhaz's name had been everywhere in the media, he was known to be the focal point within Roopbaan, and his address was listed on their events in online social networks. He was also known amongst the wider community and society for his past work with USAID and the US Embassy in Dhaka. On a more personal front, he had opened up his home to people – whether it was for Roopbaan events, or for someone from the community of sexual and gender minorities who needed a place to stay. This put a target on his back – his level of publicity made him easy to track and his openness made his life easy to infiltrate. Though Tonoy had also been a target, his murder appears to have been more opportunistic, as his presence at Xulhaz's flat had not been pre-planned.

The immediate aftermath

The deaths of Xulhaz and Tonoy created considerable turmoil. After the killings, BoB activists felt unsafe enough to suspend Project Dhee and peripheral community-building events scheduled outside Dhaka. Many other members of the community went into hiding, eschewing work, community and social media. Foreign organisations and embassies who were supportive of minority rights and had previously funded sexual minority organisations seemed sluggish in their response. They eventually collaborated either to provide safe houses for prominent activists or to aid them in leaving the country. Xulhaz's profile brought a lot of attention to his and Tonoy's deaths. There were reports in multiple newspapers around the world and a call made to Bangladeshi Prime Minister Sheikh Hasina by John Kerry, then the US Secretary of State.

The national response was complicated. Many prominent heterosexual human rights activists expressed their condolences in a personal capacity, and were willing to be named for their support. However, no expressions of support or condolences were made in an organisational capacity, including from the government's NHRC, who had previously been supportive in private. Any hope sexual minorities harboured of government support were dashed by the Home Minister Asaduzaman Khan, who responded to the murders by saying that homosexuality is not compatible with Bangladeshi society and that the government would not tolerate anyone offending people's religious sensibilities. His claim seemed incongruous, considering that Xulhaz and the other members of Roopbaan had not attempted to engage in any religious proselytisation. The minister's statement could be better seen as part of the government's attempt to appease Islamist extremists. More worryingly for wider society, Khan claimed that these most recent murders were not at all linked to the previous killings of atheists or secular activists, and were isolated events that did not point to any patterns in the country. His confident claims were followed by the Holey Artisan Bakery massacre by Islamist terrorists the following July.

The government has found itself dealing with a considerable amount of Islamist violence over the last few years. A lot of this stems from the government's decision to bring local war criminals from the Bangladesh Liberation War to justice. Many of the accused are of an Islamist bent, and the government's actions have spurred claims of persecution from Islamist groups. These groups form various factions and have differing aims, but all claim that Islam is under attack – a comment very tenuously linked to reality given that the population is 90 per cent Muslim. These groups have been lashing out against the parts of Bangladesh they deem to be anti-

Islam, such as atheist bloggers. The government has chosen not to speak out in defence of an individual's right to have no religious affiliation. In 2015, Sajeeb Wazed, the Prime Minister's son and senior advisor to the government, went as far as to tell the Reuters news agency that his mother could not publicly condemn the killing of atheists since that would run against populist sentiment in the country, and that the opposition party could use this to tear votes away from them.

These statements and reactions are what sexual minorities in the country use to ascertain the government's stance. While Islamists have now expanded their scope to target sexual minorities, making it more difficult to be open about one's sexuality in the country, no support can be expected from a government which is chasing the populist vote. Activists have thus felt unable to ask the government for protection – a process which in Bangladesh would formally begin when an individual or entity files a general report with the police after receiving threats. Many people fear that upon initiating this process, they would themselves be detained.

Detention under various pretences is not uncommon in Bangladesh, as evidenced by the government's past decisions to jail atheist and secular writers temporarily – and it would be easy for the government to apply Section 377 or other parts of the Bangladeshi Penal Code to imprison sexual minorities. Bangladesh is notorious for deaths in custody perpetrated by both the police and a special forces unit called Rapid Action Battalion (RAB) – and several cases accusing RAB of torture and extrajudicial killings are currently making their way through the courts. The government has, however, pursued the extremists on account of maintaining law and order and because of the attention garnered by the multiple deaths at the hands of Islamist terrorists. Several members of the Ansarullah Bangla Team (ABT) – a group officially banned by the government for their terrorist activities – have been arrested, and the police claim the group is linked to the murders of Xulhaz, Tonoy and Avijit Roy. There have also been 'crossfire' deaths of ABT members who were officially suspected of involvement in these crimes. The responsibility for multiple blogger and activist murders has also been claimed by AQIS, but a link between ABT and AQIS has not yet been definitively proven. From my interviews, I gathered that the police have sometimes informed victim's families of progress made with specific cases, but it is difficult to track everything that has happened accurately. The government also releases news piecemeal via traditional media, and there is no organised activist resource to follow and document either this information or the legal proceedings on those arrested. It is important to consider that while Islamist groups are often well funded, sexual minority groups are not, and it is very difficult for them to conduct their activities without money, relying solely on volunteers.

There currently isn't enough media interest in the country to pursue this further, as the Holey Artisan Bakery attacks in July 2016 by another Islamist terrorist group – Jamaat-ul-Mujahideen Bangladesh (JMB) – has displaced both national and international attention. The Islamic State (IS), or Daesh, has also claimed responsibility for this attack. Again, the link between IS and local terrorists group JMB has not yet been fully established, but international involvement here is much more obvious. The terrorists involved in Holey Artisan Bakery attacks were trained abroad in Malaysia, or in the case of the suspected Canadian-Bangladeshi mastermind, Tamim Chowdhury, allegedly in Syria. Islamist extremism has long been seen as the preserve of fringe groups like ABT or JMB, and specific political parties like Jamaat, with recruitment limited to madrasah students or the economically exploitable. But Islamists now operate more broadly, integrating themselves across various social classes. They are well funded through international sources, allowing them to wield influence in new sections of society. For example, they now operate *qawmi* madrasahs – private mosque schools that are not regulated by the government – that allow them to indoctrinate the children from wealthier families, as opposed to solely targeting the poor through charity. Also, going by the vocabulary and framing of Islamophobia that they use – which has hitherto been alien to Bangladesh – the propaganda produced by both these groups suggests an international influence. To this day, videos that could have only been recorded by the murderers of Xulhaz and Tonoy are available on YouTube, and, to me and many of the people I spoke to, the statement alongside this video very much reads like a product of Western Islamist terrorists. The government has managed to disrupt Islamist activity with its recent spate of enforcement activity. But past experience shows these organisations will regroup – JMB for example has existed since the late

1990s. Organisations entice recruits through financial assistance, as well as appeal to people's sense of being wronged, pushing the idea that Islam is threatened in Bangladesh.

Life as we have always known it

As organisations like Roopbaan, BoB and Bandhu slow down or put their activities on hold, it is important to consider where Bangladeshi society is at present. None of the aforementioned organisations have had the chance to fully engage with the public. Roopbaan may have achieved a great deal of publicity and BoB and Bandhu may have done a lot of work for specific communities, but there are vast numbers of closeted sexual minorities that no one has reached. Multiple factors such as wealth, education and gender affect these people's experiences. For many, the lack of knowledge around sexual orientation is the key issue. There will be people who genuinely believe that anything other than heterosexuality is tantamount to mental illness. And in Bangladesh, some of the people who hold these beliefs will be sexual minorities themselves, who believe that perhaps same-sex desire is something they have been 'converted' to. Alongside this, many also believe that their same-sex attractions can be cured, either through contact with the opposite sex or, for those with the financial means, through medical treatment. These are views mirrored within mainstream Bangladeshi society, and are hard to shift because of a lack of informed discussion around sexual orientation in the public sphere. Society generally views sexuality as taboo and an orientation diverging from heterosexuality as something to be fixed. It is not only the person of minority orientation who feels pressured to conform – the expectation extends to the individual's wider social circle. There are examples of families who do accept their children for who they are, yet deny this acceptance in public in the face of societal pressure. Others do not show any such acceptance.

Stories of parents sending their children to therapists and psychiatrists to deal with their sexuality are relatively common, and many in the Bangladeshi medical community continue to believe that sexual minorities are mentally ill. Prominent psychiatrists in Bangladesh such as Mohit Kamal – who enjoys a high level of publicity from his television appearances – practice conversion therapy to 'cure' people with same-sex attraction.

Others have a softer approach, where treatment involves coaching around social appropriateness coupled with a heavy regimen of 'pills'. Thankfully there are doctors in Bangladesh who are more understanding of sexual minorities, who opt instead to work with individuals to manage the stress and isolation of dealing with their sexuality.

And so, broaching the subject of one's sexuality with heterosexual people in Bangladesh can lead to varied consequences. People usually have supportive friends but hostile families. However, even here it is significant to consider that friends may think same-sex attraction is a curable illness but choose not to actively persecute someone on that basis. In many instances, the issue is brushed under the carpet and never discussed again – with many people reporting that their families act as if a discussion around sexuality never happened. And as long as the individual who 'came out' then proceeds to act as expected from society – by getting married – parents and relatives assume that the problem has gone away.

One nagging issue is that of terminology. In Bangladesh, many people are familiar with the labels used by the hijra community. The imported English acronym LGBT (lesbian, gay, bisexual and transgender) would probably be used only by urban elites. But there are other homegrown labels that have long been in existence. The word *shomokami* has always been used to identify homosexual people, and *ubhokami* to a lesser extent to identify bisexual people. In Bengali, the *kam* part of those words imply sex, which heightens the controversy when using them in Bangladeshi society. The community of sexual minorities has therefore introduced the word *shompremi*, which implies love towards someone of the same sex. This word was first made common by a lesbian group called Shawprova, and further cemented into common parlance by Roopbaan's decision to use it in print and communications. This move away from any reference to sex has resulted in greater potential for alignment with the Bangladeshi mainstream. Yet this has also divided the community amongst those who would like to conform to Bangladesh's current social norms versus those who would like to push for honest and frank appraisal of why sex is so taboo.

Also, while I have used the terms 'sexual orientation' and 'sexual identity', these are not concepts that are intelligible to many other people in Bangladesh, including some sexual minorities. Same-sex intercourse is just something they enjoy, but they consider it to be a small part of their lives. They don't see why it should prevent them from marrying the opposite sex and having a family. There are men in Bangladesh who are married to women and have children but continue to have sex with other men in secret. They are able to lead these double lives because they outwardly perform the traditional heterosexual role society expects of them. But when they are not curtailing their desires, they can often be found around the various cruising grounds in Dhaka and other parts of Bangladesh. Men meeting in this way commonly fulfil a desire that is purely physical, with no further attachments or relationships involved. For many, there are feelings of guilt attached to these actions – some view it as cheating, or draw parallels to visiting a sex worker. In my observations, if pressed, some of these men will admit to wondering why they are like this. Yes, some do enjoy sexual contact with their wives while others are frustrated about why they do not harbour any such desire. But question these men on Islam and they are unlikely to view their actions from a religious standpoint. And indeed, from what I was told by the many people I spoke with, imams themselves can be seen at cruising grounds in cities, and certain religious monuments like *mazaars* (Sufi shrines) are known to be cruising spots in the country.

Women across the social classes are less free than men, from my own observations and from what I was told. The social expectation of women is that they will get married and have children, and that they will do this quickly. Perhaps for a wealthier woman this fate is delayed as she completes her studies, but the final destination is the same – a husband and children. Families also see the country as generally unsafe for women, meaning they will often curtail women's movements. Women are thus unable to do many things, whether it be attending organised events by NGOs, or meeting other women more discreetly like many men in Bangladesh do. Self-identifying lesbians have stated that women of a certain economic class instead have emotional relationships over the phone or via the Internet – which is a marked difference from those men whose same-sex liaisons are purely physical. When I've asked them further about why this is, they talk about how society impresses upon girls and women that desiring sex is sinful, and teaches them to feel guilty about their sexual desires.

Physical meetings are less common, though a minority of women enjoy a certain level of freedom, for example female workers who live far away from family and familial judgement. These women sometimes live with same-sex partners, hidden in plain sight amongst their heterosexual counterparts in single-sex hostels. In this way, their behaviour is very similar to certain men who earn their own money and live away from family, either alone or in shared accommodation – a situation more readily acceptable in Bangladesh for men compared to women. In these scenarios, men will often be able to host other men as sexual partners, or even live with them as long-term partners, under the guise of being friends. These arrangements will usually face no scrutiny from heterosexual members of society, given the general ignorance about sexual minorities in Bangladesh. Up until recently, this meant that these men could lead quite comfortable albeit closeted lives. But with the greater exposure brought on by recent events, many feel these lifestyles of theirs will now begin to raise suspicion. I was told that some of these men have been angry with Roopbaan for drawing so much public attention to the point where some have harassed and threatened Roopbaan and BoB members themselves.

Since the murders, the members of BoB and Roopban who remain in the country have all but clammed up. They feel as though their deaths would not even be noticed, because though they are instrumental in Bangladesh's movement for sexual equality, they are not prominent or well-connected like Xulhaz. According to them, discreet parties and social events, for men at least, are still happening. But an entire generation – those who counted Xulhaz and Tonoy as friends, and those who involved themselves with Roopbaan and BoB – no longer attend these. Several gay men and lesbians who were involved in campaigning have since decided to opt for marriage to someone of the opposite sex, stepping into the ultimate closet for the sake of safety. This reversion has made some people realise there is more to be done before the community is able to rely on itself in times of need.

It has also become obvious that Islamists are not concerned with same-sex activity as such – otherwise, there would be more widespread killings at known cruising grounds and an upsurge of violence in madrasahs where same-sex activity is rife. Islamists instead target groups where members specifically express an identity based on their sexual orientation and try to build social acceptance of this phenomenon — similar to how they target vocal atheists but not quiet agnostics.

The challenges we face are not solely religious, however. Many say Bangladesh is creeping towards increasing levels of Islamic conservatism. This may be true, but in my experience people in Bangladesh are religious to fit in with the rest — not because they believe in God and wish to study doctrine seriously. Islamic criticism made by many towards same-sex activity usually derives from the perspective that there is no explicit framework for same-sex marriage in the Qur'an or hadith. This criticism is then expanded to target same-sex intercourse outside marriage and adultery by married men who have sex with other men. There may be the occasional and vague reference to the Prophet Lot, but it is unusual for that to be backed up with knowledge about the possible interpretations of those verses. The public will put their faith in scholars' interpretations, and parrot their views without question — for the heterosexual majority, especially men, these interpretations do not curb their own freedoms.

Is it really the case, then, that hostility towards sexual minorities stems from Islamic teachings, or is it that people interpret Islam in a certain way because of their pre-existing prejudices about sexuality? From my interviews, it is clear that hostility towards sexual minorities is not monopolised by Muslim or indeed religious communities in Bangladesh. It is common for non-religious or atheist Bangladeshis to reject sexual minorities as well, despite recent events where they have been cast as the progressive free-thinkers of the country. During the organised protests led by secular and atheist activists against Bangladeshi war criminals in 2013, a lot of derision was directed towards sexual minorities at a personal level. The Roopbaan members I spoke to felt that even Mukto-Mona bloggers, who describe themselves as freethinkers, atheists and secularists, can be prejudiced. It is common for them to equate sexual difference with mental illness and to fixate on the uncleanliness of anal sex, ignoring the fact that many heterosexual people partake in this activity while many sexual minorities do not. Some of the religiously-observant sexual minorities I spoke to said that many atheists will also deliberately use conservative and prejudiced interpretations of Islam to confront and taunt them. This is often in an attempt to move them away from religion, thereby creating an unnecessary amount of conflict between the two minority groups.

There is currently little to no engagement with the religious dynamic in Bangladesh from local activists, and discussions of a theology that accepts or embraces sexual diversity are not yet commonplace. It must also be recognised how intimidating it can be to engage with faith-based organisations when they are so vocal in their hatred of sexual minorities. The Islamic Foundation, for example, organised a street protest against one of the country's national heroes, Nobel Laureate Muhammad Yunus, after he made a pro-LGBT statement in 2013. Given that the foundation is a government organisation, the action was seen as state-sponsored homophobia by many of the people I spoke with. In my experience, many activists working for sexual equality are not religious themselves, and so do not feel the need to refute prejudiced religious interpretations.

The future

So where is the movement for the rights of sexual minorities now? It's true that a lot of people are still afraid, and a lot of people have left the country. But the past few years have provided a certain level of clarity. In the short term, we must come together again and organise. There is work to do on several fronts. The fact that so many people in Bangladesh believe anything other than heterosexuality is indicative of mental illness must be addressed. This must be done systematically, working first within the medical profession before raising awareness among the general population. There are allies – doctors and academics – within these quarters who are willing to help, and we should aim to deploy their expertise effectively.

It is also now undeniable that sexual minorities are the targets of Islamists, and future efforts must bear this in mind. Perhaps the days of public Facebook events are on hold for now, but that does not mean we cannot continue to organise quietly. The positive reactions from society to Roopbaan – from the general public as well as other human rights activists – has shown us that some amongst the heterosexual community do acknowledge and accept us. We need to work to increase the proportion of such people in the country. And we must admit that at some point sexual minorities will have to engage with supposedly Islamic criticisms of our existence, and we should look towards progressive Muslims, if they exist in Bangladesh, for support.

A relationship with the government looks more difficult right now, but building these bridges and eliminating the fear of losing votes is what will really move the government, and perhaps open up the question of legal equality. There is safety to be had in numbers, and we should look to form functional relationships with those individuals and organisations which have made themselves known as allies in the recent past. Together with them, we can approach the government or society at large more easily. We must also leverage differing expertise – remembering that often only local organisations will be able to help us on the ground, as only they are able to navigate within Bangladeshi society. International organisations like the UN and foreign embassies can help, but there must be caution in this approach, lest it be seen as foreign intervention. There is much to be said about barriers to funding of sexual minorities from international organisations, and perhaps we should look into alternative means of support, such as direct appeals and crowdfunding. In all of this, there must be no naivety – none of this will be easy to accomplish, and change will not come quickly. But it is what must be done if we are one day to improve the state of our lives.

BIRANGONA WOMEN

Onjali Q Raúf

How many of you have heard of the term 'Birangona', let alone know the faces described by this exceptional word? I'm guessing not many, which is sadly true even if you happen to be a Bengali – especially if you are a second or third generation British Bengali like me. Up until three years ago, I would have been puzzled by this word. Because despite declaring myself to be a feminist at the age of seven, despite having worked for human rights charities – specifically women's rights charities – locally and globally since the age of fifteen, despite being a Bengali woman whose parents and grandparents witnessed and survived the traumatic birth of the country I trace my origins from, I had never heard of this term or the hundreds of thousands of women whose faces and lives it strives to represent. A dire ignorance which, to my great shame, I was only awakened from three years ago in the most unexpected of places – a small, dark theatre in the outskirts of Wimbledon, London.

In May 2014, I was asked if I wanted to see a one-woman play called *Birangona:Women of War*. I shuddered and shook my head. I was dealing with the abuse of women in my day job – the last thing I wanted to do was spend my free time watching a play on that very topic. But after some persuasion from friends who had agreed to see the play, I gave in. It was a decision that would rock my perceptions of my ancestral homeland and its people and has since changed my life irrevocably.

The play tells the story of Moryom, a newly married village girl who is expecting her first child. War suddenly breaks out, tearing to shreds the calm and innocence of village life. Within what feels like mere moments, Moryom is captured by the Pakistani army and interned in a rape camp. As she unleashes stories of the endless murders, kidnappings and rapes now taking place around her, she clings on to vivid, simple memories of feeding her ducks and chicks, learning to swim, and falling in love with her 'tamarind man'. Archived video footage interspersed throughout the play reminds us that Moryom's stories represent living, breathing women who suffered and dared to live on.

This sixty-minute documentary theatre piece left me shell-shocked tear-streaked, long after Moryom had exited stage right, never to return. Judging from the moment of silence that resounded across the hall before rousing applause broke out, I was not alone in feeling overwhelmed by the endless names of Birangona women as they silently appeared before us like ghostly apparitions. To the audience, Moryom represented Bangladesh's everywoman – the embodiment of thousands of voices we never knew existed because they were missing from our history books, global peace conferences and women's rights platforms. A wilful omission, it seems, aimed at deleting the heart-breaking part women played in the formation of today's Bangladesh and, by extension, the dual worlds British Bengalis now reside in.

'Birangona', as I learned that night, means 'Brave Woman' or 'War Heroine'. It was coined as a mark of respect to honour the estimated 200,000 to 400,000 women and girls who were strategically raped, tortured and murdered by the Pakistani army and their Bengali collaborators during the 1971 War of Independence.

Yet somehow, I had never heard of this atrocity. Ever. Not even as a footnote in the hundreds of texts I had studied over the years concerning the histories, methods and impacts of gender-based violence. Not even though the term itself marked a first in global history – because it remains the one and only time any government in the world has not only openly acknowledged women survivors of rape in war through an honorific title, but actively encouraged their reintegration into a society that was otherwise all too willing to reject them.

To put it into context, the United Nations and our history books rightly highlight, catalogue, and continue to condemn the rapes of an estimated 200,000 women during the atrocious ten-year conflict in the Democratic Republic of Congo (DRC). And whilst the world will have heard of the outrages committed in the DRC, in Afghanistan, in Bosnia, in the Korean and Vietnam wars and in Sudan, it has – for reasons I cannot yet fathom – chosen to dismiss or ignore the victims of one of the swiftest attempts at genocide and strategic use of sexual violence ever to have taken place.

More bewilderingly still, it seems that this is a nullification of conscience that Bangladesh has also willingly chosen to partake in. Travel across Dhaka or Sylhet, traverse the tea plantations and fishing villages of the south, the town squares and farms of the north, or frequent the country's libraries and museums, and you will be hard pressed to find a plaque, statue or exhibition dedicated specifically to the Birangona women the country once claimed to honour. For whilst the roles of female Freedom Fighters (*mukti juddhas*) may continue to be glorified and highlighted by Dhaka's Liberation War Museum, the National Martyrs' Memorial and the infamous Aparajeyo Bangla statue, I have yet to encounter a national tribute designed to honour the figure of the Birangona woman alone.

Why is this? How has this been allowed to happen? Did Bengali women's lives not matter as much as those harmed in other wars? Or were the reasons purely political? Was there a conspiracy afoot to ensure the rape camps of Bangladesh stayed firmly out of sight and out of mind from our collective conscience? And most importantly, what had become of all these hundreds of thousands of women and girls?

Bewildered at my own ignorance, I returned home from the play that night burning with these questions. As with all things in my life, I looked to my mother for answers. She was just nine years old in the year Bangladesh fought for its creation and survival. She had seen rivers of dead bodies, hid with her family in ditches, faced starvation and seen her own father nearly executed no less than three times. Had she never heard of the Birangona women? Had she never seen or met them?

My questions were met with a momentary blank stare, followed by, 'Of course. Everyone knew about the Birangona. Sheikh Mujibur (the founding leader of Bangladesh) made sure we did.' Why then had she – and other members of the family – never spoken of them? After all, there were plenty of uncles and great-uncles proudly sharing stories about their heroic endeavours during 'The War'. Why was the existence of these women missing from their tales? My mother's answer shook me to my core. 'Because we don't speak of it,' she said. 'We were taught not to. We couldn't even speak about what had happened to us as women – let alone speak about them. What your grandmother went through to keep us all alive is unthinkable but she was never allowed to talk about it. The men talk. The women carry on with life.'

After a reflective pause, my mother went on to add, 'And remember, after the war was over, we were faced with famine and a new form of hell. The country was starving to death. Our grains and lands were being destroyed in front of our eyes. We just didn't have the time or energy to face the other survivors of the war. We were too busy trying to find enough food to get us through to the next day.' She later confessed there was a village nearby my grandparents' home in Bangladesh where some of the Birangona women were known to live. 'We knew they were there but no-one was allowed to talk to them. We were told to stay away. Of course, we didn't know why at the time. We were just kids ourselves, remember. It was only years later we found out the real reason. And by then it was too late. The country wanted to move on.'

As with any survivor of a sexual crime, whether it be here in London where a woman is estimated to be raped or sexually abused every three minutes, or one of the thousands of Birangona women still alive and living as outcasts across Bangladesh today, the consequences of the crime remains the same – an unjustifiable 'shame', a burden of 'honour', and an onus of silence is placed on the shoulders of the survivor alone. All of which erodes women's histories – an erosion that seems to be demanded by families, communities and, in the case of Bangladesh, an entire country, in order to enable themselves to carry on 'normally'. The ancient and unjust allocation of blame, of further isolation and humiliation, continues to be one allotted to the woman or girl who has been raped. It is a sentence she is forced to bear for life and throughout history, silently.

My awakening to the existence of the Birangona women led me to delve into a side of Bangladesh's history I had never been conscious of – its political foundations and the consequences which still resonate for all British Bengalis, both Muslim and of other faiths, regardless of the order of generation.

I learned for the first time of the Bangladeshi Collaborators (Special Tribunals) Order of 1972, established to bring to trial those Bangladeshis who had aided the Pakistani Army during the Liberation War both in terms of arms and rape. I learnt that this Order was dismantled in 1975 following Sheikh Mujibur's assassination – events that were controversial at the time and continue to be today. I learnt that the bodies of aborted babies found in rape camps were helicoptered out and dumped in nearby rivers; that women who had survived the camps and had been strong enough not to commit suicide were largely banished from their families, homes and mosques – despite the government's attempts to ensure they were accepted back – and forced to survive with just the clothes they were wearing at the time of their release or rescue; that some survivors underwent a further hell by being taken to work as servants within their rapists' family homes in Bangladesh and Pakistan; that other survivors went back to their families and surviving husbands under a vow of silence which they have not broken to this day; that compensation and psychiatric help was never given until 2015 when forty-one Birangona women were recognised as Freedom Fighters and finally given the same financial dues and care their male counterparts had been receiving for decades; and that there are Birangona women living not just in the poorest of Bangladesh's slums but also in grand estates in India, America, in plush apartments in Italy and, yes, in London. They walk amongst us but have succeeded in drowning out their own stories in order to be able to integrate fully, survive and be accepted as 'respectable' women – as the mothers, sisters, daughters, aunts, cousins, nieces and friends they want and have every right to be.

I also learned of the horrific role so-called 'Muslims' played in instigating and supporting the creation of rape camps and in selling rape as a legitimate tool of war. From the foot-soldiers who carried out the crimes to the leaders of Islamist parties who condoned them, that any man claiming to believe in God could not only commit or condone a rape but perpetrate it in the belief that Bengali women were '*gonimoter maal*' (war booty) – especially those belonging to the minority Hindu population – remains beyond my imagining or understanding. The anger, confusion and perplexity at those 'religious leaders' and the followers who participated in, and even openly supported, God-forbidden acts as a means of humiliating and eradicating an entire nation, continues to divide British Bengali Muslims and their families today. The execution of the Islamist party leader Motiur Rahman Nizami is one such example. The debates, protests and arguments unleashed by his hanging for the crimes of genocide and rape on 11 May 2016 expose just how fresh the wounds of the 1971 war are, and the potential for division it still holds. Even in 2017, as war tribunals continue and despite the evidence and testimonies of brave rape survivors, deep denial and dismissal of the extent of these war crimes continue to divide Bengali and Pakistani communities alike.

Change, however, is afoot. A growing frustration at the way Bangladesh's war heroines have been gagged and silenced for nigh on forty-six years is leading to a movement, spearheaded by the arts, to ensure this side of history is not trampled upon and forgotten. In my sphere and all those that have joined it since, Leesa Gazi's phenomenal play *Birangona:Women of War* was the beginning of that movement. As with all movements, the first and most powerful seed required is awareness. Once one is aware of an injustice, opportunities to rectify it inevitably arise, and it is our choice whether we decide to take them.

For me, that opportunity has come in many forms. Writing this article so that more people can learn of the existence of the word 'Birangona', the brave souls it represents, and its significance to the socio-political framework of Bangladesh and, consequently, British Bengali Muslims is one example. The other lies in my being fortunate enough to support Gazi in the creation of a documentary film comprised of the testimonies of the Birangona women themselves.

Entitled *Rising Silence*, this film recognises that there is a deadline to telling the truth. In today's Bangladesh, those who are openly recognised as Birangona women, and who continue to be discriminated and pushed aside as a result, are in the last stages of their lives. Many, being cast out from their homes or, having witnessed the murders of their loved ones, live in a state of poverty that is unfathomable, dealing with the trauma of what they went through alone. For others who could not abort, or refused to abort, the children they bore as a result of their rapes, the social stigma they face has transcended generations to impact their children and grandchildren. Every single woman embodies the irony that the very term created to honour them is now tantamount to a national swear-word. Yet despite ongoing attempts to silence both them and Gazi, they go on, each carrying a story of global significance that must be captured before they and their histories literally die out.

Of the more than ninety women who have come forward to be part of *Rising Silence* since filming began in 2015, twelve stories have been selected to showcase not only the breadth of experiences borne in those tragic nine months but also the strength, fortitude and beauty every survivor holds within her. We've heard stories such as those of Raju Bala who, to this day, does not know how old she is. During the 1971 war, she was forced to witness the murder of her baby daughter by the opposing army and was raped innumerable times immediately afterwards. Her husband, who tried in vain to save their child, was beaten and severely wounded for his efforts, sustaining injuries that led to his death a few years later. Four decades on, Raju Bala still honours her husband and the love they shared by singing and dancing to her own version of 'The Radha-Krishna Amour' – one of the greatest legends of love within Hindu mythology.

Women like Raju Bala are not a rarity – each and every one of the Birangona women I have come to learn of and love through this project truly represents the essence of the word that was created to honour them. They are warriors, battling not only their own memories but the unjust realities of their everyday lives with grace, humour and an unshakeable faith. Still looked upon as 'women of sin' and treated abominably by surrounding – largely Muslim – communities who, by a mere stroke of luck, did not experience the physical and psychological traumas of brutal rape themselves, they continue to fight to retain their sense of self. In other words, whilst the world surrounding them continues to define them as women of rape, they have refused to allow that word to define them.

It is time these warriors of a nation are respected in a way that befits their role in the birth of Bangladesh. But before this can be done, we must all recognise and accept their very existence and experiences. The Bangladeshi and Pakistani communities of Britain, 'back home' and beyond, and Muslim communities everywhere, have a unique window of opportunity to ensure that one of the most important parts of our collective histories is not lost. It is also a chance to recognise our past and present failings in our duty of care to all women, regardless of faith, colour, caste or creed, and reassess the roles we can each play in preventing the atrocities of rape from occurring – whether on a mass scale in war zones or on the streets in which we live.

Rising Silence will, I hope, ensure that the Birangona women of Bangladesh are never erased from the pages of our history books. I trust that it will also remind us that the crime of rape has an endless ripple effect upon not only survivors, but their families, communities, governments and nations, for a lifetime and beyond, with devastating impacts on faith, politics and history. This is true whether we are talking about the DRC, Bosnia, Korea and Vietnam, today's Syria and Yemen, or any other place in the world where a woman has been raped or abused. Only by confronting these truths and being open enough to listen to the women who have borne the unbearable, can we finally begin to fulfil our duty – our God-given duty – of making any form of sexual violence towards another human a thing of the past.

AMERICAN, BANGLADESHI, WRITER

Sharbari Z Ahmed

The day after the 2016 American Presidential election I was still in denial, which turns out is quite an American trait. I told myself it was a cosmic joke and somehow the punchline would reveal itself, like, 'Hey Americans, gotcha! You've been punked. Now continue buying your snow tyres.' As I wrote this sentence, we were a mere eleven days from truly appreciating that the joke was on us.

On 20 January 2017, Donald Trump was sworn in as the forty-fifth President of the United States of America in Washington D.C. The next day, I drove with several of my female friends to descend on the nation's capital and show the new President that we were no longer in denial and that we would resist him at every turn that required resistance. So many things have changed since then. I am now a dry-eyed pragmatist. Having Trump as president is not surreal to me any longer because every day brings with it some fresh horror. Like the appointments of Steve Bannon, the former chairman of what I assume will be our new state-controlled media outlet, the right-wing *Breitbart News*, as Trump's chief strategist, and Jeffrey Sessions – a man deemed to be too racist to be a federal judge in the Deep South and who views civil rights groups such as the American Civil Liberties Union (ACLU) as un-American – as attorney general. And the passing of a bill by a majority Republican congress to repeal the Affordable Care Act that will leave millions of Americans without health insurance.

We have entered a brazenly fascist period of American history. I use 'brazen' because for some groups America has never really been a democracy or a safe haven. For indigenous Americans and the black population, for example, America has always been a minefield of oppression, betrayal, duplicity and systematic violence – a game rigged in such a way as to see some people fail. It's the elite white liberals and what

I call white-adjacent groups – middle-class and upwardly mobile South Asians like me, for example – who were shocked that Trump's platform of intolerance, divisiveness, and overall gerrymandering was embraced by a vast swath of the white population.

I never viewed myself as someone who lived in one of the bubbles President Barack Obama spoke of in his farewell address. Yes, I live in a wealthy town that was always traditionally Republican but now voted overwhelmingly for Hillary Clinton. But I am one of the few Muslims in the town and since I am not in the fabulously wealthy demographic I am on the margins of the town social scene. My friends are more or less all 'woke', as the parlance of the day goes, meaning they are conscious of the inequities and double standards of race and class relations in this country. The face of the town is also changing. More and more South Asians – mostly upwardly mobile Indians – are moving in. Yet I must admit I too was in disbelief that Trump's inadequacies and buffoonery did not give so many Americans enough of a pause. I now see that this did not happen in a vacuum, that all the ingredients for a white supremacist storm have always been there, lying in wait to reclaim the great 'Christian nation' that had been wrested away by browns and blacks and queers and atheists. The truth is, those of us who are not white or Christian never really had a leg up, never really made headway in claiming America as our own. I am not sure we ever will, Trump or no Trump.

Many liberals point fingers at rural whites living below the poverty line or the middle-aged blue collar white man who feels his voice is being drowned out by the din of feminists and leftists as being emblematic of what the typical American racist looks like. They live in double-wides somewhere south of the Mason Dixon line, in a trailer park, with a three-legged dog tied to a stake and a rusting, disembowelled truck on cement blocks in their front yard. Or they live in a coal town carved into the side of a craggy mountain, its buildings and inhabitants perpetually covered by a scrim of coal dust and resignation that no amount of water can wash off because it's seeped into their skin. See how many stereotypes I was able to pack into one sentence. Indeed, many of Trump's supporters hail from such places but I will posit that these are merely the easiest to identify. There are bigots who hide in plain sight in this country, who are possibly even more dangerous than imbeciles like Trump and Bannon because their bigotry has been in a slow burn, masked by soft political correctness and what appears to be liberal altruism and inclusivity.

This insidious bigotry and wilful ignorance that masks itself as tolerant and expansive resides in many living rooms dotted throughout the country's liberal bastions. But it exists most noticeably in Hollywood, that powerful arbiter of public sentiment – at times even more powerful than the government. Hollywood was and still is mired in racist, simplistic stereotypes, most enduringly concerning Muslims and Arabs. It has always been business as usual, regardless of who was in office and what the atmosphere in the country was. So then is Trump's win such a surprise? And what does it mean for Muslim American writers such as myself?

To answer this, I must look back on the past eight years. Initially the election of a half-black president, educated and erudite with an equally graceful and intelligent wife, lulled me into a false sense of security. I indulged in what I now understand to be simplistic sentimentality and celebrated what I truly believed to be our model democracy. I was led to believe that the nation had finally turned a corner in terms of race relations, that, though we had some way to go, we had taken a giant step towards healing the wounds of the past 400 years.

This was short lived. As I witnessed President Obama embrace the US Drone Program I became increasingly disillusioned and heart sore. I watched him use more drones to wage war on the already beleaguered people of Afghanistan, Yemen, Libya, and Pakistan than his predecessor, George W. Bush, a man not known for his generosity towards Muslims and Arabs. In fact, the Obama administration mounted ten times the number of drone strikes than Bush, Jr did. According to the Bureau of Investigative Journalism, Obama oversaw 'more strikes in his first year than Bush carried out during his entire presidency. A total of 563 strikes, largely by drones, targeted Pakistan, Somalia and Yemen during Obama's two terms, compared to fifty-seven strikes under Bush. Between 384 and 807 civilians were killed in those countries, according to reports logged by the Bureau'.

What this means to me, what this shows me, is that President Obama was just as biased against Muslims and Arabs as his predecessors, and now his successor. I am not saying Islamic extremism doesn't exist or that the US is reacting in a vacuum but Obama's approach to the Middle East and environs smacked of 'business as usual' in casting sole blame on Muslim and Arab nations for the region's instability. Watching Obama cry for the child victims of the Newtown, Connecticut massacre, where over twenty children were gunned down, was the height of hypocrisy and skewed morality, considering that, as reported in *The Atlantic*:

> A new analysis of the data available to the public about drone strikes, conducted by the human-rights group Reprieve, indicates that even when operators target specific individuals – the most focused effort of what Barack Obama calls 'targeted killing' – they kill vastly more people than their targets, often needing to strike multiple times. Attempts to kill 41 men resulted in the deaths of an estimated 1,147 people, as of 24 November [2014].

If this was our leader's foreign policy towards Muslims abroad, how could it not have influenced the way Muslims were viewed domestically and how they were portrayed in the media, on stage, in fiction and on screen?

As a writer and artist, I had thought that having a person of colour as our leader – who knew how to pronounce Pakistan or where Bangladesh was located, who did not seem to fall at Benjamin Netanyahu's feet and whose name was Barack Hussein – would mean America would somehow shift away from bigoted portrayals of Muslims and Arabs. As time wears on, however, I see that Hollywood was and is as committed as ever to 'othering' Muslims and Arabs or just flagrantly continuing the terrorist stereotype. This industry created award-winning and critically-praised shows like *Homeland* – a show where, as journalist Lorraine Ali points out, 'the mere act of a man facing Mecca to pray is a harbinger of ominous events'.

I am genuinely embarrassed to admit my naiveté, because while President Obama settled into a seemingly graceful, confident presidency, black men and women were either being incarcerated or killed on an almost regular basis at the hands of an egregiously flawed justice system and police brutality—just as they had been from the moment Abraham Lincoln signed the Emancipation Proclamation into law and America entered one of its darkest times ever, the Jim Crow period.

Jim Crow laws were enacted in the 1870s in the South to keep Black and White Americans segregated. Blacks were excluded from earning a decent living, equal education and relegated to second-class citizenship though they were now technically free. The laws mutated as time went on to make it easier to throw people, especially black men, into jail for the smallest infraction. Black people lived in a constant state of terror, since 'lynchings were violent and public acts of torture that traumatised black people throughout the country and were largely tolerated by state and federal officials [and amounted to] terrorism'. Lynchings were public events thousands of whites attended. Sometimes they would bring picnic baskets and their children as part of a family outing. They would feast on sandwiches and pop as they watched a young black man slowly die. Thus, historically, for black Americans, white racists have always been the terrorists or the bogeymen in white bedsheets burning crosses on their front lawns. Like the Holocaust, the collective memory of this terrorism has been passed down from generation to generation and hovers in the air between blacks and whites, whether fully conscious or not.

Protagonists often make mistakes on their hero's journey, and I was no different. I ignored the entrenched past, the collective memory and the signs of impending darkness and just forged ahead without much thought. And, as with many epic tragedies, outlandish and absurd eventualities like a Trump presidency and an immigration ban for Muslims had long been foreshadowed.

Of course, the shameful spectre of slavery constantly hangs over this nation. It's hard to forget and ignore, and even Hollywood occasionally tells that story, though mostly imperfectly and almost always with too much sentimentality and with a white saviour in the centre. But the foreshadowing I am referring to was the herding of Native Americans onto reservations, setting in motion a multi-generational cycle of powerlessness, substance abuse, marginalisation and self-destruction. Later, it was the interring of Japanese Americans into camps during WWII, which Franklin Delano Roosevelt had signed into law. Japanese Americans were now viewed as the enemy, with their American identities and contributions to society and their communities disavowed and practically negated. (But German Americans were not treated in the same manner – why?) Few Americans who did not live through that era even know what happened to the Japanese Americans or Nisei. Few Americans can fathom the notion of special camps designed to contain people on this country's soil. Because wasn't that what the bad guys in Europe had done? We're nothing like the Nazis – we fought them off. We saved the world. Sure, the internment of Japanese Americans is taught in schools but I remember it being skimmed over. There was no discussion of how and why this could happen in

America. And I went to an excellent school – but even then, American history was angled heavily in favour of the white male conquerors.

Hollywood attempted to tackle the subject in the form of a decent but not heavy hitting movie, *Come See the Paradise* (1990), starring Dennis Quaid and directed by Alan Parker. It is not too maudlin and honestly portrays what life was like in the camps. But the narrative is co-opted by a white male hero who stands up for his Nisei wife and child.

Looking back, learning about the plight of first-generation Japanese Americans during that era stayed with me. The fact that it was within my parents' lifetime made a lasting impact. So much so, many years later I wrote a short story called 'Alexander Detained' (published in *Critical Muslim 22: Utopias*), about Muslim Americans being sent to internment camps. I wrote it eleven years before Trump took office and declared war on Muslims. I thought to myself, if this could happen in America in the recent past, then it can and will happen again. And we (Muslims) have been the enemy du jour for nearly 40 years, so we would be the next targets. It seems, to my dismay, my imagination does not differ widely from what has been set in motion since Trump took office.

The bright side is that with the imposition of the travel and immigration ban on Muslims, people started to talk about what happened to the Japanese and slowly became aware of the lurking darkness within our National Character. Of course, it has to take something as overt as singling out an entire religion and countries where this religion is practiced for derision and persecution to get Americans thinking and learning about their history. I am reminded of the *Saturday Night Live* skit the week of the election where African American comedians Dave Chappelle and Chris Rock played guests at an election party. They were the only black people there and when Trump won all the white guests were in disbelief that an overtly racist misogynist was elected. One character exclaimed, 'this is the most shameful thing America has ever done!' Chappelle and Rock looked at one another and burst out laughing. Two African Americans, most likely the descendants of slaves, thinking this is the most shameful thing to happen in American history? That single satirical sketch captured the reasons why no one saw a Trump victory coming, not to mention the white liberal elite's disconnect from the experiences of fellow Americans. It's the denial, the short memories, and the lack of imagination that led us here.

For a long time, generations, really, we were able to hide from the world that this nation was divided along strict class and racial lines. Or we made it seem that if there were such divides, they were justified because of the inherent evil or inferiority of certain races and classes. Hollywood contributed to that by perpetuating the myths of the 'savage Indian', murdering and pillaging their way across the vast American plains in Westerns where the invading whites were forced to defend their womenfolk and lands. In its infancy, Hollywood grounded its racist mythology with films like D.W. Griffiths' *Birth of a Nation* (1915) that portrayed African Americans as rabidly sexual and violent deviants. This contributed to the already rooted belief that black men were sexual predators and genetically violent. And before social media and cellphone camera vigilantism captured the systematic police brutality against black men and women, these narratives helped us to sell the notion that we were the ultimate democracy.

Hollywood has always been and still is about formulaic storytelling. You need a good guy, a bad guy, a pretty girl, some romance, some sex, tense conflict and a thrilling resolution that ties everything into a bundle that can then be placed neatly in a psyche that has been groomed to crave happy endings and simple ideas. Anything else might affect box office takings. What it also does is keep people in pre-designated cubbyholes and because Americans generally believe what is in front of them on a screen they carry those cubbyholes home with them. It creates an inability to relate to someone of a different race, religion or sexual orientation without being informed by those 'other types' one has been bombarded with in the media and in entertainment. The chasms caused by this 'othering' have become so vast and deep that Americans know very little, if nothing, about one another except via Hollywood and mainstream media stereotypes.

In the current socio-political climate, this is more dangerous than ever. Faulty, reductive, even fake information can come in to fill the void, dividing us further and fomenting even deeper misunderstanding, resentment and violence. This gross imbalance was always there. It just took a tangerine-tinged megalomaniac to bring it into relief. As the author Toni Morrison said, 'In this country American means white. Everybody else has to hyphenate.' Which brings me to my personal hyphenated existence as a Bangladeshi-Muslim-American.

I've always joked that one day even those who consider themselves yogis might be on the chopping block, yoga being something aggressively appropriated by middle-to-upper class whites in this country. Every non-white, non-traditionally Christian group has had its moment of being the 'villain du jour'. But some groups get the dubious honour of being the Big Baddie, the one who must be vanquished at all costs using the militarised bodies of our young men and women and our tax dollars. For decades, besides the Communists, it's been the Muslims who fill that role. Suddenly now, more than ever, being Muslim-American, and further, being a Muslim-American writer means something different to me, other than always being cast as a terrorist in Hollywood. This is a new development – one I have been almost forced to acknowledge as imperative because of the current socio-political circumstances. Initially, I was not open to exploring these themes because I was focused on developing my craft.

And so, even though I am of Muslim descent, the other part of my hyphenated identity took centre stage for most of my life. My parents were of a generation that saw East Pakistan become Bangladesh, a nation that was envisioned as a secular democracy. Three million Bangladeshi lives were claimed in pursuit of self-determination and independence from the oppressive spectre of West Pakistan. West Pakistan was a theocracy and we, as Bengalis still in touch with our West Bengal, Hindu roots, rejected the notion that our identities were dictated by Islam. Islam was part of our culture in a powerful way, but so was just being Bengali. People had fought and died to maintain Bangla as the mother tongue as opposed to Urdu, which was being imposed on us. Bangladeshi women still wore midriff baring saris and bindis – a Hindu symbol of marriage. This did not conflict with their Muslim identities.

Then at fifteen, I heard about the 'Dotbusters', a hate group prowling the streets of Jersey City, New Jersey, looking for South Asians, primarily Indian immigrants, to beat up and threaten. I feared for my mother, who always insisted on wearing saris and bindis no matter how long she had lived here. We did not live in Jersey City – in fact at the time my parents were in Beijing where my father, a UN diplomat had been assigned. Yet the fear was acute because it was the first time I had heard of a group that specifically targeted my people, that wanted to hurt us, maybe even kill us. I had dealt with my fair share of ignorance and being consistently 'othered', but this was pure hatred. It was the first time I felt vulnerable in my own country, a feeling African Americans have lived with for centuries, which at that age did not occur to me. The knowledge of the existence of such groups forced me to realise that to some of my fellow Americans, I was the enemy.

Then there is the exotification factor. If I am not having racial epithets hurled at me, I am dealing with well-meaning liberals casting me as the fascinating foreigner. When I was starting out as a writer in the late 1990s, I was enrolled in the NYU Graduate Creative Writing program. I was unaware of how competitive it was, which turned out to be a blessing. I was possibly the only Muslim in the programme and one of three South Asians. This was two years prior to Jhumpa Lahiri's big debut, when the most famous South Asian writer in the American consciousness was Salman Rushdie – we were still by and large an unknown and more importantly untested quantity. I did not start by thinking I was a Muslim or a Bangladeshi writer. My voice has always been, if anything, unabashedly American, both in humour and expression. What I discovered immediately was that my appearance and name brought expectations from my fellow students about what kind of story I would tell and how I would tell it. I wrote a story about the troubled relationship between a woman and her mother-in-law. It was set in Bangladesh but I didn't play it up, in that I did not dwell on details about the natural surroundings or present an exotic picture of the culture. There is nothing exotic about mothers-in-law and their fraught relationships with their sons' wives, a dynamic that transcends culture and religion. But the notes I received were, can you talk a bit more about the arranged marriage and what kind of saris the mother-in-law wore? Nothing about the relationship between these two women. The mostly white students wanted the exotica.

I do not think the majority of American readers or agents and publishers have evolved out of this notion as quickly as I hoped. And there is no shortage of South Asian female writers providing the exotica for them. I have been asked to write more about straddling my Muslim/South Asian/American identities and the conflict that comes with that and I have refused because writing about it has never come naturally. I was more interested and still am in stories that are character driven and do not want to be limited to characters of one ethnicity or religion simply because I happen to be of that ethnicity or religion. To me, this would be creatively and emotionally stifling.

But when I was writing for the TV show *Quantico*, I was brought in primarily because of my South Asian heritage since the star of the show, Priyanka Chopra, is Indian. The episodes I wrote had nothing to do with that, which suited me fine. I did not want to be viewed as the token South Asian writer on the team even though that was why I was there. However, there were also two Muslim characters on the show and sometimes I was asked specific questions about them. Yet if the nuances I provided did not serve the bigger storyline or plot they were scrapped. I look back on Season One with a certain regret, wishing I had pushed harder for those nuances and spoken up, especially given the moment when the show was first aired – the beginning of the Trump campaign. I simply did not have enough influence creatively, something I am hoping to change. There are very few Muslims in positions of power in Hollywood and very few Muslim writers in the Writer's Guild of America. This is forcing me to think of myself as a Muslim writer and not just a writer. It is unfortunate and unfair because white writers do not have the burden of representation the rest of us do, especially at times like these.

The reality is that being Muslim and American has become dangerous and my loyalty to my country is brought into question. Politicians on both sides of the aisle ask us to prove our fealty regularly because we are the villain du jour now. This is something I can no longer ignore, something I must address in my work, not just to combat this juggernaut of hatred being directed at us by Trump and his emboldened neo-Nazi constituency but also to place Islamic extremism under the microscope which is undeniably part of the bigger problem. To me, America's two biggest allies in the Middle East, Israel and Saudi Arabia, are violently oppressive theocracies. To deny that America's links with Wahhabism and Zionism are not fuelling much of the instability in the region would be as myopic and foolish as to think that having a black president for eight years would somehow destroy the racial divide. I know that America worked with the Taliban to fight Soviet control of Afghanistan and created a monster there. I know that by supporting the Saudi regime America is essentially supporting Islamic extremism to the detriment of Muslims the world over, including me. I also know this is by specific design. I must explore these disconcerting things in my creative work so I can make sense of the world I am now living in but also because there must be a variety of nuanced voices bearing witness to this latest dark night of the American soul. As a first-generation immigrant, I must share my story because the voice of the immigrant is being silenced by the current administration. If I – if we – don't share it, it will be lost and we will be doomed to repeat history. We are in the throes of this now – war is on the horizon, new wars with new enemies. As a writer, I am obliged to keep turning things over and examining them.

I am also in a unique position as an artist. The spotlight, though nefarious, is on Muslim artists and there will be interest in our voices and perspectives. We are de rigueur. If I sound cynical, let me explain. What I have experienced is that yes, our voices and talents are sought after in these moments, because this will sell. But rest assured it will be the most palatable and already established voices that will be given the dais. The rest of us, who don't pander, who don't couch things in a familiar, non-startling way to appeal to the sensitive white liberal palate, will get less air time. I have thought about packaging my identity to make it easier for the American mainstream to relate to, to make myself small and unthreatening. I think about Brent Staples' seminal essay, 'Just Walk on By', about how he, a six-foot-plus black man with a PhD, must physically negotiate white spaces so he doesn't frighten anyone. He whistles Beethoven or tries to keep as much distance as possible to make others comfortable. He has to, as the physical personification of the Scary Black Man. I think many Muslim American writers, artists, and pundits are doing that now, making themselves 'safe'. But I also know that Revolution doesn't happen in times of great comfort. People need to be jarred into facing the injustice and inequities of their time. So, it's not my job to make anyone feel comfortable – we are not living in comfortable times.

ARTS AND LETTERS

THE GROUND THAT BEARS MY WEIGHT

Sadaf Saaz

Those words went round in my head as I reeled from the descriptions coming out of the attack at Holey Artisan Bakery Café, in Dhaka in July 2016. I had learnt about the Holocaust, and the rise of Nazism in Germany. In the safe, sanitised first world upbringing I had at Queen Edith Junior school in Cambridge. Easy to feel righteous in that pristine, beautiful, cloistered environment. The words resounded in my head...and I couldn't get away from them. I remember thinking then – how could a people just keep quiet? It was incomprehensible that citizens had not raised their voices as people had been removed, one by one. As depicted in Martin Neimöller's poem, which we all grew up internalising, 'First they came for the Socialists, and I did not speak out, Because I was not a Socialist.'

Dhaka had just suffered the country's worst terrorist attack. The cold-blooded clinical way it was carried out jolted me, and the entire country, as nothing ever had before. The dots connected in a flash – with a gnawing, sinking realisation. The apparent random deaths; the Italian in Gulshan the previous year, the lone Japanese person in Khulna, the priests, the pacifist Bauls with their renouncement of worldly possessions – many of these were probably connected – the horror of a Poirot-like revelation. That all the signs were there but we chose not to look. Connecting them would mean that the terror of Islamic State was here. In some form. As a virtual tenuous connection with local groups, a franchise, or even an actual physical presence. Whatever the model of engagement, they were influencing our events. Even if the government chose to still deny it. We were not below the radar. We were not immune – to carry on carefree, far away from the 'war on terror'.

Since 2013 there had been an epidemic of execution murders. Writers, publishers and others, in a land described as having a 'moderate' Muslim Bangla majority population, had been brutally killed, mostly by hacking off their throats, for doing or representing something which purported to be against a type of fundamentalist ideal. As publishers, bloggers, and then minority and gay activists were killed, there was a distancing – of us and them. In a country that we had known to be accepting and encompassing, relaxed with its diversity, we were suddenly relieved that we were not them. Those initially targeted asked for justice of war criminals. Until the death list was extended to progressive writers. Until the attack at Holey, which hit us all. With full force. Now we were in a space where we had already lost a lot, because of our nonchalance, our inherent prejudice, the smugness within our protected battlements. We had enabled this.

We have always had upheavals, political rivalry, strikes, blockades, and unrest. We were used to animosity between our two rival parties, the Awami League (AL) and the Bangladesh Nationalist Party (BNP), due to deep historical reasons. It all seemed part of normal existence in Dhaka – not a real threat to its future. The frustrations of a third world country usually didn't get to me. I had alternatives in place for any particular scenario, personal and professional. Being able to adapt to anything – whether dinner plans, being stuck in traffic for hours, appointments, sudden strikes and disruptions – were all elements one could cope with, in fact were to be expected. One flexibly manoeuvred around them all, or fit them in. I was always on a high about the possibilities of our potential, the enterprising spirit, the continuous innovations, the drive for a better life. On a normal day, Dhaka buzzes with activity; a boy with a cage of chickens on his head, a man pushing a cart with long steel rods for a construction site, a battered, overflowing bus stuck, executives crammed in a CNG auto-rickshaw, schoolchildren overflowing a rickshaw, the ubiquitous Toyota car filling spaces. There is something going on. Always. Young men on motorbikes, beggars, and hawkers with pirated books, weaving their way through the gridlock. Markets, restaurants busy with business – Chinese, Korean, Thai, Indian, Italian, Japanese, you name it. North end coffee, which a famous Australian sports writer who had come to Dhaka tweeted as being the best coffee in Asia. Normally one can't find a free table for a morning meeting.

Suddenly, nearly deserted eateries and cafes. An ominous stillness in the normal bustling spiritedness of the diplomatic area – concomitantly, the government had started an ill-timed drive to clamp down on commercial enterprises housed in 'residential areas', even though licenses had been given to many. Small coffee stops were under threat along with the upmarket boutique hotels and guest houses. Misguided, it seemed that at a time when people were terrified to come out of their homes, gatherings and communities coming together was more important than ever. This strange move by the government served to alienate us further. I needed to talk to and be with those to whom I was closest. I had felt I was going down, down to a place with no way out. This attack was different. Would I be able to take foreigners with no security around Bangladesh? I had flashbacks of the previous year, wandering around Sirajganj town with a few foreigners, with the minimum of fuss. Would I ever be able to stage a play in a provincial town, Jhenaidah, voicing women's sexuality without thinking twice, or thrice? I used to wake up at night in a sweat; that feeling that we had lost our country, that this precious beautiful space had been invaded by aliens. Young boys, Bangladeshi boys, from affluent English-educated backgrounds, had managed to coolly kill. Young people who had been brought up here – the boy in the flat below, the boy who played football with people I knew, students of my friends. Who could be turned into a killing sociopathic machine in a such a short time? They had not seen war first-hand for years, as a Palestinian in Gaza, or an Iraqi youth. Who had enough rage or social media '15 seconds of going viral' ambition, to stab a young woman multiple times? The type of person that spoke softly, with a slightly American affliction, calmly reciting Arabic and declaring a distorted idea of a utopian 'Muslim state' as their goal.

For days afterwards, we were silently making sure we knew our *suras* (when the rumour went around that those had been spared knew their *suras*). Would I have given in and put a headscarf on, to save my life, to pacify them, these young Turks? Would I start to dress differently now?

I run the International literary festival in Dhaka – the Dhaka Lit Fest, with my dearest friends Ahsan Akbar and K Anis Ahmed. The year before, we had fought to keep this literary space, despite dire security warnings from foreign embassies, at a time when we had nineteen cancellations, Facebook was shut down the first day of our festival, and the hangings of two notorious war criminals took place on the last day of the festival. This year was different, the stakes were much higher, as news kept coming out about the Holey Bakery incident of how they died, what they said, what they did. Footage emerged for the world to see, as young men were shown to be casually sitting around, with no sign that they had just killed multiple people, stabbed and mutilated them, and put them up on the internet for all to see, played out in a movie-like surreal setting, where uploading gruesome photos was as calmly done as selfies from a Gulshan party. The connection with the Islamist State and our fundamentalists. It left me with despair and encompassing fear and grief. We knew now, the lengths that Bangladeshis were prepared to go for this 'cause'. A suicide mission like this had never happened before in Bangladesh. We could not ever go back to a normal life. This was it. No more meeting social development goals, having skill development programmes, without a nagging feeling at the back of our minds. We were at the centre of it, as CNN and other international channels showed us all live. Some were saying that we, I, were devastated due to the fact the attacks had hit right to the heart of our bubble – at a place we went to all the time, where you would be bound to bump into many people you know. That, that was why we were so affected. Yes, no doubt on one level – but the real reason was we no longer had the option to deny that there was a force out there, albeit small, to destroy all we stood for. To make their ideology a reality. It could have taken the form of fascism, communism – any totalitarianism. For us, now, it called itself Islamic. More than forty-six souls had lost their lives to date before this attack. Any one of us that didn't subscribe to their 'vision' for Bangladesh could be targeted. There was an overwhelming feeling of loss, dread and self-reflection. It would come up on me, the inconsolable sadness of losing my country. I normally went everywhere, and anywhere. Going to villages and listening to all night performances of folk ballads, sitting in on spiritual forays with maestros singing about universal truths, the wooden boat on a small river in the moonlight listening to *ektara* being played by a boatman's assistant in Ramu, Lauren Moriaty the former US ambassador's wife, spontaneously performing a Hawaiian dance under the tree in Shazadpur where Tagore wrote his famous poem 'Sonar Tori', the energy and possibilities at one of our women's get-togethers, where high on our own endorphins (and nothing else!), women from all districts danced to folk-fusion technobeats. All these images flashed before me. I could suddenly feel a deep empathy and understanding of the pain of having to leave one's home. Of not being able to write. Those I had pitied, sympathised with. Refugees. Writers-in-exile. Immigrants. We had been on a slow sliding path into hell. Yet, I had not wanted to see it.

Aborted

My pen freezes
With ink pressing long-hand,
on crisp, thick page
Thoughts, sieved through mindful edits
Could bring death
Or its shadow, hovering.

Words escape
Revealing my truths

Will it be that I am teleported
to a far-away land, where I have
no wish to be
Exhausted
A struggling migrant community
Rebuilding fragments of a life.

Through boats, containers, ports, high seas
Jetties, danger, camps, bureaucracies
Shoved, cordoned, isolated, interrogated
Frozen, battered, near-drowned, embattled
Refused, denied, entry and movement
Seeking refuge
Beggars of abode.

Or just walk in, via that coveted
red or blue pass-port,
an immigrant.

Bearing disintegrated dignities.
Truncated memories.
Castrated histories.

Pouring my potency and strength
To this new land
Where I am pitied, despised, justified
Leaving the old-betrothed
To vultures.

As I metamorphose into
a statistic

I start anew.

Or stay and stand for
ideals in a battle, perhaps, already lost
Where there are no rules, anymore.

The creeping Saudi-isation of our Islam. It's as if I had suddenly opened my eyes to see a new Bangladesh that I never noticed before. One day, soon after the attack, while shopping in an upmarket mall, I was outnumbered as every other person I saw seemed to be wearing the hijab. Shops were selling cheap versions of designer-looking versions and other 'modest' (read: Arabic type) outfits. I had been noticing a change, yet suddenly it seemed glaring. The separate headscarf has not been part of Bengali culture. It is normal to have an *orna* (or *dupatta*, the name that has come from North India), with the Shalwar Kameez, or the sari *aachol*, its end, can be pulled over the head, during *azaan* (the call to prayer). Appearing in my mind were black and white photos of our mothers and grandmothers – with sleeveless blouses, no conflict with their pious ways and deep faith – with the sari length over their heads when saying *dua* or prayers. Not these polyester head-to-toe gowns, totally unsuitable for our weather, which were suddenly part of our landscape. Or, matching outfits with long dress-like attire made of knit jersey, body-clinging, with headgear of layers piled high attached with a bling brooch, framing a heavily made-up face. I found out that women were buying less saris. Not due to the influence of Star TV, replaced by shalwar/churidar kameez, or a *fatua* and jeans. This was due to women buying Arabic maxis, in urban and rural areas. I did respect that many women may want to put on a hijab, or head scarf or burqa. More and more, women were saying that they felt more comfortable, or safer, or that they were being better Muslims than those who didn't wear these items. On the other hand, others were finding sexual harassment increased while fully covering themselves, as if it was assumed that their voices had been silenced too. A three-year research project that I had led for Naripokkho, on the perceptions of male perpetrators of violence, revealed that men felt just as willing to commit acts of violence whatever the attire, blaming both covering up and non-covering on women! The position, as feminists, that we had taken earlier was to maintain the secular and democratic nature of Bangladesh – that we would not fight for feminism based on what Islam said or not, as some of our Malaysian Muslim friends had done. Now, I felt we had to engage on a deeper level, as it increasingly had spilled out to affect our everyday lives. We had already been fighting, very unsuccessfully, to challenge personal law, which had to be followed according to one's religion, in matters such as inheritance and guardianship. In addition, those who regarded themselves as Muslim feminists were not united in their thinking. Some felt that the essence of Islam was being viewed through patriarchal or a 'Wahhabi'-fied lens, and needed reinterpretation (i.e. many Muslims feel that the Qur'an doesn't call for covering of the head). Others thought that Islam already gave women the rights they deserved. While I respect the right for a woman to wear what she wanted, I didn't want Bangladesh to be a place where a woman could be negatively judged for not wearing a headscarf. To be blamed for what they wore or didn't. The shifting of this paradigm to a very public expression of what was acceptable attire for a woman needed to be addressed, yet there was very little critical analysis of this.

I recall all those years ago as a teenager going to Chittagong College, a state Bangla-medium college. Those breezy rickshaw rides. Feeling suffocated by what I considered then to be so conservative. The importance of going around with the *orna* to hide one's breasts from the male gaze. In provincial Chittagong, even if you didn't cover yourself it should still be there, part of the outfit. Such that till today I find myself reluctant to leave my *orna* behind when I go out, even if symbolically draped over my shoulder. I remember though, that rhythmic hysterical chanting of Shibir marches, the student wing of Jamaat-i-Islami, through the streets. It used to fill me with fear, with stories of their intolerance, raping women, cutting of veins. More than twenty-five years ago. It was contained, then. Those days before 'global extremist Islam'.

Today's women in the early morning and night, fill roads and pathways, putting Bangladesh on the global map. Emerging to work outside the home, to live on their own and make decisions over their lives, carving out their destinies. In Dhaka and Chittagong, hundreds of thousands, in their myriad colours, on the go, with saris and kameezes. I suddenly had a haunting vision of the future; this moving mass mutating into forms covered in black, slits for eyes, hiding all underneath. Unimaginable, it seemed. But then, the unimaginable had happened.

I was grieving for a Bangladesh that we would never have again. Who knew what the new reality would be? I clung to those I cared about. I just would weep, talk with friends, Skype, WhatsApp, text and occasionally meet up. No one wanted to go to a coffee house. Those conversations and friendships got me through those dark days. It was a time for just connecting, reaffirming our bonds. Something had died and been lost forever in Bangladesh that day.

Nostalgia

I feel the brick red soil
Moist under my bare feet
As it carries me
That of ancient terracotta friezes, with sunset-orange red
The familiar vestige of 2-storeys, earth's-colours
Framed with Bougainvillea shade.

Dhaka's half built constructions
Mis-match modern scrawl, boasting Asia's biggest mall
Glass palaces, steel green, with pseudo-Greek

Patched-up, ugliness, with modern sleek
Tin shanties, incessant inflow, every inch packed
Spanking new flyovers and burgeoning slum-shacks
Scraggly tree dividers, waiting to grow
Wide avenues, sewage pipes, BMWs on show
Jammed buses, rickshaws, pick-ups, push-carts
Ciggie-vendors, hawkers, rejuvenated parks
Potholes fixed within dug-up roads
People bustling busy, earning livelihoods
Patchwork mess of the urban hue
Sights and smells, span my view
Stench-infused jasmine
Women in and out of home
African raintrees and Krishnachura flame
Shaded avenues, open gutters and crooked paves.

Home.
This place
Usurped by this Cancer. A Trojan tragedy
Unfolding.

I can well up with despair
Native Americans
The Aborigines
The Incas at Machu Pichu
Countless colonised.
Unable to withstand the onslaught
Of the powerful few.
Destroyed, in their own lands.

The faith I grew up with
Distorted
Infiltrated
An alien fungus, into fissures, alleyways
their extreme tentacles
demanding to take parasitic root

via that perfectly-oiled global machine
through brain-dead foot soldiers
Exiled from our beings
Supported by democracies and dictators alike
What is too high a price.

To keep fighting for
Every space
to breathe my words.

The ground that bears my weight
As I have nurtured it
Passionately, selflessly, with love
Fertilises my roots.

Desensitised, with breaking news
unpalatable.
We shake our heads
Cold, pity, indifference
carrying on our own
Far-off bombing, families torn
Arm dealers gaining, rubble-wrecked lives
Overturned jeeps and drone attack surprise
On our smug LED screens, their worlds intrude ours
For that 3 seconds.

Memories at every corner and road
This cauldron I hate to love
Where I am invisible as I am visible
A petri-dish of exponential multiplicity
This dense metropolis
(Once) full of promise
Removed from suffocating provinciality
Capitulating to the narrow confines
of nationalisms and Islamisms.

The elusive intangible
We were the place
Of Jibanananda, Manasha, Maizbhandari
The land of Lalon, Tagore, Pritilota
Rebellion and syncretism.

As I hold the earth in my hands
Each grain slips through my fingers
Water from my eyes nourish
A soil where anything green will grow
Ideas, as rivers, have freely flowed
injustice always had a champion.

The spirits integral to nourished lands
Our people take calamity hand in hand
To accept fate, yet innovate.

Where cultures, beliefs forged
the identity, which we fought
to keep.

They are not me, those in
Distant places and counter-terrorist
Trucks, embedded crew, grotesque grief
Selectively hiding beneath
World games at play
Conspiracy theories
Mossad, MI6, CIA.

Till one day
I'm caught in the crossfire
The naïve shock
That the well from which I drink
Is poisoned
I look around me
like a surreal Dr Who episode

Dalek-like bodies
Surround me.

As it crumbles underneath
I let go of nurturing something
Lasting
Dreams fall away before me
And everything tangible
Dissipates.

While I try to hold on.

What if this is not my country anymore? This was our moment of reckoning – we would speak up, we would claim our country back. It was not too late to fight for everything we believed in. Every generation has its moment.

My co-directors of Dhaka Literary Festival and I were steadfast in our belief of the need to put on the festival, though in those first weeks after the attack, we gave ourselves time to process it all. The offices of Jatrik, my arts management company which produces the Dhaka Lit Fest, is on the first floor of what was originally meant to be a residential building – built several years ago, the exterior looks unimpressive and shoddy, painted a murky beige, with no signboard on the outside. The gate is not 'manned' by slick guard – there is a guy who acts as such sparingly; normally nowhere to be found, running errands for others. It feels comfortable and relaxed. Our space on the first floor means it's cooler on a hot day; no need to use the claustrophobic small lift that a friend of mine got stuck in for forty-five minutes. Performers, artists, curators, directors, musicians, graphic designers, cinematographers, students, writers, vendors, come and go – for meetings, rehearsals (we had just put on a South Asian adaptation of JB Priestley's *An Inspector Calls*). The accessibility, the constant comings and goings, that organic creative energy, was something we took for granted. Anyone could, and often did, walk in. Last year I had constructed an ugly partition forming an ad-hoc reception area, suggested to give a barrier to anyone entering. Now, we did what we had to do – CCTV, expensive 24-hour security, carefully checking those who enter. Shortly after the

Holey attack I sat down with the Jatrik team. Their reaction touched me — they were aware of the obvious risks. They all felt strongly that cancelling the Literary Festival was not an option: we could never give in. At risk of their lives, we must go ahead with the festival. As I saw my own thoughts, reflected in the resoluteness in their eyes, it gave me hope, along with a realisation of the terrifying enormity of the responsibility, that we had for the lives of the team, the writers, the audiences, to my family, to all who took part. It was July. A month earlier, the play we had put on, with foreigners in the audience, seemed light years away. It seemed unthinkable that we would be able to get back to that 'place' ever again. In August, barely a month and a half after the attacks, we went ahead with the Shaone Dala Festival on the last day of the rainy season, in honour of Manasha the snake goddess, animist in origin, in Tangail, a district, a couple of hours north of Dhaka by car. The festival rituals, performed largely by Muslim elders and artists, were enthusiastically and devotedly attended by huge numbers of the community.

Fast forward to Dhaka Lit Fest in November — in a packed tent, Bangladeshi-Spanish artist Monirul Islam talks about his life works in art, with the Spanish ambassador on the stage, and the US ambassador and head of USAID in the front row. The grounds are filled, all five stages are packed. The previous day hundreds turn up to see one of the world's greatest living writers, VS Naipaul. More than sixty international authors, alongside Bangladeshi writers and poets, take part in animated discussions on a wide range of subjects. Yes, it was terrifying, taking on the decision to put on the literary festival — but not going ahead would have been one more step to losing our country.

Going ahead with the Festival, despite the huge challenges ahead, was our only option. We were not going to succumb to fear. A major bank that had committed to being a key sponsor pulled out, not wanting them to 'risk' their brand image if there was an attack at the Festival. Another sponsor stepped in, believing that what we were doing was important. The government wanted to give the clear message that Bangladesh was not going to give into this radical terrorist threat. This was the time to bring out elements of our pluralistic and rich heritage, and the essence of Islam in Bengal. To counter the pervading narrative of rigid doctrines.

At the back of my mind, I dreaded a headline that would make the news around the world. I don't think I could eat or sleep for months, leading up to and during the event; a knot of tension in the pit of my heart, constantly. We were working intensely to communicate with authors, confirm the programme, doing all the big and little things for the event. Ahsan mainly in the UK, Anis and I in Dhaka. Well aware that no one had yet breached proper first level security, and yet, the new element of suicide missions meant a whole different level of planning.

The recent epidemic of killings of writers had started with the Shahbag movement in 2013, though there had been sporadic threats on writers since 1973, an attack on the Poet Shamsur Rahman in the late 1990s, and a fatal attack on Humayun Azad in 2004. In 2012, the government proceeded with the prosecution of the war criminals who had collaborated with the Pakistan army during the Liberation War. There was widespread support for this step, despite certain reservations on the exact process. There was a national need for healing and closure. The AL had largely been voted in on a mandate to ensure the trial of the perpetrators. During early 2013, the word got around about a possible clandestine plot of the government with Jamaat-i-Islami, the party who had many members facing trial. This sparked off a spontaneous gathering, when one of the collaborators was given a sentence less than the maximum, and he marked it with a 'V for Victory' hand signal. The rumour circulated that those convicted of war crimes would not get the sentences they deserved, due to this underhand deal. Before long there were hundreds of protestors at Shahbag junction.

'*Fashi chai*' ('We want hanging'). I heard the irresistible slogan chanting, catchy as the charged-up movement gained momentum, as I arrived late one night at 2am. It had a carnival atmosphere, with face painting, caricatures of the rogues on public moveable toilet doors, candlelit vigils with flower petal alpana designs and group chants of slogans, often coalescing to mega-crowds, chanting in unison in their thousands. The hay day of bloggers – it was the promise of the anti-apathy of a new generation. Hundreds of thousands came together over those days in early February 2013. It was a spontaneous cry for justice – those initial heady days captured a Woodstock feeling, mixed with a mob-like ferocity reminiscent of descriptions of the Ku Klux Klan. Initially safe for women, later the atmosphere mood changed, and those harassed and groped kept quiet lest they endanger 'the cause'. There was hope that a seemingly disengaged and apathetic youth cared, and that the founding principles were still very much alive. Bizarrely many human rights activists joined in chants of '*fashi chai*'. The authorities felt the pulse and didn't attempt to regain control of one of the major intersections, at the heart of the city. Later on, they tried to cash in. Thousands turned up in support for the *janaza* (funerary prayer) of the blogger Rajib Haider, brutally killed after threats on his life, due to his atheist views. Little did we realise then – it was the start of the spate of murders of those described as 'secular'. The term secular has been associated in the West with a separation of religion and state, as seen by liberal progressives. However, in Bangladesh it was practised as a way to acknowledge all faiths – for example, starting a function with recitations from all of the major religions, rather than none. This demonising of the word 'secular' was a frightening development.

For the first time in many years we heard the phrase '*Joi Bangla*' ('Victory for Bangla') being voiced in a non-partisan way. It was associated integrally with the liberation movement; those who had heard it then said it used to make one's hair stand on end, such was the emotion it evoked. In fact, many of the most rousing war slogans were resurrected during that February at Shahbag. The rhythmic sing-song like continuous repetition of these refrains by huge crowds collectively, day and night, along with synchronised clapping, led by one or two of the main leaders, became a mainstay of the gathering. It was almost like a '24/7 rave party', addictive and mesmerising. As unnerving as the calls for hanging, one popular slogan stood out as particularly troubling, '*ekta duta Shibir dhor, dhore dhore jobai kor*' ('catch one, two Shibir members, catch them and slaughter them'). The Shahbag movement had always been hailed as being a peaceful protest. I wondered at the time, what would have happened if anyone had declared themselves to be a Shibir member in this crowd. Tragically, for the next three years, many of those who believed in a progressive Bangladesh were slaughtered, one by one.

There was no concrete ideology following on from the emotions of the Shahbag cause. Those few liberals who started questioning what was going on, or criticised the focus on 'hanging', were berated for being collaborators of the war, till most fell silent. Then suddenly, the tide turned. I was on the internet one night in a private Facebook chat. And there I saw it, an attack on bloggers as being against Islam. The widespread backlash on social media against the leaders of the Shahbag movement was effective. 'Blogger' became an untenable label. Within hours and days, the whole movement was portrayed as battle between believers versus non-believers. 'Secular' was suddenly associated with 'anti-religious', atheism unacceptable. In a country which had started with a strong socialist ethos, atheism, which had been tolerated, suddenly took on a strong anti-Islamic symbolism. By deflecting focus on them, the targets shifted. Pro-Islamist groups and individuals, from across the spectrum, condemned those associated with the Shahbag movement – some asking for death sentences from the state, and arrests, with others declaring direct death threats. A death wish-list was released, by Ansarul Bangla Team, the banned South Asian wing of Al Qaeda, of those who were 'against Islam', many of whom were bloggers or active on social media. This initial list was actually aimed at those who had been calling for bringing the criminals to justice. Society at large distanced itself. The government, not wanting to come across as anti-Islamic, fell into that binary, and seemed to blame the victims for their writing, more than the killers. Many stopped engaging on Facebook, left the country and stopped writing. Others are still under threat for their lives to this day, with the government slow to take any action.

After the Holey attack in July 2016, the government finally woke up – and found hiding places, hide-outs, conducted raids which were 'successful', killing suspected terrorists in 'crossfire'. Lists of 'missing' young men and women were drawn up. The bodies of the terrorists were not claimed by their families, languishing for days in the morgue, while the attacks were condemned in mosques around the country. That certainly gave us hope – that for a country with a majority of Muslims of deep faith, these chilling murders were widely abhorred and condemned. At the same time the government itself was becoming more authoritarian, and clamping down on dissent in various ways. There had been disappearances and harassment of those linked to the opposition. The terrifying threat of the extremism for a while, however, drowned all else out.

Keen to ensure its vote bank and pander to elements it feels are non-violent, the government is making seemingly unnecessary concessions to those who envisage an Islamic shariah state – for example with Hefazat, the network of heads of *qawmi* madrasahs (private religious schools). After a government clamp-down during a huge peaceful sit-in by Hefazat and its supporters in Motijheel, the country's financial centre, in May 2013, soon after the Shahbag movement, where a number were killed by government forces, some kind of behind-the-scenes truce appears to have been reached. There are ferocious anti-secular sermons on mobiles that are listened to in the slums, with the Islamisation of school text books and the continuing proliferation of 'Talim apas' in different neighbourhoods, preaching orthodoxy. The paradox of Bangladesh comes through. On the one hand screaming preachers condemn Begum Rokeya, a champion of women's rights, for educating girls. Conversely, we continue to make all sorts of strides in women's empowerment, by excelling in girls' football and cricket, and in leading South Asia in tackling gender equity. The beautiful message of divine love, equality and brotherhood, the mystical elements of Islam brought here by Sufi sages over the centuries, don't seem to have much traction against this recent tsunami of Wahhabi Islam. Since 1971, madrasa education in Bangladesh has increased 20-fold, compared to doubling schools for primary education. Eighty percent of madrasahs in Bangladesh are known as *qawmi* madrasahs, funded by private entities, including funds from countries like Saudi Arabia, which export a Wahhabi variant of Islam. The doctrines taught are often not compatible with the secular principles, or the pluralistic nature of Bangla identity. The violence due to the most extreme expression of this orthodox trend has had an effect. Influences from our migrant communities who are in the Middle East in their thousands, also have a deepening impact, as they bring home ideas from the lands in which they have toiled. Our supposedly liberal Muslim country has been deplorable in its unwillingness to speak up or act against intolerant and communal forces. As a Muslim culturally, I am reluctant to write anything about Islam, which I resent. It's the big elephant in the room. To avoid it is to ignore the fabric of the life around me. To write about it runs the risk of one's words being extracted and battered around as dangerous sound-bites. I had grown up loving *milads*, and the beauty of collective singing of '*ya nabi salam alaika*' in rejoice of the Prophet (Peace Be Upon Him), and felt I was always protected by the powerful *duas* taught me by my mother, who has deep faith in Islam. I also remember the wondrous unity I felt meeting Muslims from many different countries at Eid prayers, while growing up in the UK. I had learnt my *suras* in Arabic, along with their meaning, at the Sunday school in Cambridge, from Brother Nazir, a gentle-voiced Syrian student who was studying at the University. Later, I read the Qur'an taught by our Bihari *Malvisaab*. I recently heard a Sudanese-Australian friend talk about her struggle with her Christian upbringing, which was brought into her birthplace by zealous white missionaries, along with brutal white colonisers, who had no respect for their indigenous culture. She told me of how she had learnt of the personal journey of divine love with God, and devotion to spiritual peace and respect for humans of all faiths, from her African-American partner, who was Muslim. I despaired that the spirituality of Sufi Islam, which we always boasted as engendering a tolerant and a deeper spiritual backdrop to our culture, did not seem to be able to counter the prejudice and bigotry surfacing. I know how close I feel to the divine not only when I sing *khayals* based on Sufi philosophies, but also Kabir *bhajans*, and *kirtaans*, which are still rendered at the Kantaji temple in Dinajpur. Bengal's rural communities had essentially imbibed different waves of belief systems over the ages. Even today a Muslim who prays five times a day would not feel any contradiction in hedging his bets and paying his respects to a female deity to protect his crops. Before British rule, communities were not categorised into distinct official religious blocks. The British strategically adopted a 'divide and rule' policy, systematically categorising and playing different groups against each other. Wahhabi-style orthodoxy, which had never taken hold in Bengal, had originally been brought into the region in the nineteenth century by Haji Shariatullah, after he had spent time in Arabia, and Titumir, who had led a peasant revolt against the Hindu *zamindars* (landowners), and the British. (Titumir was trained in the traditional martial arts of *lathi*, where bamboo sticks were used for combat.) Their movements, which were brutally suppressed, had originated in response to the terrible conditions of the Muslims under colonial rule.

The Dhaka Lit Fest was filled with families with kids, young people, writers and readers. Once inside, after traversing the all-important security check posts, it was an intellectual sanctuary of free discourse and dialogue that we really had feared we lost. People thronged in their thousands – Bangladeshis as resilient as ever. We didn't ask any of the authors to censor what they said – and those attending, Bangladeshi and others, spoke freely on a range of topics including religion, spiritual truth and government hegemony. Rural oral performances with Muslim influence telling the stories of Hasan and Hussein through the popular theatre form *jarigaan*, women performing legends of river goddesses, which are normally performed by men, dance fusions performed by women and men, using classical, folk and contemporary forms, which depict over 600 years of Sufi influence, a poetic sparring called *palagaan* (traditionally enacted all night in villages), with a debate about orthodox Islam between a mystic and a cleric, philosophical ballads with traditional instruments with Sufi-influenced lyrics, beautifully worded *puthi* melodic reciting of Islamic tales – all oral renditions which have gone back centuries, were performed at Dhaka Lit Fest that year. There are over 220 forms of intangible cultural practices, rooted in religion, indigenous beliefs and secular traditions. Presentation of these forms served to counter the myth of a dichotomy between Islam and our Bangla culture. The festival was a strong reaffirmation for our writers and poets. That there was hope, and all was not lost. That there was scope to not self-censor, if we continued to stand by our truths.

The death of a foreigner in September 2015 rang alarm bells that we didn't listen to – historically less than a handful of foreigners had been killed in our forty-five-year-old history, and none by terrorists. Famed for our hospitality to strangers, the sheer beauty, resilience, warmth and tolerance of our country was thought to be enough to protect it. Only a couple of years before I had been in Lahore, where a friend told me, 'Don't let what happened with the fundamentalists in Pakistan happen in Bangladesh.' I naively thought that day would never come. That the centuries of amalgamation of beliefs and rituals woven into the tapestry of our history could not be purged so quickly. We had fought a war for it. It was that very essence in rural Bangladesh that had given me the hope, not an idea that an urban middle class would be the vanguard of upholding our beliefs. Ironically, it was those from the elite privileged, disenchanted and disengaged, who went missing, not solely to join to fight the war in Syria or Iraq, but to arm to attack their own. Culture is dynamic, constantly changing. How long would it take for a hegemonic fundamentalist force to change sensibilities? Also, things weren't as innocuous as they seemed. I did not forget the fact that Jamaat-i-Islami, who had been on the side of Pakistan during the war, was able to gain a footing and build up their power and wealth in Bangladesh, as we let them. It seems that this and other incestuous extremist off-shoots may have been biding their time since 1971, to end a secular Bangladesh, and purge it of its pluralist cultural elements. Discovering links of events in Bangladesh to the Pakistan military who continued to deny the genocide was unnerving. I saw the self-styled Pakistan Defence site being one of the first to carry anti-blogger propaganda during the Shahbag movement. Just after the Holey attack, the grandson of Monem Khan, the governor of erstwhile East Pakistan, was killed in a raid on a Jamaat-ul-Mujahideen (JMB) terror cell. Sinister signs of pro-Pakistani forces still trying to destabilise us, all these years later. Years after independence the Pakistan government made comments about our war crime trials, an internal matter for Bangladesh. This was even more unacceptable considering Pakistan has never officially apologised for the genocide, or mass rapes by their soldiers. Recently a Pakistan Defence video was circulated on social media, which denied the genocide of the war. A Pakistani poet who I had always thought to be a friend of Bangladesh, appeared in this anti-Bangladesh video. I wrote to her, telling her of my shock at her appearance in this grossly inaccurate portrayal. She never replied. On the other hand, other Pakistanis had expressed a deep sorrow for what happened during the war, and the complicity of silence then, while a sizeable number of the population is perhaps unaware of what happened, due to lack of discussion and acknowledgement of this part of their history. In Bangladesh, we were also faced with the development of a zealous missionary breed of British-Asian Muslims, trying to bring their brand of orthodox Islam to Bangladesh.

There is no scope, therefore, to feel complacent, or relieved. At least twenty-nine deaths have been claimed by Islamic State to date, whatever their local involvement and engagement. This March, suicide bombers attacked police outposts, the Islamic State's name was inscribed in Bangla in a suspected terrorist den in Sitakundu, and for the first time a suicide attack was aimed at a crowd, in Sylhet. Terror cells in various districts have been raided, linked possibly to a new incarnation of JMB. Yes, we have to fight this, in every way possible.

Innocent no more

Was it the day

When they slaughtered Rajib
Who blogged, questioning god and after-life
Accused, falsely or not, who knows
Of pornographic caricatures of the prophet (PBUH)
As they were circulated on a Pakistani Defence website
Calling him an atheist
As if that justified his gruesome murder
The desperate push-back of slipping power
after his janaza attracted thousands
Stopping traffic
At the busiest junction in Dhaka.

Was it the day

When Silence was my comforter and companion

And they arrested those for 'hurting religious sentiment', even
As they were on a death list, being executed one by one, when the nation
Stood by in complicity.

When was the day

When Abhijit was butchered, despite warnings, he
came to launch his book at Bangla academy, and we didn't shout as we
should have done, Protesting, feebly when others said he shouldn't have
written those things.

Was it the day

When Silence was my refuge

And I didn't use words

as weapons of choice
When they killed
The Hindu priests
The Buddhist monks
The gay activists
The Baul singers
The lovers of music
The lone foreigners
The Sufi sages.

Was it the day

When Silence was demanded of progressive writers and poets, liberals
and thinkers,
And yet they were still not brought to justice.

Was it the day

When five, barely men
Soft spoken, entered our neighbourhood café, sort of
boys next door, casually wearing black t-shirts, with backpacks,
Mobiles, toting guns and savagely stabbed a pregnant woman
dozens of times in her womb, executing Japanese and Italians,
while terrified Sri Lankans hid in the pizza oven,
and my vibrant spunky dear friend was already dead....

Was it the day

When the deadliest organisation on earth, without remorse,
came to our doorstep, and through our children we let them be
part of our history, spinning our trajectory
into mindlessness.

Was it the day

When after howling and crying at the loss of my world, I saw sparkling eyes of young hearts before me ready to risk their lives, to fight for the word.

Was it the day

When I choked. Murdered those words before they were born.
Euthanised the spirit in me to be a vassal of the cloned masses.
Bought into creature comforts
While others were thrown in jail
Ostracised, penalised
Or drained of blood red.

Will it be the day

When I am dragged out
As a woman who dared,
with armies gathering in around me, who will not say a word.

Will it be the day

When I realise

Silence is the enemy.

NIGHT, BEFORE DAWN

Rajib Rahman

Jamil: Just Another Night

Every time Jamil has a night shift, he feels like quitting his job. Staying up all night, two nights in a week! Sleeping during the day is just not the same thing. But this is his own doing. When he studied Hotel Management, he knew night shifts were common in hotel jobs. He is like a woman who elopes with her lover, his thoughts echo ironically. When the passion gets depleted, she can neither put up with the burdens of the relationship, nor go back to her parents with grievances about her husband and in-laws.

A little before eleven Jamil starts his shift. He glances at the PC and sighs, relieved to see there are no new arrivals that night. It will not be a busy night.

It is twenty minutes after midnight. The lobby of the five-star hotel is quiet tonight; more so than other nights. Then Jamil remembers it is Friday night. The bar is closed on Fridays. No wonder there are hardly any people. Only six people scattered throughout the vast lobby. Jamil and Faisal are at the Front Desk. A little further away is the Duty Manager Nasir's desk; Night Porter Rosario is at the Concierge desk; the Security Officer is posted next to him. The most conspicuous person tonight is a young girl in a magenta sari with a silver ream. She sits huddled on a corner sofa. She is not particularly striking, but well dressed and personable. She has a purse and a carry-on case. It is difficult to say how old she is. But then, Jamil can never gauge a girl's age! Perhaps she is in her mid-twenties? Jamil had noticed her when he came on duty, so she must have been sitting here for a long time. She keeps fiddling with her mobile phone, keeps calling someone intermittently. She speaks in a subdued voice; at times she looks agitated, at times vexed; and then for long moments she is silent. After a long break, she dials a number again, but she does not seem to be speaking to anyone anymore. Perhaps no one wants to answer their phone so late at night!

Time crawls, but does not halt the proceedings of the night. Jamil and Faisal complete their tasks for the night. Just when it's time to take a tea break, the girl walks up to the Reception. 'Excuse me, can you please look after my bag? I'll be right back.' Without waiting for a reply, she walks off towards the Ladies', fixing the creases of her sari.

The Duty Manager looks at her from the corner of his eyes. He picks up the phone on his desk and calls Faisal to enquire about the girl.

Faisal: She asked us to keep an eye on her bag; she's gone to the washroom. There aren't even any arrivals tonight. Nasir Bhai, will you see what's going on with this girl...she has been sitting here for ages...

After a few minutes the girl returns to her former seat. Nasir summons the Security Officer on his walkie-talkie. As soon as he appears, Nasir approaches the girl.

Nasir: Excuse me, Madam! Are you waiting for someone?

The girl looks annoyed and turns the other way.

Nasir: Madam, are you listening to me? I'm the Duty Manager, Nasir. Actually, one can't just keep sitting here in the lobby indefinitely. Can I help you in any way?

No reply comes from the girl.

Security Officer: Madam, can you hear us?

Girl: Why are you all bothering me? I haven't done......

She starts to weep mid-sentence and startles both Nasir and the Security Officer. She calms down in a bit and walks towards the Reception.

Girl: Excuse me Bhai, what is the room tariff for one night?

Jamil: $170 for a deluxe room. It comes to $195 including VAT, service charge, etc.

Girl: That seems like a lot of money. How much does that come to in Taka? Is that your cheapest room?

Jamil starts to press the buttons of his calculator and says: Yes, Madam, it is. It comes to about 16,000 Taka.

Girl: That much?!

She stops to think something and bursts out in tears again. Nasir comes up to the Reception.

Jamil: Madam, please sit. Let me see what I can do.

The girl walks back towards the sofa and rummages through her purse, looking for something. Perhaps she is checking to see how much money she has!

Jamil: Nasir Bhai, what do we do? It's obvious that she can't afford to take a room. And I can see that she is not lying.

Nasir: This is the problem with you young people! You get swayed easily by a woman's tears!

Jamil: What rubbish! Think positive for a minute, will you? The question is, what do we do now? After all, there is something called humanity.

Nasir: Yes, yes, I know. But what can I do if she cannot afford a room? I can give a discount of maximum $45, but I doubt that will help matters.

Jamil: At least we can let her sit here until morning, can't we? We can't just ask her to leave in the middle of the night!

Nasir gives Jamil a wary glance. He asks the Security Officer to keep an eye on the girl and returns to his own desk. Jamil walks up to where the girl sits. He doesn't mention the $45 discount.

Jamil: Madam, if you wish, you can sit here until light. No one will bother you anymore.

The girl looks up at Jamil. The look of gratitude is clear through her tears. Jamil is amazed by how vividly one's expressions can portray one's emotions.

The night is dark and still, not only outside the hotel, but inside too. Time trudges on in its own pace. The Concierge is mumbling incoherently about something or the other while newspapers are being sorted by the Security Officer and Rosario. The Duty Manager is slumped on his desk, napping. Faisal watches TV in the telephone operator's office. Jamil stands alone at the Reception and reads his book, Sunil Ganguli's Moner Manush. It's such a good read! He regrets not watching Goutam Ghose's movie which was based on this book.

Joya: The Unending Night

She reflects, so many times she has walked past this hotel, but never seen what it's like inside. Well, she had entered it but only been up to the foyer and the ballroom to visit the various trade fairs taking place there. She is mesmerised by the splendour this evening, when she walks in with Mirza and their two friends. They come to the hotel straight from the marriage bureau to dine at the restaurant here. She feels as though a movie scene is unfolding in front of her...the doorman's suave welcome, the glittering lobby strikingly beautiful, people speaking in hushed tones. The hostess at the restaurant looks far lovelier than some of our top models, she observes, highly impressed. She is, however, taken aback by the sky-high price of the buffet meal – four thousand per person, excluding tax and VAT! But she does not stop Mirza. Let him spend as he wishes tonight, she feels, even though he can hardly spare such a huge amount. It is, after all, their wedding day! It's true they did not have a proper wedding with grand arrangements, but it is and will always remain, very special in their memories...

Time flies while they chat and laugh and share jokes, and before long it's past 10pm. Their friends leave as they had left their baby with his grandparents. Mirza's phone rings as soon as they leave and he walks away from the table to answer the call. Joya wonders who he is speaking with, but she can't hear anything from so far. Joya goes back to enjoying her dessert. Such delicious ice cream they have here! The feeling resembles something like falling in love for the first time! Why can't we get ice cream like this in shops? Or maybe I've never been to shops that sell it, Joya thinks.

Mirza pays the bill and hurries back to the table. 'Joya, I need to go right now, there has been a huge crisis....'

Even before he can finish speaking Joya says, 'What do you mean, what's happened? Why are you so worried?'

Mirza: 'I don't have time to explain anything now. I'll be back really soon. You can sit in the lobby or somewhere. Please don't be mad, I won't take long.' Mirza rushes off without saying anything more. The other diners turn and stare at Joya as she calls out after him 'Mirza wait, Mirza...!' Joya composes herself; even in this state of mind she realises one is not supposed to be so loud in a posh place like this.

So many terrifying thoughts go through her mind as she waits in the lobby. She cannot stop worrying. It's almost midnight and Mirza is still not back. She keeps calling him but there is no reply on his cell phone. Maybe he has lost his phone in his hurry. She informs the friends who had had dinner with them. They try to contact Mirza too, but to no avail. He is nowhere to be found.

Meanwhile, two men decked up in suits come and ask Joya if she needs any help. Oh, what a nuisance at a time like this! How on earth could they help her in such a situation? Is she supposed to say, 'Yes, please help me find the man whom I got married to a few hours ago, who has left me here, disappeared, and is nowhere to be found?' Her eyes tear up in frustration and fear. She rushes toward the Reception and gathers enough courage to ask about the room rates. She might as well get a room for the night. As soon as she hears the reply her confidence crumbles. There is no way she can afford such an expensive room! She wonders if they will ask her to leave the hotel and instantly tears run down her cheeks. She rummages through her bag and finds she has around 8,000 taka and a few small gold jewellery. She is not sure they will keep the cash and the gold and let her take a room, and she doesn't feel like asking either. She has an inkling things don't work like that here. Dejected, she returns to the sofa.

She finds herself going numb with worry. She feels helpless and lost, doesn't know what to do now. She presses her mouth with her hands to keep herself from sobbing out loud. She didn't know she had so many tears stored inside her. A little while later the young Receptionist comes up to her and informs her that she can sit in the lobby until sunrise. 'No one will bother you.' Joya is jolted back into reality. His words bring immense relief to her and she wants to thank him with a smile, but she is still in a daze. He, too, doesn't give her a chance to speak and walks back towards the Front Desk. She puts her phone in her purse and huddles in a corner of the sofa. She is curious and thinks to herself, 'Do they lower the temperature at night or is it cooler because there is hardly anyone in the lobby?'

Her thoughts are jumbled: What is she doing here? Where is Mirza right now and what is happening there? She looks all around her in search of a clock. How come there is no clock here? How will she tell the time? Then she remembers she can always check her phone for the time. But she doesn't feel like looking at her phone, or the time. It's not as if anyone is waiting for her. Strange thing, time. When you need it most, you can't find any. And when you have plenty of time to kill, it just doesn't seem to pass.

The day's events catch up with Joya and she dozes off, exhausted. She has no idea how much time has passed but suddenly she can hear the muezzin's voice carrying the *azaan* to her ears, and she wakes up with a start. She goes to the Ladies' and freshens up a bit. She is startled to see her reflection in the mirror – her features look distorted; puffy eyes and face from crying and fatigue, she guesses. She hurries out and goes to the reception. The young Receptionist is still there, reading something. She walks out of the hotel's glass doors. It's still dark outside but she can hear the birds waking up, chirping. There is a cool breeze blowing, and Joya shivers, not so much from the cold as from apprehension – where will she go from here?! She has no parents; she used to live with her uncle, but yesterday she had left a note to them saying she was leaving for good and would not return to their house. Mirza used to live with a couple of colleagues in a flat in Kolabagan, but she doesn't know the address as she has never been there! Last night they were supposed to move into a small two-room apartment. Mirza had wanted to surprise her on their wedding night, so he had not taken her there before. She knows the area but again, doesn't have the exact address. Joya takes out her mobile phone from her purse; no missed calls. Should she try calling Mirza again?

Dawn is breaking. She starts to feel a new confidence being born inside her. Without knowing where she is headed, she starts walking. In this huge big world full of billions of people, is there not even a small space for her?

Mirza: The Last Night

It is almost four in the afternoon. Mirza realises he must hurry and step into the shower if he is to reach the Marriage Bureau by six. He glances at the room one last time to check if everything looks alright; but he doesn't know himself what it is supposed to look like! Yes, his new bride will be coming here today, but he has made no great arrangements. He has just moved into a small white-walled two-room apartment. The curtains are off-white coloured, the bed sheets a brilliant white with e few red roses in one corner of the bed. He has downloaded some of Joya's favourite songs on his laptop.

His mobile starts to ring in the next room – who could that be now? Yes, he knew it. It's Ahona. His only close friend. Since their first days at university together, they have been friends. So many things have happened since then, so many things have changed. Even their friendship has changed. It is as deep now as it was casual then. There is just one problem – Joya does not like Ahona at all! Strange, considering it was Ahona who had introduced Joya and Mirza to each other.

Ahona: Hi! Why did it take you so long to pick up the phone? Has my driver reached your place?

Mirza: You've already sent him? But I won't start until five or quarter past.

Ahona: I know, but have you forgotten that you are bringing your new bride home today? What if she is hungry or thirsty in the middle of the night?

Mirza says nothing, knowing she will continue talking.

Ahona: Listen, I've sent the maid with my driver. She has some fruits, sweets and dry food that she will keep in your fridge. The driver can drop her back home and then go pick you up around five.

Mirza: But Ahona, why did you have to...

Ahona doesn't let him finish: And I hope you've visited the pharmacy. You don't want to do anything stupid and become a daddy the first night!

Laughing loudly, she hangs up without waiting for Mirza's reply.

Mirza feels slightly melancholic. His best friend will not be present on his big day. She is in the third trimester of her pregnancy. Two years ago, she had had a miscarriage and was being extra cautious this time. On top of that her husband Shabbir is not in town; his office has sent him to Bangalore for some training.

Mirza is pulled from his thoughts at the sound of the doorbell. It must be the driver and the maid.

There is hardly any traffic as it is a Friday. Everything goes smoothly, uninterrupted, starting from the signing at the Marriage Bureau to dinner at the hotel with friends. The problem began after that. Mirza's phone rings and when he sees Ahona's name on the screen he leaves the table to answer it. Mirza is startled to hear Ahona screaming in the background. Ahona's maid is sobbing on the phone and what she tells Mirza is horrifying.

Ahona had slipped on the stairs of her duplex apartment. She was bleeding all over the place. The driver had left a little before ten and Shabbir is out of the country. The maid didn't know what to do so she had called Mirza.

Mirza hangs up and glances towards their table. Joya is enjoying her ice cream, busy with her own thoughts. There is a serene and almost naive look on her face. Who could tell this is the same girl who has run away from home and eloped with Mirza? Mirza suddenly feels like he is the luckiest man alive.

As he approaches the table Mirza starts to think fast. He needs to leave right now. If anything happens to Ahona he will never forgive himself. But will Joya let him go like this? She is a bride steeped in dreams of her wedding night; how could she just let him go? If he starts to explain now, to convince her to let him go, it will take him a long time. No, he will call Joya and tell her everything once he has taken Joya to the hospital. He will send Ahona's car to pick up Joya, if he can get hold of the driver, that is.

Mirza steps out of the hotel, and immediately calls Ahona's driver, asking him to come to Ahona's place as soon as possible. He is lucky to find three auto rickshaws parked right outside the hotel. He hops onto one and asks the driver to rush to Dhanmondi Road 32. The driver asks for thirty takas more and Mirza yells at him to hurry. He will give him whatever he wants.

Mirza starts to make one call after the other from the auto rickshaw. First he calls Ahona's brother. Then he calls a common doctor friend of theirs to ask for the number of Mother Care Clinic. Then he calls Ahona's in laws. Meanwhile, he doesn't notice that the driver has turned from Panthapath to Cresent Road. He realises when the auto rickshaw pulls over.

Mirza: What happened? Why have you stopped? Don't tell me you've run out of gas? And why have you come here?

The driver jumps off the vehicle even before Mirza has finished talking. Mirza feels a cold wave wash over him. Something is wrong. He struggles with the door and finally gets out. As soon as he does he sees five or six young men come and stop next to him on two bikes. They get off and before Mirza can protest they start beating him up. They punch him in his face, his head, his stomach, everywhere they can. They snatch his mobile phone, his wallet and his watch. They seal his mouth with tape. Mirza tries to get away and this seems to agitate the goons even more. A couple of

them bang his head against a wall, and then against a lamp post. He feels a
wetness in the back of his head. His body becomes numb.

He can vaguely hear: Is he dead?
Another voice: Don't be daft, he's just unconscious!
Someone else: Start the bike, hurry!

The hijackers disappear in a cloud of smoke.

Epilogue

Jamil sees the girl from last night at the bus stop when he gets there at
quarter past seven the next morning. She is sitting in a corner, her head
tilted to one side, her gaze somewhere far away. Jamil feels sad but he
doesn't know why. It's not as if he knows her. Still…

As soon as the bus comes, Jamil takes it and gets off at Kalabagan. There
he takes a rickshaw. As soon as he enters the lane where he lives on Cresent
Road, he has to let the rickshaw go because there is a huge crowd of
people. He pushes his way among eighteen, twenty people and then sees a
dead body of a young man. (He doesn't know why he thinks it's a dead
body. The fellow could be unconscious.) There are bruises all over his face
and body. There are flies buzzing around his blood clotted head. The police
are here. Everyone seems to be asking the same question: is the man alive?
Jamil doesn't want to know; if he is alive then good. But what if he is not?
This morning looks ugly to Jamil.

When Jamil gets home he sees everyone celebrating. His mother's cousin
Ahona, who had had a miscarriage last time, has just given birth to a
beautiful baby girl. Mum is searching for a name with 'A'.

A strange sensation seeps into Jamil.

Translated from the Bengali by Mehreen Rahman

SORTED

Ahsan Akbar

Growing up in Dhaka in the eighties, at a time when English novels – if not Shakespeare, Dickens or Kipling – were gold dust, my small collection of books made me a literary boy about town. Not an accolade to be proud of. I'm talking about a town where books equated to boredom: the loner's saviour, the nerd's respite from memorising textbooks. Every now and then I would request my father to buy us more books from his trips abroad. He would nod in agreement but without much assurance. He appeared quite content with the weekend supplements he would religiously devour. Until one day when Sohail, my brother, and I felt a mixture of astonishment, excitement and reverence because our father had brought home a special book. It was wrapped in linen and he diligently placed it on top of our bookshelf. It was the Holy Qur'an in English and Sohail slapped my wrist when I tried to touch it: 'Oi you think you're clean, eh? Ablution first.'

I never challenged my brother – he was my senior by two years. 'Respecting elders... part and parcel of being a good boy,' my mother would always remind me before she passed away in a tragic car accident five years ago. Five years ago, I was only eleven and Sohail thirteen, but he would show immense maturity and grace, especially when softly wiping the rolling tears off my cheeks. 'Boys don't cry,' he would whisper, carefully hiding his own misty eyes.

Five years passed, and it wasn't at all rosy but it was a happy moment for Sohail. His passport got the American visa stamped, which he couldn't stop placing under sunlight, and he curiously examined the watermarks. He was a brilliant student and his high SAT score awarded him a scholarship at the University of Chicago. Sohail had a newsprint image of Milton Friedman from his scrapbook days. He wanted to be an economist for as long as I remembered and also to win a Nobel Prize like Friedman. That was all he wanted. He would occasionally bore me with his nonsensical views on Friedman's monetary policy. I had no interest in economics so it was the wrong Friedman for me; but I loved Marty Friedman, the lead guitarist of my favourite band Megadeth. I knew mother would have been proud of Sohail, and perhaps pleased with me too as I prepared to leave for London. I was nowhere as brilliant as my brother but I was blessed with a British passport. 'British by birth,' my father would say to the High Commission staff in Dhaka, when we would be there every five years for passport renewal. It meant little to me, but I could fathom the sense of pride in his voice.

I was allowed to take the Qur'an in English with me, and I had carefully kept its linen cover. It baffled me, though, for I could not understand the language, even though it was English. Sohail told me the Qur'an is like poetry. You read it with your eyes but you had to feel with your heart. I failed miserably, and I felt awful. When I approached father to help me out, his advice was Zen-like: to keep reading until I would be granted the knowledge from Allah to really understand. 'Rabbi-zidni-ilma, try repeating it five times a day, every day after your prayers,' my father said with a smile and walked away. He was always a man of brevity. He didn't know that I only went for the Friday prayers, which was to be in the mosque with friends, but I learnt the three-worded prayer by heart. I also learnt it roughly translated as O Lord increase my knowledge. And it became my absolute favourite for exam-and-other-pressure type situations.

***

With no one willing to be my legal guardian in London, there was no option but to look beyond the Big Smoke, or as locals would say 'outside of the M25'. A friend of my father agreed to be my faux parent, thankfully. He was a restaurateur in Nottingham. He wanted me to help him with his tax calculations ('it's all very simple, just adding and dividing', he proclaimed) and teach Bangla alphabets to his children in the weekends. In return for the favour, he would sign mandatory forms, attend obligatory meetings in school, and generally pretend to be my 'uncle' although we were not related by even some long shot.

Landing in Heathrow and greeted by no one but the heat wave, I quickly checked whether I had actually arrived in Britain or some Mediterranean destination. Boarding a National Express coach, by evening I made my way into a town I knew little about. Yes, the fables of Sherwood Forest. In my mind, I was thrilled that I would be writing to my friends back home about it. I couldn't wait to find the record stores, the bookshops, the cinemas, and sadly, even the thought of going into a McDonald's excited me. I was following detailed instructions my father had written down on the back of an A-Z map book. Finally, I took a short taxi ride from Broadmarsh bus station, in the heart of Nottingham, to reach Thurland Balti House. I recited rabbi-zidni-ilma three times before walking in there. And many, many times throughout the journey.

'Is Mr Saliq here, please?' one couldn't go wrong with the extra 'please' and 'thank you' on this turf. A dwarfish waiter grinned and showed me to a table right at the back of the box-shaped restaurant, which strangely resembled a cargo ship. Seeing me, Mr Saliq stood up a little, but struggling with his paunch, quickly sat down yet he held his hand forward with his head tilted modestly. It meant both 'hello' and 'welcome'. I shook his sweaty palm and sat facing him but I kept my gaze lowered and unknowingly I recited my little prayer again. I knew he was staring at me, assessing my suitability to be his nouveau-nephew. After a few seconds of awkward silence, I produced a letter my father had written to him. It was in Bangla and after a cursory glance, he said he needed to concentrate to read it. Folding it abruptly, he said 'letter later' and first he must 'sort me out'. He looked like someone who could talk all night with the right company, but his heavy-lidded eyes gave him a perpetual look of seriousness.

'My Spanish is now better than my Bangla. Isn't that funny?' he said and laughed a little which made him cough a little.

'Right, wow, very good.' I was hoping he liked me enough to 'sort me out' and I was aware of his Spanish connection, his first wife was Catalan.

'Do you know Bhayt?' he pointed to the table, messy with papers, and I could see letters from the Inland Revenue.

'Yes, I do,' I said confidently. What a moronic question, I thought, how could anyone not know of Value Added Tax? Besides, he discussed this matter with my father on a long-distance phone call just two weeks ago. My father, sitting by our home landline, shouted throughout the call even though the line appeared clear. It was my father's reflex from his student days in England when long distance phone communication suffered from sounds of sea waves and popcorn cracklings.

'Do you know how to calculate Bhayt returns?' he looked solemn through his gold-rimmed Cartier glasses.

'Yes,' I lied and I quickly tried to offset it by reciting the three-worded prayer in my head. More than ever I needed the knowledge, and I needed the confidence.

'Excellent! Hmm, very good chap you are, just like your dad when he was your age. You look a bit like him, but your skin tone is darker. Okay, so I'll provide you with lodging in a shared house with three other students from Nottingham Trent. It's a very serious house; very serious - everyone works very hard, studying day and night. The loft is perfect for you. You are so lucky.' He spoke like a running train and I listened patiently like a passenger waiting for the last ride home.

'That is perfect. Thank you so much.'

'Forty pounds per week. All-inclusive. Electricity and telephone on top.'

'Thank you, uncle, thank you.' Beggars cannot be choosers, and I wanted to ingratiate myself so I stopped myself from being prickly. Only Mr Uncle knew what he meant by 'all inclusive'.

***

'Sorting me out' also meant finding a school for me. I had done some initial research using the stuffy library of British Council in Dhaka. There were three names I jotted down under Nottingham. And fifty-five under London. I was hoping against hope to find an angel, in the form of a guardian in the great capital of Great Britain. That was all I really wanted.

Before the other residents of the house could wake up, I took a quick shower, skipped breakfast and put the crumply bit of paper in my blazer pocket and gently closed the main door. I had not met my studious housemates yet and I liked it that way. In the hallway, I saw miniatures of at least three Hindu gods: Gyanesh, Durga and Kali and maybe half a dozen Buddhas. Next to them were empty wine bottles, used as candleholders. Someone had tried to give the student house a certain charm and serious character.

Mr. Uncle lived down the road from the serious house. Answering the door, he seemed happy to see me, and offered tea by simply pointing to his mug. I was anxious about the schools and did not want any drink, hot or cold. We needed to sort that out before anything. As a hint, I passed him the piece of paper and kept silent. He looked at the names and had a scowling expression.

'All bogus. Bogus, bogus,' he rebuffed.

'But I found them in a directory at the British Council.'

'Don't trust anything from Bangladesh.' This was his fatwa of the day.

'Right,' I said and giggled to show support. I pinched a corner of my left arm very hard to prevent myself from bursting out in laughter. Nothing could be more British than the British Council, surely a remnant of our colonial past!

He showed me the way Brits do things. Dusting a little, he lifted a directory from underneath a coffee table. It was electric blue in colour and had Thomson Local written in big bold letters. He had this snappish energy, as he started dialling numbers. At letter 'B', we struck gold. Beaufort RC School had a place. We needed to rush over before it went. The school didn't take reservations; the restaurateur tried.

In the car, I was reciting prayers. Silently. I was aware Mr Uncle would be irritated with my showing of weakness. 'People pray when they feel weak,' our physics teacher in school told us over and over again. He was a proud atheist. This newly acquainted Mr Uncle reminded me of Mr Physics, though I had no clue about his beliefs apart from a point he made about his restaurant serving only halal meat. 'Halal Frankfurters', he joked last night, when a plate of sheekh kebab appeared in front of me. I also had a glass of Coke, which was flat but made slightly drinkable with two slices of lemon and three cubes of ice in it. Mr Uncle asked for 'half-a-lager', and one of the waiters kept refilling his glass twice or thrice. His beer belly made sense to me and it nearly touched the steering wheel. The radio in the car distracted me. It was UB40. 'Kingston Town'. I could hear him humming, and it was apparent he did not know a single word - apart from the chorus line - of the song.

At Beaufort, I got curious glances from teachers and students alike. The RC in the name stood for Roman Catholic. I read that twice walking through the large main doors. 'Does that mean one has to be Catholic to be admitted?' I had asked Mr Uncle and because responded with 'let's see', I knew he wasn't entirely sure. We were waiting outside the Headmaster's room. On a wooden removable plaque, it read: 'Douglas Fitzgerald, MA (Oxon)'. I read it at least twenty times before being called into the room. Mr Uncle was asked to stay behind. The school secretary tut-tutted at him when he almost forced his right leg past the door, like a wily salesman. She then went about her affairs as I was asked to sit on a stiff wooden chair. I felt the nerves. Rabbi-zidni-ilma, it was my subconscious.

'So you come from the subcontinent.' Mr Fitzgerald was smiling while looking at my O Level grades and certificates from school.

'Yes, sir. From Bangladesh sir,' I said and stole a little confidence from his smile. I was hoping my grades would be my saving grace.

'Look. Just call me Douglas. Cut the sir business.'

'Sure, sure sir. I mean Douglas.' I quickly responded and I let out a nervous laugh.

'Tell me something. Have you ever taken the Rajdhani Express?'

'No. Not yet.' I was taken aback by the randomness of this question.

'Ah, I see. My favourite train ride was from Delhi to Pondi.' He looked wistful saying that.

'You have been to India?' My lashes jumped up as though I had met a fellow Martian.

'I was born there. British Raj. Long story. But for now, young man, please be present tomorrow at eight o'clock sharp. It will be your induction and we will start with morning prayers.'

'So I go now?'

'Yes, on your way. And do close the door as you leave. Cheerio.'

I nearly jumped with joy but outside the Headmaster's room, Mr Uncle's face appeared grim. Was he being a typical Bangladeshi, upset at not being allowed in the room? He should have been pleased that I got a place in a faith-based school in spite of being from a different background. He crowed and made it clear: 'this school... too many girls, too many,' and 'must concentrate on your studies'. In the same breath, he told me 'no hanky-panky' and that he would take me to the 'top night club' in town to celebrate my eighteenth birthday if I do well and be a 'good boy'. Carrot and stick, I thought, and a wait of a little under two years.

It was a pleasant surprise that Mr Uncle was spot on. The school was brimming with girls, beautiful girls, for sure, and there were only two of us who looked 'foreign'. I calculated my competition during the morning prayers, which was mandatory for all. The other was Dede Romero, straight out of Rio de Janeiro; his mother pursued a PhD at Nottingham University, which I came to learn was the 'proper' one, unlike my housemates' alma mater 'Trent', an ex-polytechnic. It was when I began to understand snobbery existed in every sphere of the British society. Starting with your accent to where you went to school, somehow it all mattered, and especially if you wanted to be part of the upper echelon of this defined class structure.

In school Dede was far more popular than I would have liked. In fact, it was no competition. Boys were in love with the Brazilian football stars, and many of the girls would go COPA-COPA-CABANA in chorus and do a mini-choreographed dance during recess. Dede would encourage them by clapping and shaking his hips. And me, I was just in admiration of my classmates. There was time and place for everything for them, from prayers to studies to sports to parties. They all arranged their minds into neatly compartmentalised sections. I marvelled at this skill that everyone seemed to have.

The girls all loved Dede and we all loved Latin American culture – the bossa nova, the samba. They liked me too, but there was no samba for me. It was all doom and gloom. 'Bangladesh - you guys get a lot of floods, innit?' was the standard remark. It got worse, as I became more approachable: 'do you live in mud huts back there?' and 'do you eat curry with naan bread every day?' It was this unease of an impoverished screen behind me, an image that I did nothing to build but got bestowed with. Bangladesh was simply unsexy next to Brazil. In my defiance, I couldn't care less, though I secretly vied for attention from the girls. And I didn't think rabbi-zidni-ilma would work for these kinds of pursuits. Dede soon started dating Gemma, who was the cutest girl in our year. Within a couple of weeks, every boy in my class seemed to have found someone to go out with. Going out on Friday and Saturday night to get 'lashed, trashed and laid' before coming back to Monday, starting with morning prayers in the school church with Mr Fitzgerald leading the sermon. Everything worked like clockwork.

My weekends were lame in comparison. I listened to a lot of BBC radio and I finally had access to all the books I wanted to read. Aside from the school library, the local council had a decent collection – a paradise for someone like me – and best of all: the membership was free. The two bookshops in the city centre were often my afternoon wonderland; I would be happy to simply browse and memorise titles from the colourful shelves to later look up in the library. On Sundays, I wrote long letters to my brother in Chicago and a few friends in Bangladesh who would respond by sending beautiful cards and letters. The letters were filled with love and hope: '*inshallah* I will see you soon' and 'we miss you but *mashallah* you're doing alright'. This was my culture, the bits of Arabic influence in our communication, and it was always more culture than religious practice for us. Much like my little prayer, in a way. And Beaufort and Nottingham celebrated a different culture. My English friends were not religious but 'Catholics prefer Catholics,' I consoled myself by repeating this in my head, at times when I felt lonely. Beyond that, I had no complaints, for I had my loft abode, my books, my buzzy radio, and housemates so serious that I never saw them, and I had my place in a school full of friendly characters. And as long as I knew my little my prayer, I knew I was sorted for everything else.

TWO SONGS OF LALON

Lalon Shah

Lalon Shah, a.k.a. Lalon Fakir or Lalon Shain (c. 1772–1890), was the greatest of the Bauls, the mystic minstrels of Bengal who preached – and practised – a homegrown humanism and egalitarianism infused with a mix of the Sufi and Bhakti traditions. Legend has it that he was born a Hindu, and on the way back from a pilgrimage to the Jagannath Temple in Puri came down with smallpox and was abandoned by his companions. A Muslim weaver and his wife found him and nursed him back to health, but he lost one eye to the dreaded disease. He could not return home since he had lost caste through intimacy with Muslims. The weaver gave him land to build a house where he embarked on his new life as a mystic singer-composer. A Baul guru called Siraj Shain, who lived in the same village, initiated him into the cult. Lalon has had far-reaching influence on poetry and South Asian culture as a whole. Kazi Nazrul Islam and Allen Ginsberg owe a debt to him; as does Rabindranath Tagore whose Oxford lectures, published as *The Religion of Man,* are infused with Baul philosophy. Lalon's shrine in Kushtia, Bangladesh, draws large numbers of pilgrims and Baul aficionados. The sole likeness of Lalon is a drawing by Jyotirindranath Tagore, the poet's elder brother.

The Mysterious Neighbour

In a mirror city
Close by
Lives a neighbour
I've never seen

Though I long to see him
How can I reach him

Being like an islander
Amidst endless water –
No boat in sight

Of my curious neighbour
What can I say, for
He has neither limbs nor
Head and shoulders

One moment he's soaring in space
And floating in water the next

If only he'd touch me once
All fear of death would disappear

He lives where Lalon lives
And yet is a million miles away

Strange Bird of Passage

A strange bird of passage
Flits in and out of the cage –
God knows how

If only I could catch it
I'd put on its feet
The fetters of consciousness

Eight rooms and nine doors
And little windows piercing the walls
The assembly room right on top's
                                a hall of mirrors

What is it but my hard luck
That the bird's so contrary
It has flown its cage

And hides in the woods

O Heart, beguiled by your cage
You don't see it's built of green bamboo

Lalon says 'Beware! It will fall apart any day.'

Translated from the Bengali by Kaiser Haq

RAIN, RAIN

Shaheed Quaderi

Shaheed Quaderi (1940–2016) is one of the most important Bengali poets of his generation. Born in Calcutta (now Kolkata), he migrated with his family to Dhaka after Partition, and from the late 1950s he and his friends consolidated the modernist movement in Bangladeshi poetry. A lifelong bohemian, he was an engaging conversationalist and at the same time a fastidious poet. He published four collections in his lifetime, and a posthumous collection is under preparation. He was self-exiled since 1977, first in Cologne, then in London, and since 1982 in the USA.

Sudden panic sends colourful homebound crowds –
Even drowsy ones – scuttling
Like scared red roaches every which way
As if someone in cold forbidding tones,
Tolling familiar bells,
Had come to warn of imminent plague,
Emptying homes and city squares

And then
A flying harpoon of lightning rips through
The rounded whale's belly of the sky.
Deafening thunder and hail and rain
As if circular saws had roared into ceaseless motion
While a million lathes let out a whine of torment.

Dusk brings on electric storms –
Nervy, peevish – and more
Clouds and water and wind –
With a chromatic scream

Like a peacock's rainbow tail –
How imperilled our dwellings –
Doors and windows desperate to take wing –
The old house heaving like a tyrannosaur –
Flash floods sweeping through crowded neighbourhoods
And gleaming, abandoned avenues
And swirling round the city's knees.

Through dusk rent by apocalyptic gusts –
As if the wind were Israfel's OM! –
Rain falls aslant on parked cars –
Passengers sit in silence, heads bowed

In anxiety and apprehension, and startled,
Look up to see
Only water,
Swift and fierce,
Flowing ceaselessly
And willy-nilly hear
The sound of lamentation
Resounding in their own hearts
And in the weird, vagrant monsoon's sterile dithyramb.

Tonight in this downpour, on city thoroughfares
Tramp and drifter, homeless youth and lifelong beggar,
Spy, thief and the half-crazed
Come into their own,
Theirs is the kingdom in the rain tonight.
The revenue collectors
Always to be seen carefully counting
Money they pocket every day
Have fled in terror.

They burst into lusty song – dark
Festival hall and drunken placard flapping on the wall,

Twisted telephone pole at whose tip swings
An old dented signboard blown thither by a gust
While the city's countless shutters keep time
With a relentless clatter,
For the constable on the beat,
The sentry and the taxman
Have all fled in terror.

And these too – the wise and the wealthy
And all their sidekicks and sycophants –
They too have slipped away unnoticed –
The torrent has washed away all footprints
And will carry only a few miserable mementos
As it rushes, merry as a civic procession,
Towards cascading town drains:

A cigarette tin floats by with a sound like tambourines,
And broken glass, torn wire, envelopes,
Blue air letters, yellow laundry slips,
Doctors' prescriptions, a white medicine box,
A broken button from a favourite shirt
And miscellaneous keepsakes
From the varicoloured days of civilised existence.

O Lord, amidst the lightning-lit deluge
In this dark city, barefoot and alone
In tattered pantaloons, inside
A shirt billowing like a sail,
I am a shiny little ark –
In the lonely turmoil of my flesh-and-blood existence
Smoulders Noah's restless, red-hot, wrathful soul
But not a single creature, man or beast,
Stirs in response, though scudding waters
Carry the sound of breathing,
The wind wafts anguished cries –
Exalted by what ardour, towards

Which city shall I drift,
Lured by these seductive waters?

Translated from the Bengali by Kaiser Haq

TWO POEMS

Kaiser Haq

Eid Mubarak

At sixty-plus
one doesn't look forward
to festivals –
and further proof
of the inadequacies
of the pocketbook

Preferable by far
is the view
in the rearview mirror

Summertime Ramadan
when fasting was a rite of passage
sweetened by lemonade
chilled with ice
at 2 annas a seer

20-20 eyes on the lookout
for the elusive
Eid moon's
thin-lipped
seductive smile

Henna leaves
ground to a paste

and copiously applied

The bustle in the kitchen
the syrupy sweet dish
and the chicken-pilau

The early morning bathe
the new clothes
with their pleasant factory smell
and cotton wads
soused in attar of roses
in the ear

The calisthenics
of collective prayer
the criss-cross hugs
to a count of three
the coins dispensed
to chanting beggars

The cheerful visits
around the neighbourhood
and naïve delight in company –
the pretty girls prettier
the plain ones less plain

At day's end
a brazen moon
flaunts a saucy smile
a boy runs through clean air
across fields of fresh grass –

from his joyous heart
as I remember it
let me send you
through heavily polluted air

the heartiest of
greetings this Eid
though admittedly
it's only
a teetotallers' carnival

Pariah

Growing up with strays one learns their ways,
making friends with the dust of hostile streets,
wary behind the nonchalant gaze, quick to turn
the silence of a greeting into warning growls,
ready to turn tail, skitter down dark alleys
and bark, bark, bark
as if Qiyamat had come.

Afternoons, back from Anglophone school,
I whipped off my tie and joined the local pack,
mid-ranking member of a motley crew.
Our leader, just years older,
carried neither knife nor knuckle-duster:
armed with a wicked sense of humour
he could turn anyone into a laughing stock;
we were always in stitches;
neighbourhood mothers looked askance.

One summer hols he turned serious for a lark,
a tin shack estivating between one tenant
and the next became a makeshift mosque,
I gave the call to prayer, God is great, great, great,
a fusion of raga and rock, he led as imam;
the neighbourhood rejoiced in the power
that lies coiled in disciplined devotion.

Hols ended, recipient of a Higher Secondary Certificate,
he got a job in his dead father's office; after hours

regaled us with workplace jokes and caricatures,
awed us with plans to acquire higher power:
at dead of moonless night in a cemetery, stark
naked, he'd recite backward from scriptures,
and such power would then accrue, he said,
whipping out a dirty hanky and letting it swing,
that if he wished he could make Earth swing like that;
we joined in his laughter, more manic than ever.

He was out of his job soon after, his humour
of no avail, in fact a liability; rummaging
Wanted columns with growing desperation
forgot to laugh, grew morose, glazed eyes refusing
recognition to disciple and detractor alike.
One day he was ambulanced to hospital bleeding
through the throat. He'll be alright now,
neighbourhood mothers said, he's losing
the bad blood that made him sick,
but from overheard whispers we knew
he'd tried to kill himself. Thank God,
the whispers said, it was with safety blade,
not cut-throat razor. I began missing my prayers.
The dog catchers came on their periodic rounds,
caught a local stray and left; I dreamt
they were coming to catch me as well.

He came back a different being, put up
with attempts at a cure with good grace
until doctor, utterly out of depth, and family
sighed in mutual sympathy
and wrote him off as a lost case.

The rest of the story is easy to sum up
for nothing else happened in his life
as far as one could tell,
he became the local lunatic,

avoided people's eyes and vice versa
as if he had a Gorgon's stare,
grew skeletal in dirty rags, smoked
thrown-away cigarette butts
and in the depth of night
raged with inarticulate guttural roars and
hammered the steps he sat on with a brick
and alternately broke into hideous laughter

while the strays ran around
playing their own game of survival
and demonstrators ran into police bullets
and genocidal wars spread like brush fire
and refugees filled up maps
and independence lit up the sky with fireworks
and varieties of misrule flourished
and slums grew like leaves in spring
and trade and manufacture sped up like falling meteors
and every outfit grew a thousand eyes like Indra
to keep an eye on what was or wasn't going on
and people scattered like autumn leaves
and periodically dog catchers came round armed
with warrants of arrest or deportation

and everyone forgot about him, my sometime imam,
until one day driving around the old neighbourhood
I spot him at a local shop waiting for someone
to drop a cigarette butt, and too late wish I'd stopped
to buy him a pack. No one has heard of him since
but reading or watching the news I often think of him
as of one who understood the desire for power
and the despair of not having it, and though I'll not
take his name, fancying a dread taboo on it,
hear again his manic rage and manic laughter
as valid commentary on all there was or is or will be.

HOMEBOUND

Maria Chaudhuri

There was a time in my life when the question 'where is home?' would have been an absurd one. Born and raised in Dhaka, Bangladesh, I had never been on an international flight until after high school (save a short trip to Calcutta by road in tenth grade). Dhaka was the only home I knew. At eighteen, I prepared to go the US for my undergraduate studies, without an inkling, that I might be opening my heart and my life up to another home. I was sure I would finish college and return to Dhaka. I never would have believed that the pursuit of a foreign education could alter my psychological bearings, unhinge my physical associations and tug at the very roots of my being.

In college, where I looked, talked and thought differently from most of my peers, the first thing which rapidly came under scrutiny was the matter of where I was from. It was no longer just a city I had physically inhabited but an invisible badge of identity permanently stuck on me, sometimes to my detriment. Are you from India? No, I'm from Bangladesh. Is that in India? Well it's right next to India. Do you speak Hindi? Do you walk barefoot? Do you wear the dot? India evoked a world that was far beyond a place; it was a complex organism that dictated every part of a person who claimed to hail from there – their skin, their language, their food, their religion and even 'the dot' on their foreheads. To make matters worse, I didn't even belong to India but some godforsaken little spot on the world map, wedged between India and Myanmar. Some lumped me together with Indians anyway while others decided that Bangladesh, being one third the size of Texas, simply didn't deserve so much attention unless perhaps I admitted to living on a tree. It didn't matter whether a few years down the line, I felt at home in the little town of South Hadley and a few years later still, I fell in love with New York City hard enough to tattoo a Big Apple across my body. What mattered was that I was not expected to.

Clearly, the term home carried multiple layers of meaning. Although my liberal American education continually pushed me to stand my ground, to rely on my own opinion and to value my rights, I never could shake off the feeling that when it came to calling a place home, much of it had to do with how others perceived me. That's why, perhaps, I never claimed the American soil with as much conviction as I did my American ideas, even when I finally held my American passport in my hands. Did it mean that I still thought of Dhaka as home, no matter where I was? Not quite, certainly not always. What it meant was that I had embarked on a lifelong battle with the idea of home, a battle that I still quietly fight in my head, a battle where I am unable to pick a side.

Looking back, I can only say that the act of making a new home is as vast and uncontainable as leaving the old one. As the solid ground slowly recedes from underneath one's feet, it feels as if it is being replaced by quicksand. While I often ache for clear low skies and the harsh cawing of crows at daybreak, I also recall, with affection, walking in the blinding New England snow, hand in hand, with my dearest friend Maya, as she tried to regale my shivering soul with stories of spring time in her hometown in Bulgaria. I remember my heart opening like lotus petals as I walked across the sprawling green into the majestic red structure called Skinner Hall where I would take most of my Philosophy and Religion classes during my undergraduate years. Something in me knew that what I would learn within the old walls of that building would be far more precious than anything I had learned thus far. And I remember the night when I participated in an Indian Dance routine as part of a South Asian Festival, an affair meant to celebrate and comfort the likes of me who had left their homes to come this far. Towards the end of the dance, my gaze suddenly fell on a head of flaming red hair and a pair of piercing blue eyes belonging to a boy who I had fleetingly met at a music class and whimsically invited to the South Asian Show. That he would actually turn up, just for me, was beyond my expectation. But in that moment, donning a haphazardly wrapped sari, garish costume jewellery and a mountain of trinkets on my hair, I felt more alienated from my own skin than ever before. I wanted nothing more than to strip off the layers of shimmer and shine and stand before him to show him that I, with my dark hair and dark eyes, was not all that different from him. I remember lying on a bed of crocuses under the Spring sunshine by a gurgling brook behind my dormitory, reading Emily Dickinson's poetry, some of which she had written on those very grounds, and wondering if I had, finally, come home. But side by side with those momentous images of what had felt most like home were also the fondest memories of all the sights, sounds and smells of Dhaka that I never stopped missing. My heart had expanded to inhabit not one but two homes.

Just as leaving home is never an absolute parting, so also, building a new one has never a complete ending. Now, two decades after leaving Dhaka, I've lived in two different continents and three different countries. What took me many years to fathom and embrace – the acceptance of multiple homes or the renouncement of one home – my two children seem to grasp with perfect ease. Born in Hong Kong to Bangladeshi parents, equipped with American passports and Hong Kong resident cards, attending International schools with diverse student bodies, breezing through Mandarin lessons and travelling to foreign destinations on school holidays, my six-year old son Elan is nonplussed by the duality that constantly plagues me. At the end of each holiday we take, he refuses to return to Hong Kong, where we presently live. Why can't we just stay here? he asks each time. Because we don't live here, I emphasise. Then Rei and I will stay, he says, speaking for his one-and-a-half-year-old sister who thrives equally well in new environments. And what of our home...? my voice trails uncertainly as I am suddenly infected by his childish sentiments, the dull skies and steely skyscrapers of Hong Kong floating gloomily up to my mind's eye. Desperately, I try to find the right words and images which will evoke the love and comfort that the word home necessitates. Don't you miss your room, your toys, your friends? He shakes his head vigorously at the mention of his room and toys, ponders about his friends for a second and then shakes his head again. I have friends everywhere, he says confidently. Indeed, he does. And not only because he is a child and a friendly one. But mostly because I have never clearly defined for him where or what he belongs to. He faces the world everyday with the intention of fitting in, of finding his place in it among the familiar thoroughfare of foreign faces. He is a lilac shrub, shallow rooted and fragrant, adaptable, and easily placed in gardens, balconies or coffee tables. Compared to him, I am a gnarled old oak, roots so deep, they strap me tight and drag me down by the weight of their history.

Sometimes I wonder if I am depriving my children of a sense of belonging (call it home, nation, culture or religion) that is essential to their being. That's when I desperately reach back into my own childhood and pull out rituals and habits — irrelevant as they might seem — and try to reinstate them in my children's lives. I dress them in red and white for Bengali New Year and take them to the lone mosque in the city for Eid Prayers. Yet somehow, these rituals never feel the same anymore, the drive behind them weaker than it had been during my own childhood. Donning a red mickey mouse t-shirt and white jeans do not correlate to the serenity of wearing a red kurta and white shalwar. Eating halal dim sum at the mosque canteen with wooden chopsticks can never be the same as devouring, with one's bare hands, a sumptuous mutton biriyani.

Uprooting takes its toll. You can only re-pot a plant so many times before it starts to shrivel and die. Redefining home, time and again, leaves it without a definition. As the years unfold, this yearning for home falls into a pattern, finds a rhythm, starts to feel natural. I catch a sudden glimpse of Dhaka in the fiery petals of the stray gulmohar tree in my West Kowloon neighbourhood, I smell her in the tall jars of spices in my kitchen cabinet, I see her in the darkening of the sky before one of those fierce Hong Kong typhoons in July, and I can hear her, ever so clearly, in the notes of the Bengali folk music I constantly play on my iPhone when I go for my evening walks. These yearnings lull me into a kind of dreamlike state, shush me into a bubble of nostalgia that haunts me but doesn't disrupt my existence. With each passing day, I am less compelled to leave this modern, efficient, religiously-neutral and culturally-diverse metropolis — whose official language I do not even speak — to run back to the blazing chaos of Dhaka.

Even New York, my second and more recent home, feels more like a longing than a compulsive urge these days. I miss it as I miss my younger days — deeply and intensely — without ever seeking, in any real way, to return to it. I defend it valiantly to those who vilify it, my breath catches when I hear of any trouble in the city, my eyes mist with love when I remember the well-trodden streets and wide avenues that took me 'home' again and again. But here I remain, stationary, seemingly satisfied, in a quiet corner of this small Chinese-British city, to which I am connected by neither clan nor plan.

What has happened to me? What have I settled for when I have never before felt more unsettled than I do now? Where is the horizon? Or have I simply forgotten what I'm looking for? I cannot imagine I will stay in Hong Kong forever. Just as I knew that I would not remain in Japan either. Japan was the third place I had moved to, right after New York and right before Hong Kong. It was during this move I realised that something in me had wilted, become smaller, less visible; some warm and moist part of me had grown a hard crust. I do not mean to say that I was not amazed by the wonder that is Japan; I cannot say that I was not spellbound by the subtle beauty that pervades every corner of Japan — from the futuristic magnificence of Tokyo to the more exquisite temples and flawless Japanese gardens of Kyoto. Never in my life had all five of my senses been so alive, so stimulated and yet so alienated as in those three years in Japan. Never had I felt so alert and so lonely. The part of my soul that needed to grow into its habitat and claim it as my home — much like a seedling spreads its shoots into the soil — seemed to have been lost forever. It was in the Gion district of Kyoto, late one night, walking hand in hand with my husband, that we suddenly glimpsed the tiny figure of a Geisha scurrying along in her resplendent silken robes, disappearing behind the dark wooden door of a ryokan as quickly as she had appeared, the interior of which would remain as much a mystery to us as the person hidden behind the startling white paint on the Geisha's statuesque face. In that moment, I was struck by the poetry that was so abundant in Kyoto, the low moon, the delicate cherry blossoms lending a gentle perfume to the spring night and the fleeting image of the fabled Geisha that could almost have been a figment of our sake-infused imagination. And I remember thinking, if only I could call this home. If only I could call some place home.

REVIEWS

RELIGIOUS MEDLEY

Giles Goddard

It is an oft-noted irony that the religions that want to heal and save us seem so frequently to be riven by conflict. In Christianity, the first major row took place within ten years of Jesus's death. According to the Book of the Acts of the Apostles and attested in the letters of Paul, a serious disagreement erupted between Peter and Paul over whether it was necessary for non-Jewish followers of Christ to adopt the Jewish legal requirements – circumcision, avoidance of pork and so on – or whether they could retain their Gentile customs.

A Council was called in Jerusalem, attended by Peter, whose authority was derived from the fact that he had been with Jesus, and by Paul, who claimed the authority of his conversion. The two camps were unable to agree. It was finally decided that Peter and his followers would remain in Jerusalem working with the Jews, and Paul and his followers would go to the Gentiles.

Suleiman Mourad, *The Mosaic of Islam: A Conversation with Perry Anderson*, Verso, London, 2016.

The internal history of Christianity from then until now is one of disagreements, arguments, battles and slaughter. For example, St Augustine's fourth-century writings were forged in the crucible of struggles against followers of the Donatist heresy in his hometown of Hippo, in North Africa. The thirteenth century Albigensian Crusade against the Cathars in south-eastern France can be considered 'the first ideological genocide' which gave rise to the Inquisition – an institution which developed many of the techniques of persecution that are still in wide use today. And Christianity's relations with members of other faith traditions have been no better, as exemplified both by the Crusades and the later history of Christianity as an agent of colonialism.

There are three dominant strands of Christianity – the Orthodox, found predominantly in Eastern Europe and the Slavic states and tracing its origins back to the early Fathers who lived in the pre-mediaeval period; Roman Catholicism, deriving its authority from the supposedly continuous line of Bishops of Rome now known as Popes; and Protestantism, which traces its history back to Martin Luther's famous nailing of his 95 Theses to the door of a church in Wittenburg, Germany, 500 years ago this September. The Centre for the Study of Global Christianity at the Gordon-Conwell Theological Seminary – one of the largest evangelical seminaries in North America – estimates that in total, there are now approximately 45,000 Christian denominations.

Within those denominations are small groups, particularly in the US, of 'Millenarian' evangelical Christians who stockpile arms and prepare for the final battle, quoting the famous saying attributed to Jesus in the Gospel of Matthew (10:34-39):

> Do not think that I have come to bring peace to the earth; I have not come to bring peace, but a sword. For I have come to set a man against his father, and a daughter against her mother and a daughter-in-law against her mother-in-law; and one's foes will be members of one's own household.

This quote has, along with others, been used to justify intra-Christian violence as well as violence against non-Christians throughout the history of Christianity.

It would be a challenging task to elucidate the origins and current state of the various strands of Christianity in a short book of clear and simple prose. Islam is struggling under even greater geo-political pressures, as well as the horrors provoked by what some refer to – rightly or wrongly – as 'radical fundamentalist Islam'. It is all the more admirable that Suleiman Mourad has produced, in conversation with the British historian Perry Anderson, a calm and accessible explanation in 150 pages of the origins and current state of *The Mosaic of Islam*.

Mourad is a historian of distinction, born to a modest Sunni family in the mountains of south Lebanon in the late 1960s and now professor of religion at Smith College in Massachusetts. His speciality is the development of Islam during the mediaeval period – including innovative studies of the interweaving of the stories of Mary and Jesus in early Islamic texts – but he is also fluently in command of contemporary Muslim politics, particularly in the Arab world.

Coincidentally, at the time of writing this review I was also reading Ibn Khaldûn's *Muqqadima*, a work written in the late fourteenth century which is remarkable in its scope. Many see it as the first historiographical work, a forerunner to the sociology of religion and indeed of Karl Marx's theories on profit and surplus value. Ibn Khaldûn's intentions are more all-encompassing than Mourad's, but his attempt to codify and categorise the breadth of Muslim tradition as he understood it in the fourteenth century has strong resonances with *The Mosaic of Islam*. Both identify the initial roots of the divergences within the Islamic tradition in the differing manuscript traditions and interpretations of the Qur'an; both speak at length of the origins of the Sunni-Shia split and the emergence of Sufism; and both seek to identify and explain the roots and characteristics of the different jurisprudential or *fiqh* traditions. Most importantly, although separated by more than 700 years, both attempt to analyse the dynamics of Muslim societies through empirical evidence and not solely on divine revelation.

Ibn Khaldûn was writing for a predominantly Muslim audience towards the end of the so-called Golden Age of Islam. He had little interest in Christians in Europe who were, in his world-view, backward and largely irrelevant. Mourad on the other hand is addressing a Muslim and non-Muslim audience at a time of resurgent Far Right nationalism, xenophobia and Islamophobia in Europe and the US. It is now nearly a century after the dissolution of the Ottoman Empire, with US-led Western powers occupying or dominating large sections of the Middle East and North Africa. And violent Islamist groups continue emerging globally, with their ever-mutating interpretations of jihad to wage war against not only unbelievers but Muslims whom they consider traitors or apostates. Mourad has the harder task, and his achievement is very great.

To me, the parallels between the Christian and Muslim traditions are manifold. For example, there is an influential part of contemporary Christianity – the conservative evangelical tradition often identified with the Religious Right in the US – which displays little understanding of the history of the interpretation of Christian scriptures. This faction leads the field in terms of opposition to what it perceives to be modern and unjustifiable developments in Christian practice such as the inclusion of women in leadership and the welcoming of lesbian, gay, bisexual, transgender and other (LGBT+) Christians. Their arguments are, ostensibly, based on a literal reading of scripture which is taken to be authoritative, traced directly back to the first Christians. The free, allegorical use of scripture during the Patristic period, by the Fathers of the Church such as St Gregory of Nazianzus or St Irenaeus, or indeed St Augustine, or the importance of tradition, intellect and experience in interpreting scriptural texts is rarely acknowledged.

Similarly, Mourad opens his book by outlining the development of the various texts of the Qur'an which emerged shortly after the Prophet's death. He tells us that 'instead of causing a split among Muslims by insisting on just one reading, scholars decided in the eighth century to incorporate seven readings as canonical, and even to tolerate other less important readings as well'. But, he continues, 'in the early twentieth century, a committee in Egypt produced a Qur'an for modern Muslims with the aim of unifying the world of Islam. With wide distribution and mass production, that version became pretty much used everywhere ... in that sense, most contemporary Muslims do not understand Islam correctly'.

As the Vicar of St John's Waterloo, a progressive Anglican church in Central London, I have been involved in work across faith traditions here and in my previous parish. My work is very much driven by my personal approach to spirituality. I have enjoyed, for example, creating an 'interfaith table' in the hallway of my home which began when an acquaintance gave me a miniature copy of the Qur'an. The table has grown over the years and now includes a tiny statue of the Hindu god Lord Murugan, Buddhist prayer beads made from the bones of a Buddhist monk (a good if unconventional memento mori during meditation), and several images of Christian saints. The most recent addition is a menorah bought from the Portuguese Synagogue in Amsterdam.

The house is religiously plural as it consists currently of a Christian (me), a Muslim and a Jew – all religiously observant in their own way. For a while we had a Hindu lodger, too. We light candles for Hanukkah and Advent and last year we lit up the entire house for Diwali to welcome the goddess Lakshmi. And breaking fast during Ramadan is something I look forward to even if I have not fasted for quite the whole day. My work has also led me to support the Inclusive Mosque Initiative (IMI) and attend events organised by other groups, including Rumi's Circle and the Muslim Institute.

For me, the diversity of traditions is a celebration of the gifts of God to the world. But at St John's I have found myself at the sharp end of conflicts within Christianity both in terms of the inclusion of LGBT+ Christians and also our relationship with other faith traditions, particularly Islam. In March 2015, St John's was privileged to host a congregational Jummah (Friday) prayer organised by IMI and led by Professor Amina Wadud, a noted African-American female scholar, who also delivered the *khutbah* (sermon). I discovered that by welcoming IMI to pray at St John's, I had unwittingly strayed into a hornet's nest. There was an eruption of outrage, predominantly from conservative evangelical Christians who were horrified that Muslim prayers had been held in a church – despite the fact that there are shared prayer spaces throughout the UK, particularly in prisons, hospitals and airports – and in the end I was required by the Church of England to issue a public apology.

I deeply regret the impression that must have been given to my Muslim brothers and sisters, that the Christian church does not welcome Muslims to pray; but it is also, in this context, important to note that we were hosting the prayers because no mosque could be found which was willing to be publicly supportive of IMI's aims or to host mixed-gender prayers led by a woman. So, this particular event simultaneously highlighted the current conflicts in both traditions.

There are certainly elements within both Christianity and Islam that have sought to create an exclusionary orthodoxy which claims foundational authority – from Christ and the scriptures on the one hand and from the Qur'an and hadith on the other. The final chapter of *The Mosaic of Islam* – 'Salafism and Militant Islam' – provides a helpfully lucid explanation of the current influence of militant Islamic traditions. Mourad outlines the origins of Salafism – meaning originally simply a reverence for the founders of Islam, the Prophet and his early companions. He identifies the various strands – initially, Salafism was 'rather liberal' but it has, in the last fifty years, come to mean something very different: 'Salafis today try to relive precisely how they imagine the Prophet Muhammad, his companions and a very few others once lived … Muslims who do not adhere to this model are errant followers of innovations that have no religious legitimacy'. Mourad goes on to explain the importance of the notion of apostasy within Salafi theology: 'the mechanism of *takfir* (apostasy) is crucial to Salafism. You do not need any fatwa to kill infidels. But for Muslims … you need [a fatwa] explaining why they are no longer Muslims and what they have done that has made them apostates'.

Yet Mourad also carefully highlights the diversity within Salafism – from quietist to more aggressive versions – and violent Islamism. Towards the end of the book, the different manifestations of Salafi and militant Islam begin to feel like London buses, all arriving at once. There are so many variations on the theme that it is hard to keep track of them. As he puts it: 'modernist trends in Islam are all over the shop in terms of intellectual coherence and objectives'.

In Christianity, the struggle between the progressive and the conservative wings is being played out within all three of its dominant strands – the Pope is facing strong opposition from within the Vatican to his attempts to open up Roman Catholicism; there is an ongoing battle between 'conservative' and 'open' evangelicals in the Protestant tradition; and the Anglican Communion, of which St John's is part, is only just being held together by historic loyalty to the office and person of the Archbishop of Canterbury.

The challenge within Islam is urgent but it would be a mistake to think that this is unique to Islam. This kind of exceptionalism is what breeds Islamophobia and militant Islamism. This is why *The Mosaic of Islam* is such an excellent contribution to the debate. Mourad point out that 'the head of the Law School at the University of Qatar once said the only way Islamic terrorism can be defeated is by understanding its theology and producing a counter to it. As long as we deny this, there is no way we can gain the upper hand over militant Islam'.

During the height of the IMI controversy at St John's, some of my fellow Christians questioned my understanding and commitment to my faith – some resorted to the Anglican equivalent of *takfir*, if you like. But the apology I was eventually made to issue has not convinced me that my immersion in Christian theology is misguided in any way, especially as a priest with more than two decades of experience in running diverse inner-city parishes. My vision of Christianity is simply inclusive and I am committed to upholding equality, diversity and social justice. I expect I will continue being criticised or condemned by some Christians and perhaps some non-Christians, too – this is where we all have our work cut out for us.

YUNA, HERSELF

Laych Koh

Her road to success reads like a modern millennial story. A young girl in Malaysia teaches herself to play the guitar via YouTube. She starts performing in public, offering her songs on MySpace, and gains enough attention to land a record deal with an American music label. But Yunalis Mat Zara'ai, better known as Yuna, is different from others who have found fame this way. She studied law. She is a Muslim, who believes in dressing according to her beliefs. Her image and music have remained in her control, unlike other young stars who have been coerced into glossy pop makeovers. And after years of striving to break the US market, the 29-year-old singer is now global. She is an artist whose most recent album *Chapters* has been chosen by *Rolling Stone* magazine as among the top R&B albums of 2016. She has collaborated with music big-timers Usher and Pharrell Williams, boasts celebrities Kendall Jenner and Gigi Hadid as her fans, and has been on successful tours in the United States and Europe.

Attention surrounding Yuna, whether in her homeland or in the US, where she is now based, tend to revolve around her faith and her modest but fashionable style. She fights an intriguing double-fronted battle: she has said she faces calls from Westerners to remove her 'oppressive' headscarf while tackling criticism from her Muslim fans that she is not covering herself enough. When her star began rising in Malaysia, her fans loved her humble and folksy style – her songs were as gentle and saccharine as her personality itself. The attention and expectations would intensify as her fame grew.

She moved to Los Angeles in 2011 after being signed to American music label Fader. It was a significant development for an artist in that region, as many have traversed the path Yuna has taken – trying to make it in the tough US market yet getting nowhere. In her first years in America, she was already a source of intense curiosity for her long-time fans – how would she navigate this big bad world of Western celebrity? How would she handle free and easy Hollywood and LA culture? The songwriter had a model as a boyfriend at one point – his social media feed often flaunting his all-American lifestyle and carefree skater boy approach. Always careful to be discreet in her relationships, this particular romance was watched with interest by her fans, probably just as much as it was curiously observed by those in the West, more used to stereotypical views and examples of Muslim women donning the hijab or niqab.

Yuna has always faced up to such prurience and questions about her private life with an ease akin to a smile and shrug. In an interview with *Time Out* Kuala Lumpur, she explained: 'A lot of people ask me, "Oh, you're in Hollywood now. How is it trying to be in the fashion and music scene and you're a Muslim?" It's really not a huge struggle. I just do what I do. Whatever I'm not comfortable with I don't do. I'm not really a party girl. I don't smoke or go out at night. I don't drink. I don't do all of these things that maybe the Western industry scene is so huge and famous for. A lot of people like to have fun within the music scene, which is fine, but it's not really my scene. It's possible to just be the way that I am and still be in the music industry.'

Not everything was so smooth-sailing however, as Yuna's relationship with her American boyfriend eventually crumbled – the results of which are laid bare in the pivotal chapters, essentially a break-up album, which she said was written with raw honesty. 'I didn't want to hold back at all. For a long time in both my relationships and also musically, I was holding back a little bit.'

During her sold-out London concert held in September 2016, the long queue of people outside the Scala was as diverse as the city itself – from 'hijabsters' to hipsters, afros to silver haired folk. Unmissable too were the young Muslim women with their turbans tied with chic sharpness, in the fashion of the songstress they were here to see. There were also plenty of tell-tale accents betraying the legion of Malaysians eager to see their compatriot.

Her onstage banter – while poised and cheerful – was simple and consisted mostly of appreciative thanks to her fans for coming to the show. But a more self-assured Yuna was evident – when she asked if there were any Malaysians in the house and they replied thunderously, she playfully asked them to take it down a notch because 'everyone is watching us'. This cheekiness was also in full affect when she announced super star Usher was present to duet 'Crush' with her, later admitting however that this was not the case. A less adoring crowd may not have let her off with such a tease. It has taken a while for Yuna to reach this level of ease and confidence with her legions of fans.

Back home in Malaysia, an oft-cited country of Islamic moderation, an increasingly conservative Islamic landscape has seen heightened religious policing and a steady intensification of the influence and powers of state religious councils. Despite widespread corruption and the mammoth 1 Malaysia Development Bhd financial scandal involving the government, many Malay-Muslims, the majority of the population, have found it easier to focus on less complicated targets to berate – often female celebrities or individuals in the limelight. These women find that their attire or behaviour is subject to judgement and criticism, frequently from other women. 'It is our duty as Muslims to *tegur* (admonish) one another if you have done wrong,' is a common barb aimed at these celebrities. Yuna has received ample criticism in this guise through the years, but she has refused to play victim to the mob – as her years and experience grow, so does her tendency to offer stinging rebukes to those who attack her.

She has told off some of her Malaysian fans who have opined negatively on her choice of dress. 'Don't be judgmental over what others wear, even if it is different from what you wear,' she once replied to one such fan online. When some Malaysians lashed out at her for accepting a hug onstage from Usher, her 'Crush' collaborator, Yuna did not hold back. Her reply, posted on her Instagram account alongside a photograph of her in a Barney's campaign, was defiant, proud, and worth reading in full:

(This is a) throwback from when I was on Barney's campaign 2014 celebrating cultural differences, shot by Bruce Weber. I remember when this first came out, I was so scared of posting it because I knew the extremely rude conservative Malays (mind you I'm conservative too) would attack me for revealing my neck. Honestly. At this moment I was comfortable. The stylists from Barney's were kind and respectful of my beliefs and let me wear this beautiful shirt dress. I get to pose with this lovely Punjabi couple, along with a fellow half-Malaysian model who later became my friend. People ask me what ethnicity I am, I tell them I am Malay. Why can't you wear a short dress? I tell them I am Muslim.

Someone once told me my experience is mine. No one else is living it. No one has lived it. Outsiders have the illusion that they can tell you how to live your life because they have lived theirs letting other people tell them how to live. My father always told me 'You make your own decision. You can think. Why do you have to listen to other people?' Isn't it weird, the biggest racism and discrimination that I've ever faced, was never from the Americans – it was from my own race. There I've said it. They call me '*perempuan sampah*' (trash) and tell me [I] 'might as well go naked'. The worst, hurtful and sexist things I've ever had thrown to me, were from the lips of the Malays. All I can do is be patient. Allah is great. And Alhamdulillah (thanks be to Allah) for everything. So this is me. I will wear whatever I want. I will show my appreciation whether it's a handshake, or a hug, to my friends, this is me. Save your mediocre downgrading religious [preaching] to yourself, they have no meaning to me.

I have some Americans telling me to take my hijab off, and I tell them no. I have some Malays (telling) me to take my hijab off because 'from wearing a turban (you) might as well take off your hijab', I tell them no too. I am me. Tada! Expect more candidness from your fun, happy Yuna. May it inspire you to be yourself too without letting the toxic people around you define you or how you should be. No regrets, no hard feelings, I will continue to empower women and men everywhere as long as I live *inshaAllah* (God willing). *Lepas ni* (After this)…no filter! Yay!!

This 'no-filtering' assertiveness has made Yuna even more intriguing to watch. As her journey continues, she conveys to the world her multi-layered identity. She has her own style and thoughts on fashion, culminating in her creating her own fashion line called November Culture. She recently launched a vibrant clothing brand with designer Hatta Dolmat, and she has modelled for campaigns by Uniqlo and G-Star. She is passionate about modest clothing, but says her dressing is not 'really conservative'. Her style is anything but boring, and in a testament to her status as a fashion icon she has been featured in magazines such as *Elle* and *Vogue*.

Like many members of her generation, Yuna is enamoured by social media and Snapchat. She utilises these platforms in an attempt to control the narrative that seeks to define her, by issuing her own statements. She embraced the power of technology early, starting from her days of sharing her music through YouTube. As succinct and unembellished as her onstage banter is, she is accessible, honest and open on social media and her interviews. She is as in touch with the modern world as any millennial, while steering clear of Kim-Kardashian-style titillation.

It is her hope that the focus will eventually steer away from her religion and private life to just her music. However, it is exactly what she says outside of her songs that is so noteworthy. Her female, Muslim celebrity peers in Malaysia seldom comment on issues deemed sensitive such as race, religion or politics. Fewer still speak on issues such as women's rights or feminism, for fear of alienating their conservative fan base or attracting negative attention. Yuna has chosen to speak out on such topics without fear of damaging her image - a confidence in her convictions she attributes to her upbringing and her parents' unconditional love and support.

When she was still in Malaysia in 2010, I interviewed her for an article looking at her heritage and background. She discussed her alma mater – Universiti Teknologi MARA – a public university that only admits Bumiputera students (defined as Malaysians of the Malay or indigenous races). She is possibly one of its only well-known alumni to question this race-based policy publicly, saying: 'Am I supposed to feel or think in a certain way because I am Malay? We live with other people and they have the same rights. I believe that other races deserve the same privilege. I studied in UiTM and I am proud to be a UiTM product. But there was one time (the Selangor Menteri Besar Tan Sri Khalid Ibrahim) wanted to open [10 percent] [of the university's] enrolment to other races. There were people against it, saying this is "hak Melayu" (rights of Malays). I am a firm believer that education should be free for everyone. We are Malaysians in Malaysia. Why couldn't we give this [10 per cent]?'

The majority of Muslim female celebrities in Malaysia refuse to call themselves feminists. Malaysian Muslim feminist group Sisters in Islam (SIS) have been vilified repeatedly over the years, despite their long and hard work supporting women's rights. They have been labelled as 'liberals', a derogatory term in Malaysia, and are subject of a fatwa by a state religious council as an organisation deviating from Islamic teachings. The women of SIS have also been attacked by the women's wing of Islamist group Ikatan Muslimin Malaysia (Malaysian Muslim Solidarity), who are unwavering critics of feminism.

But all this has not deterred Yuna. She acknowledges that Malaysia's women face challenges - 'we live in a man's world', she has said – but she maintains that Western misconceptions of Muslim women not having any rights or education must also be corrected. While she has not publicly made a stand on red hot controversies in Malaysia such as the SIS fatwa or incidences regarding women's rights, she has said that she wants to play a part in changing the environment for girls growing up in a country where men are still 'super conservative' and 'are controlling their women'.

Her approach to inspiring change seems to be showcasing a kind of feminism that she says is in a style of her own. To her audience in the West, her key message is that modesty is just as bold as sexiness.

If you want to show your skin or be sexy, great, but at the same time, on the other end of the spectrum, there's someone like me who's promoting modesty of a Muslim culture where we don't really show off our hair or skin. But, that doesn't mean we're oppressed. We practice our rights, and it's my choice to stay covered and not reveal my hair. I'm a Muslim woman, but I have the same talent. I can sing, write music and tell stories. I think it's a different story I'm telling in a very feminist way. I hope that people can appreciate that.

To her audience back home in Asia, she reminds young women to go for their dreams – 'don't be scared of the community you live in, just be brave and strong and do you.'

With an internationally recognised album, a fashion business, and a personal style that grows more assured and bold, Yuna has done what no Asian artist has done in the quest to crack the American music market. Unlike Korean K-pop stars like Rain and Psy who have tried to do this by taking on either outlandish catchiness or unabashed appropriation of black culture, she has kept her Muslim faith in full view. She may find musical inspiration from icons like Lauryn Hill and Aaliyah, but she doesn't do sexy 'twerking' like CL (Chaelin Lee), another K-pop star hoping to make it in the US. She remains herself – still sharing meals with friends and fans, yet traverses her way through the world of stars and celebrities with ease. She continues to experiment melding her soulful songwriting with more edgy production styles. She is based in the West, but is a regularly visitor to Malaysia. Her parents are often at her shows; and she often points them out during her performances. At one point during the London show her mother unceremoniously made her way into the crowd to hug a friend.

The complexity Yuna encapsulates, her modesty and feistiness, navigating between East and West, and negotiating local and foreign expectations, all add to her allure. But instead of shying away from the responsibility of being an icon, she grasps the opportunity to use her fame to speak out. The *New York Times* has called her a 'poster girl for young hijabsters' and the *LA Weekly* has labelled her 'the Muslim pop star'. She says that they are apt labels: 'It's perfect actually. It shows that people care about the person that you are, and with me, I don't have a persona when I'm on stage – it's just me, I don't know how to be another person'. As she sings repeatedly in her song, 'Lights and Camera':

> Cause these lights won't kill me now
> Saying these clothes won't change me now
> Saying these words won't scare me now
> Saying I will be myself
> I will be myself

In being herself, Yuna is showing that there is no one quite like her. Her breezy independence knocks out the notion of oppressed Muslim woman. She says that in America people are now getting used to her as a musician, and that the Muslim-related questions have lessened. However, as her fame increases and she becomes more well-known in a polarised post-Brexit, President Trump world, this interest may continue just a little bit longer.

DO TELL US

Tamim Sadikali

I contemplated the bold red cover and turned over the pages. At that moment the words of Sabrina Mahfouz jumped out at me. 'It never fails to surprise me how much representation can empower and how much non- or mis-representation can disempower.' I was propelled back to a memory that continues to unsettle. 'Daddy, what colour am I?' I don't remember the answer I gave to my then four year-old daughter, but I do recall being blindsided – feeling utterly unprepared for the question. Not being one to take things at face value, she came up with a follow up just a few days later. 'Daddy, am I "wheatish"?' Soon thereafter, I remember us bumping into a neighbour in the park, a Hindu, and my daughter, happily swinging away, suddenly interrogating her about language, and whether we spoke the same one. Instinct made me rebuke her, but in hindsight, there was no need – her questions weren't rude, just born out of a burning curiosity – something which I'd never wish to dampen in her. Already feeling somewhat inept, it wasn't long before my little girl dealt me her coup de gras: 'Daddy, am I Muslim? Is Mariyah Muslim? Why is no-one else in my class Muslim?'

Sabrina Mahfouz, editor, *The Things I Would Tell You*, Saqi Books, London, 2017

As adults, we recognise that yearning for terra firma – sure-footing within one's milieux. But throw any deviation into the mix and, as my daughter was clearly finding out, the ground beneath you can feel less supportive. Ethnicity, nationality, gender, sexuality, language, skin colour, religion – how many of us are forever shuffling our deck, and wondering which card to play next? Alliances form and then dissolve; points of meeting end up morphing into fissures. For some, this ever-changing landscape is a thing of beauty – an opportunity. For others, the fight for purchase on this brittle earth is hugely disorientating. Give or take, I was thirty-five before I felt comfortable in my own skin. So how will the dice roll for my daughter? Insight into possible futures can be gleaned from *The Things I Would Tell You*, an anthology of writing by British Muslim women. With contributions in poetry as well as prose, fiction and non-fiction, and covering weave and weft in the tapestry of female British Muslim experience, this is a hugely ambitious project that Sabrina Mahfouz has spent nearly two years working on.

For those few who'll ask, 'but why only women?', the trite answer would be we've heard enough from the men. But there's subtext here, pushing through in almost every single word of this collection, that needs surfacing – that for an army of reasons, (now is not the time...), there are few more dishevelled, dysfunctional and discredited groups in society, than British Muslim men. But disproportionately, it is their women picking up the mess, and the hijabis absorbing the lion's share of hate. Which is all bad enough, but then after playing their part in effing up the world, the menfolk promptly slink off home and eff things up there too. The end sum of which is that (British) Muslim women have long been pincered – by Muslim men on one side, and wider society on the other. And if stoicism were once a virtue, the women featured in this collection are all too happy to disembowel stoicism, and leave its entrails hanging on the city gates.

Shaista Aziz's visceral and damning story on honour killing in Pakistan is a good example. Sania was killed by her own brother for bringing 'shame' upon the family for allegedly 'looking' at a man. That's it: just looking at a man! With unbridled viciousness she was stabbed over and over again. Sania's brother killed her in the family home and nobody did a thing to stop him. The police arrested him but released him a few days later because their mother had forgiven him. Aziz's reportage leaves no room for ifs, buts or whataboutery, merely laying bare a 'toxic, patriarchal culture that deems women and girls as subhuman, property owned by men who can be discarded and tossed away in the blink of an eye.' I must confess, my native instinct is to scream 'but not all of us!'. I wanted to tell the world about the achievements of my own wife who hails from a lower-middle class family from Karachi, and of whom I am unabashedly proud. How she owned an events-management company and became a TV actress, and that I am her biggest fan. But in the face of such a chorus of female anguish, I stymied my own self absorption and recognised that in this moment perhaps it's better to simply listen.

The key to a collection, any collection, is to never let the readers settle – to keep wrong-footing them, throwing them that curveball. And to that end, Mahfouz has edited the book with real skill. With each contribution, the gaze shifts – from looking inward, onto one's own family and community, to outwards, and the totemic subjects of Iraq, Israel/Palestine and Islamophobia. And the writers range from fourteen-year-old first-timers to established big-hitters, and straddle the racial kaleidoscope, as well as regions of the globe they can call home. It's a rich, exotic and heady brew that keeps the reader thirsty.

The Bantustan of today's Palestine, or the Iraq wars and everything after, are at once necessary, and yet low-hanging fruit: any related art can muster a sympathetic audience. But real art speaks to more than the packed galleries – it can reach even those with their backs turned. Selma Dabbagh's stories on the West Bank wall and the raising of Jenin succeed because, first and foremost, they are compelling works of short fiction. The main characters are rounded human beings, not simply mouthpieces for the writer. 'The memory of his arm behind my waist pulling me down onto him – that alone could floor me for what felt like weeks,' recalls one protagonist, her mind running off in tangents as tanks fire and bulldozers raise the earth around her. If fiction dealing with such political events are to leave a mark, it will be in humanising the 'other' – in reclaiming territory that terms like 'collateral damage' have stolen. And through obliquity, avoidance of saccharine-sweet emoting, natural dialogue and even the universal recognition of mundane domesticity, Dabbagh achieves this. And the very same can be said of Shazea Quraishi's poem, titled 'Fallujah, Basrah'.

According to modern-day Paki-bashers, Islam is not a race. Indeed, some scholars and writers have argued that Islamophobia – fear of Islam – cannot be pinned to the coat-tails of 'traditional' racism. And yet for those on the receiving end, Islamophobia's expressions, its manifestations, look and feel exactly like old-school Paki-bashing. So where might the truth lie? Aisha Mirza, or rather her mum, gives an idea of how one might just have informed the other. A first-generation Pakistani living in North London, she was just sixteen when she won a writing competition in

1980. In her winning essay, entitled 'An Event of Importance to my Community' she wrote:

> Today it is unsafe for any Asian person to walk down the street without his colour, speech or dress being made fun of. You, the readers, may think that I am exaggerating, but the truth of the matter is, that no-one has yet realised the seriousness of racial prejudice... I fear that by the time we grow up, we will be too full of bitterness simply to sit down and talk things over. If anything isn't done, we are going to explode and you will explode with us.

All of which suggests how crucial the 'Grey Zone' is – that liminal space targeted by ISIS, wherein different peoples intermingle on an equal footing, not as a sop, 'they put our heads on sticks and call it multiculturalism', as Mirza wryly observes, but in genuine mutual respect and for the exchange of ideas. Ahdaf Soueif writes about the very same concept, 'this ground valued precisely for being a meeting-point for many cultures and traditions', which she calls the 'Mezzaterra'. Strikingly, she wrote her piece not post-ISIS gifting us the 'Grey Zone' label, but rather in 2004 – and about her formative years. She writes movingly about how her once open and verdant landscape withered and shrunk, before concluding, 'but in today's world, a separatist option does not exist; a version of this common ground is where we all, finally, must live, if we are to live at all.'

An 'irregular' but fascinating contribution comes from the journalist Samira Shackle, and her on-off search for not-quite-love for Pakistan. With an English father and Pakistani mother, she recounts a trip to Pakistan with her mother after many years of absence, wherein both mother and daughter seemed to be working out their relationship with the country. For someone in her position it would be easy to soft-peddle or even drop the 'ethnic' side to her makeup, but early on she shows that this is not who she is. Neither Ms Shackle nor her mother 'go native', but she soon finds herself returning. 'I spent a year there in all, working, travelling, figuring out my place in this complicated land and putting back together the two "halves" of my identity, halves I hadn't realised were fractured. I've been back every year since. It's not home, but there is a place for me.'

Jerry Hall's mother is claimed to have famously declared that a lady should be a chef in the kitchen, a maid in the living room and a whore in the bedroom. Arguably, the aphorism today might even make some (Western) women laugh. Reading Kamila Shamsie's short story though, 'The Girl Next Door', one can only assume that it's all but a graduation requirement for Pakistani women. That instead of being some pithy observation from a bygone era, in Pakistan, it's actually reinforced with a fourth clause: ...and a scarf-wearing good-girl in public. But other writers in this anthology find no humour in such conditions. Again and again, their most acrid bile is reserved not for the totemic West, but for cultural norms they consider misogynistic, and Muslim men. 'When a man comes to view your house it must be clean,' writes Amina Jama euphemistically, conjuring up a mother-figure instructing her daughter on womanly duties in 'Home, to a Man'. 'Don't just sweep that dirt under the carpet. Trim that rug.' Trim that rug indeed, 'Brown Girl' as Azra Tabassum mesmerises in her poetry contribution.

While Jama and Tabassum hide their invective behind poetic form, Triska Hamid's interviews of women in the Muslim dating scene is more direct. Women descry the seeming failure of British Muslim men to succeed academically, professionally, emotionally, socially. But the pièce de résistance is not the hurt Muslim woman or the angry Muslim woman or even the 'woke' Muslim woman – it's the sexual Muslim woman. If agency is the privilege of control, including control of others, then to some extent, Mahfouz's book serves as something of a restorative; a corrective – for she has deliberately chosen to celebrate the British Muslim woman not as British, not even as Muslim, but first and foremost, as woman. Imtiaz Dharker and Nafeesa Hamid respectively give the lie to the de-sexed Muslim woman. Instead they celebrate the fullness of the experience of Muslim women, refusing to shy away from sexuality and sensuality.

There's a hijabi meme currently doing the rounds – a burqa-clad woman and a blonde wearing nothing but sunglasses and a bikini cross paths in the street, each throwing the other a disdainful look as they walk away: 'Everything covered but her eyes,' thinks the blonde. 'What a cruel, male-dominated culture!' And from the woman in the burqa: 'Nothing covered but her eyes...what a cruel, male-dominated culture!' Two women, standing just a few feet from each other, but worlds apart.

Today's (British) Muslim women must not so much run this virtual gauntlet, as permanently live within it. Layer on top of that the inequities that all women can face, as well as the tensions that a religious identity carries in an increasingly secular world, and it's a tough place to be. The likelihood of coming unstuck, of suffering real psychic harm, may well be greater than any other segment of British society. So assuming these fault-lines persist, the question then becomes: how does one not only survive, but thrive, whilst in a permanent state of revolution? *The Things I Would Tell You* does not offer a simple answer or a single message – but that's the point. The writers in the anthology have adopted various strategies: embrace religion, reject religion, embrace race, politics, activism, intellectualism, sex... As with the rest of us, there's a smorgasbord of designs for life to choose from – and it's a buyer's market. If boiled right down, the keynote is that British Muslim women are done with being pincered – with being disenfranchised and disavowed, regardless of by whom.

We named our daughter Shehrebanu. It's an historic name, awkward for a British tongue and 'heavy' – but I don't regret my choice. She's now five years-old and loved at home, cared for at school, and excited anew for each day. Eventually, the fault-line between the worlds she straddles will hurt her, but I hope she keeps a firm foot in each. My role as a father is simply to immerse her in the best of both worlds, and right from now. It's possible that Ahdaf Soueif's 'Mezzaterra' will make a strong comeback, but I doubt it. Nevertheless, I share Soueif's view that, mutually assured destruction aside, it's surely the only possible future – and one that I hope my daughter grows up to embrace.

ET CETERA

ON NADIYA HUSSAIN

Samia Rahman

Oh Nadiya. How we love you. I mean, like, everyone. Over 13 million people watched you win, rooted for you to win. You were invited to bake the Queen's ninetieth birthday cake. A slightly 'leaning tower of Pisa-esque' orange drizzle cake, designed and created by your solitary self. Who would have thought? You were the plucky girl-next-door who stole the nation's heart. *The Great British Bake-Off* Muslim woman winning in hijab. Your self-deprecation and stumbling self-belief won us all over. You grew in confidence in front of our very eyes and week by nail-biting week we rejoiced when, convinced you would be voted off the show, you survived to make it through to the next round. For some viewers, you became probably the only British-Bangladeshi hijabi Muslim they will ever consider something akin to a friend. You were sweet and funny and real. You hugged a gay man and kissed your husband in front of everyone and without a care in the world. Nadiya, you made women who wrap their hijab real.

I was a little late to the party, I must confess, but I loved you too. This is despite never having watched a single episode of *Bake-Off* before. Eventually the buzz around you was all too seductive and I sneaked the occasional peek, instantly and willingly surrendering myself to fandom. You were single-handedly procuring the hearts of the masses. Resolutely visible in your headscarf, you held the coveted trophy aloft and declared that you would spend the rest of your life refusing to be restricted by self-imposed boundaries. There was not a dry eye in the tent and, in that moment, you were an emblem of self-belief to women everywhere.

After emerging from obscurity and sweeping the nation into a tumult of exultation, we find that now you're, well, everywhere. Ubiquity is a double-edged sword and as your star rose I began to sense the inevitable snipers in the shadows. The whispers were harsh. Was your success down to the fact that what you present is the 'acceptable' face of British Islam? Never without a smile on your face, except when crying tears of joy, your humble demeanour made you oh so inoffensive. With your sparkling personality, there was much scoffing that you were the epitome of the 'good Muslim' – eager to please and contort your foreign-ness in an effort to win over the twinset and pearls brigade.

Swathes of Middle Englanders, despite their Tory and Brexit leanings, took to you. Your openness had the effect of penetrating even the hardest veneer. You crept into the emotional core of those who began to almost imagine you, yes someone like you, as their neighbour, chatting over the garden fence about the pesky foxes digging up otherwise immaculate lawns. With a thrill they could envisage the scene, encapsulating deep-seated Nadiya fantasies. How you would bring your famed clementine and cod curry, cooked according to your grandmother's very own recipe, along to a dinner party they were hosting. You would be introduced to everyone gleefully as the lovely scarf-wearing Muslim lady, and you would all sit down to feast and partake in earnest and worthy conversations. You were not anyone's token Muslim friend in hijab of course. That would just be crass. The unthinkable was happening – even these people loved you. Their idea of you and all that you represent as a woman who covers her hair, a self-professed second-generation practising Muslim.

You are an icon, a role model, an inspiration and every young (Muslim) baker's aspiration. But, and it seems almost sacrilegious to repeat, do you hear what they say? Asking, could it be that you've set the bar so very high on what it takes for a Muslim to be accepted by society? Some of us, after all, just cannot live up to your impossibly impeccable credentials. Do you have to be so adorably personable? Sometimes even the most burden-conscious, representing, hijab-wearing, Muslim can be prone to a grumpy and sullen demeanour during their morning commute. Your diffidence is a charm but does it set a precedent for the more confident and strident 'sisters' who are just not so, well, grateful for every opportunity society deems fit to throw their way?

Reality television is such an unforgiving force, scrutinising, rating and commenting on every aspect of your appearance and behaviour. It requires the strongest of characters to endure the relentless amplification of your every single flaw. But you, the nation's sweetheart, were thankfully spared the cruelty of tabloid dissection. Your emotive facial expressions were deemed thoroughly delightful, there were no cruel barbs about your appearance or attire (and rightly so!). Your wearing of a headscarf was viewed paradoxically as a non-event by some yet simultaneously slated as the factor that made your win so momentous by others. You turned your diminutive stature into a tower of strength. In your own words, you walked into the tent feeling so small, the teeniest contestant to have ever competed, yet walked out feeling empowered and tall. The adjectives used to summarise your appearance and manner were kindly and benign. There were no jibes or taunts about attractiveness or physical appearance. You were cute and sweet and just lovely. Society seemed actually able to have a grown-up appreciation of you.

Yet that only led to the objectification being directed elsewhere. While you were patted on the head simply for being adorable, all eyes were fixed on your dream-boat husband! Let's face it, Bangladeshi men have been somewhat neglected when it comes to being ranked in the hotness stakes. Middle England suddenly went doe-eyed over this unsuspecting Bangladeshi Muslim IT worker. Twittersphere, populated by the Nadiya-adulating #Nadiyators, was alive with comments about his ethereal skin and handsome form. I like to think you both brushed off the furore with a chuckle and carried on as normal. Perhaps you felt a little uncomfortable with all the lascivious attention. But isn't it ironic that you seemingly redeemed the archetypal Muslim man who otherwise dominates the headlines for being a terrorist, grooming underage girls, committing honour crimes and every other hateful outrage. Is this really what redemption looks like? Aesthetic appeal, an overly humble disposition, sheer inoffensiveness all seem to be the key to public acceptance. It appears you are all these things but I hope you don't lose sight of the fact that you are also so much more.

After all, you were born in Luton into one of those same communities that social commentators love to demonise. You attended a majority-Muslim school and according to some newspaper reports you didn't have a single white friend. Luton is so ghettoised, haven't you heard? Such a traditional and patriarchal Muslim community to be found there. The women all veiled and kept indoors, barely speaking English. The men steeped in misogyny and everyone sadly lacking in the British values department. Much hand-wringing about social cohesion in Luton seems to be abound. Would you and your family fulfil all the expectations of those who call for Muslims to make a greater effort to integrate into British society, Nadiya? Are you so very different to all the other everyday Muslim women in Luton, or in Leeds, where you now live? How does it feel to be exceptionalised for no other reason than appearing so agreeable on TV?

Such opprobrium seems unnecessarily caustic and I hope none of it dents your optimism and zest. Your quality was precisely your ability to win at being unique, unprecedented, and truly yourself. But such is the fate of the reality television victor that it seems almost impossible to preserve all agency. However much we didn't want to believe it, Nadiya, you were always destined to embrace the machine. Fame comes at a price and there was likely no other path available to you. Winning *Bake-Off* was just the beginning. From that moment, you would be destined to the same dark place, to be commodified and marketed to the nth degree. The GBBO's advisory team must have thought they had hit the jackpot when they realised your bankability. Such a nice young woman with the potential to earn exponentially on the back of her cuddly Muslim-ness. How they must have conjured up all manner of schemes and projects to eke out your fame. I'm sure you were reneged with all the wondrous possibilities you could turn your hand to. A cook book – tick. A presenting gig – tick. A newspaper column – tick. How about a work of fiction? 'You never claimed to be a writer but we have a way to get around this small detail.' I wonder if that was how the conversation went. Yet it still came as something of a surprise to me when I read that you had branched into novel-writing, among other things of course. I hear that your effort is a perfectly passable tome. Did you toil away, crafting your characters and cultivating your plot with the agony and exhilaration that is the experience of every writer? It did pique my interest to learn that you were encouraged to employ the skills of a consultant, or perhaps a less vague euphemism would be 'ghost-writer'. That's perfectly fine – don't let anyone tell you otherwise.

People can be unkind, however. And it seems they are telling you otherwise. Wasn't the *Guardian's* review of your novel, *The Secret Lives of the Amir Sisters*, just a little mean-spirited? After all, the reviewer was implying that you, a baker, had no business pretending at being a novelist just because of your new-found fame. She didn't get much truck with her ideas and at least one commenter pointed out that in exactly the same vein it could be asked why she, a novelist, was playing at being a book reviewer and a journalist? It's not as if I don't understand the cynicism. It must be galling to see a flash in the pan reality television celebrity get that all-too-elusive book deal that you spent your entire life striving for. What was problematic, though, was her reasoning. The reviewer – chick-lit novelist Jenny Colgan – seemed to have read your novel in the hope that she would 'gain insights into a culture I don't understand,' only to be disappointed to find that according to your novel, 'big noisy religious families are all more or less the same, which... didn't add much for this Irish/Italian Catholic'. Well, my deepest apologies that Muslims are not the exotic freak-show she was hoping for! How deceitful of you, Nadiya, to imply that actually, we are not so different to the rest of the human race!

This is the burden that you carry, Nadiya, whether you chose it or not. The onus has fallen on you to embrace the double-edged dagger of being a British-Bangladeshi hijab-wearing national treasure. You navigate the cultural minefield of identity politics with the grace that endeared you to so many. I know you would prefer not to be defined by your faith or gender or background or the piece of cloth that covers your hair. But it seems as if you just can't win. Right-wing critics declare that you won because it suits the BBC's love-affair with so-called 'political correctness'. Some are adamant that your triumph has been co-opted by the liberal agenda and is not any form of litmus test on the state of multiculturalism in today's post-Brexit Britain. Right-wing Muslims are also keen to have their say, moralising and pecking away at your breathtaking achievement, criticising you for wearing the poppy hijab on the one hand and bemoaning your penchant for free mixing on the other. Then there are those who project their own jealousies and insecurities on to your success. With the world of publishing so achingly white, it is somewhat incongruous that a middle-class white female author who has published more than twenty books should be calling out an under-represented minority writer for daring to prise a little room on the bookshelf and give voice to her imagination, 'consultant' or no 'consultant'.

Colgan said she wanted you to invite her into uncharted territories. Well what luck. It was your mesmerising expedition of gastronomy to Bangladesh that sealed my already buoyant veneration. With poise and openness, you introduced viewers to a part of the world that was unknown, oblivious to its lush nature and ethereal beauty. The dynamism of the small, South Asian country was made vivid through your enthusiasm and passion. You showed us that this corner of earth was more than images of flooded villages and grinding poverty. When you said that food isn't just fuel, and that it should be emotionally nourishing too, you summarised the attitude that Bangladeshis have towards eating. Food is at the centre of every aspect of social life and is an expression of love, hospitality, respect and familial ties. Meeting members of your family was an unexpected delight, particularly because they were as captivating as you with their disarming humour and winsome appeal. Everyone together, eating, cooking, partaking in *gupshup* and laughing at tales of the past. Watching you explore and re-connect with your roots made us all adore you even more.

You took care to point out that your experiences and memories represent merely that – your experiences and memories as a woman whose family hail from the Sylhet region of Bangladesh. This was not enough for some compatriots and fellow British Bangladeshis who took umbrage at the finer details contained in your recall of previous trips to the motherland. How dare you assume that eating on the floor was due to a lack of chairs and how could you possibly insist that Bangladesh suffers the absence of dessert dishes, which meant you never had the luxury of a wedding cake. Sylhet is not the sum total of Bangladesh, they berate, chastising you for misleading generalisations about the country's traditions and customs. 'The Chronicles of Nadiya' rendered such faux outrage entirely limp. Nadiya, your voice to tell your story was your own and no one else's.

Therein lies the rub. You are not just any reality television star, Nadiya. Why don't we hold you to the same standard as other celebrities instead of demanding your attainment be even higher? You won without enjoying those privileges and advantages that society bestowed upon previous winners and your fellow contestants. Why can't we all acknowledge that? Instead we place a plethora of burdens upon your shoulders. The expectations we impose surpass all that you could possibly hope to assuage. Isn't it time everyone stood down their keyboard arms and supported you for being you – a tenacious baker who lights up a room with her smile and geniality? I hope you don't listen to the detractors or allow them to tarnish your distinctive shine. Grasp the authenticity of your truth and that way you can ensure no one else has the power to loot it from you. Take a moment to push away the weight of representation and simply be by seizing every opportunity that comes your way and supports the potential of your talent. Nadiya, you promised you would never be limited by boundaries again. Be true to that promise and we will love you all the more for it.

TEN BANGLADESHI CULTURAL DELIGHTS

One recurring theme in this issue of *Critical Muslim* is that it is impossible to discuss Bangladesh without getting drawn into the larger and longer history of Bengal and the Indian subcontinent. It also makes little sense to separate the 'real' Bangladesh from its diaspora, or its Muslim from its Hindu heritage. At the same time, what it means to be Bengali has been profoundly shaped by British colonialism, the partition of India and Bangladesh's War of Liberation from Pakistan. Hence, another recurring theme is that there are intertwining yet competing versions of the story and history of Bangladesh and what it means to be Bangladeshi. Bearing this in mind, we present an eclectic list of entries that we hope will be useful for newbies while resonating with our Bengali readers, especially in Britain and Bangladesh – wherever and whatever they consider *desh* (home) and *bidesh* (foreign lands) to be.

1. *The Sylheti Language Revival*

The language that the vast majority of London-based Bangladeshis use is mutually unintelligible with standard Bengali. They speak Sylheti, the main language of the Surma and Kushiara valleys of Sylhet Division in Bangladesh and the Barak valley region of Assam, India. There are an estimated 10 million Sylheti speakers worldwide. Although it is related to Assamese and the rural dialects of eastern Bengal, Sylheti has numerous words derived from Persian and Arabic and its own distinct grammar. Its written script, Sylheti Nagri, is now seeing a revival in Bangladesh, Bengal (in India) and the UK, as new generations question the disconnect between what they speak at home and how they communicate in public.

Sylheti Nagri started declining from around a century ago for a combination of reasons, including British colonialism, the partition of India and the birth of Bangladesh. As a result, a standardised form of Bengali emerged. Yet proponents of Sylheti would argue that it is a language in its own right and not a colloquial or 'peasant' corruption of Bengali. Also, the region of Sylhet has a rich canon of literature in the Sylheti Nagri script, going back at least 200 years, in the form of *puthis*, or poetic religious or fairy tales. The Sylheti revival is inspired by these and other related aspects of South Asian history. Some of this was explored by the British Bangladeshi visual artist and designer, Saif Osmani, in his 2017 exhibition, 'Bangla is Not My Mother Tongue'.

2. Akram Khan

The opening ceremony of the 2012 London Olympic Games was an artistic spectacle directed by British Oscar winner Danny Boyle. It also sparked an infamous response by the Conservative MP Aidan Burley, who labelled it 'leftie multiculturalist crap'. The ceremony featured a segment with Akram Khan and his dance company performing to 'Abide With Me', sung by Emeli Sandé, in tribute to the victims of the London bombings of 7 July 2005. 'Leftie multicultural crap' ostensibly included this artistic response to terrorism, led by a British Bangladeshi dancer-choreographer and supported by a Scottish singer-songwriter of English and Zambian parentage singing a well-known Anglican hymn. But Khan is not just any dancer or choreographer – he is practically an institution in the performing arts in Britain. Born in London in 1974 to a family originally from Dhaka, Khan began training in the South Asian classical dance form of *kathak* when he was seven. His work has won him multiple awards in Britain and beyond. Apart from Boyle and Sandé, he has also collaborated with Kylie Minogue, Hanif Kureishi and Juliette Binoche. These accolades, however, meant nothing to NBC, the US broadcaster of the 2012 Olympics, who cut Khan's sequence and replaced it with an interview of swimmer Michael Phelps by Ryan Seacrest, host of *American Idol*. Khan admitted that this had upset him, but suggested that perhaps American viewers might not have been able to handle a work that was 'too truthful'. Ouch.

3. Bangla Stories

After the independence of India in 1947, more than 20 million people – Muslims and Hindus – left their homes in the Bengal delta region to move across borders and settle in a new country. A small number moved further, to Europe and the Middle East. All migrated for varying, complex reasons, including to escape war, communal conflicts or natural disasters, for work, or for marriage. A team of researchers from the London School of Economics and the University of Cambridge conducted a three-year project, involving over 180 life history interviews, to understand the experiences of first-generation migrants living in India, Bangladesh and the UK. It focused on Bengali Muslims – the largest group to settle in Britain. Their findings are presented in *Bangla Stories*, a website that showcases eight core interviews in detail, alongside a wealth of other resources that delve into the rich and extraordinary stories of the Bengali Muslim diaspora.

4. The Bengal Tiger

It's the national animal of India, appears on Bangladeshi banknotes and – through the character of Richard Parker – was the lead character in the Booker Prize-winning novel and Oscar-winning film, *Life of Pi*. According to the World Wildlife Fund (WWF), the Bengal tiger is also the most numerous tiger sub-species, with more than 2,500 left in the wild. Yet, for all its political symbolism and cultural ubiquity, the Bengal tiger is under threat from poaching to meet rising demand in Asia, including for tiger bone wine in China. Furthermore, the Sundarbans – shared between India and Bangladesh and one of the tigers' major habitats – are the only mangrove forests in the world that are home to tigers. Yet, despite protests from local and international environmentalists, the Bangladesh government appears keen to develop coal plants next to this World Heritage-listed ecosystem. The effect upon the Sundarbans would be devastating, say activists. In the light of this, saving the Bengal tiger is not merely symbolic, nor should it be the trendy preserve of soft-hearted celebrities. According to the WWF, protecting just one tiger means protecting around 25,000 acres of forests. And this means protecting the lives of those people who rely on the Sundarbans for clean water, food and their livelihoods.

5. Baul Songs

Elsewhere in this issue, we have showcased the poetry of the nineteenth century mystic and philosopher Lalon Shah, who is also considered a Baul saint. The Bauls are described by the United Nations Educational, Scientific and Cultural Organisation (UNESCO) as 'mystic minstrels' living in rural Bangladesh and West Bengal, India. They have historically drawn upon Hinduism, Buddhism and Sufism to produce a unique, unorthodox tradition which is devoted to – and centred upon – making music. Although they have always been relatively marginalised, Bauls are an intrinsic part of Bengali culture, notably influencing the compositions of the Nobel laureate Rabindranath Tagore. UNESCO includes Baul songs in its Representative List of the Intangible Cultural Heritage of Humanity and notes that the tradition is regaining popularity in rural parts of Bangladesh. The Baul tradition has also been popularised in the world music scene through artists such as Purna Das Baul and Bapi Das Baul.

6. Rickshaw Art

Rickshaw art, or auto art, is not exclusive to Bangladesh. In many parts of South Asia, elaborate paintings adorn trucks or the rears and canvas roofs of three-wheeled pedicabs, or rickshaws. There are subtle variations across the region, however. Truck art is more prevalent in Pakistan, especially in cities like Karachi, Lahore and Rawalpindi, while rickshaw art is much more visible in Bangladesh, notably in Dhaka, the 'rickshaw capital of the world'. The country has an estimated million rickshaws, which millions of people rely on for transport every single day. Well decorated vehicles attract better business, and owners will hire artists for good money – up to $200 – to paint the Taj Mahal, for example. Others might request peacocks, pigeons or generic landscapes.

7. Hilsa or Elish Fish

Stereotypes be damned. Bangladesh has a national fish – which many refer to as the king of fish – the hilsa or elish fish. A species within the herring family, it contributes up to twelve per cent of the country's total fish production and approximately one per cent of its GDP. It is eaten for breakfast during Pohela Boishakhi (see below) and, among Bengali Hindus, a pair of fishes is usually offered on auspicious days, for example Saraswati Puja and Lakshmi Puja. Part of Bengali wedding ceremonies also involves an elaborate gift exchange, or tatwa, which often includes a pair of elish fish dressed as bride and groom. (Cue Google Images search now.) Unfortunately, however, the species is now overfished and reserves are dwindling due to the impacts of climate change. In October 2016, the Bangladesh government had to impose a twenty-two-day ban on hilsa fishing in twenty-seven districts and compensated the affected fishermen with rice. This conjures another variant of the Bangladesh Paradox – if you want to keep enjoying hilsa fish, you'd better not cook it or even order it when you visit a Bengali restaurant.

8. The Dhaka Art Summit

Since the 1990s, Dhaka has developed a vibrant art market and galleries, along with a circuit of curators, critics, collectors and artists. This scene has grown to become part of a web of private entrepreneurs, multinational companies, government officials and political parties who all play a part in the patronage of the arts. In 2012, the Dhaka Art Summit was founded by the Samdani Art Foundation – a private, Dhaka-based body established by the collector couple Nadia and Rajeeb Samdani – in collaboration with Bangladesh's Ministry of Cultural Affairs. The summit is hosted every two years at the state-run Shilpakala Academy. The third Summit in 2016 attracted more than 138,000 local and 800 international visitors. The next summit will be held on 2-10 February 2018.

Alongside its burgeoning arts scene, Dhaka is also a literary hub. The Dhaka Literary Festival, founded in 2011, is held during November each year. There is also the month-long Ekushey Book Fair or Ekushey Boi Mela, which takes place every February.

9. Bengali New Year

The Bengali year is based on a solar calendar. A revised version is used as the national and official calendar of Bangladesh while an earlier version is followed in the Indian states of West Bengal, Tripura and Assam. The

Bengali New Year is known as Pohela Boishakh (or Pahela Bhaishakh) or, more popularly in the UK, as Boishakhi Mela. It falls on 14 April and is a national holiday in Bangladesh, and either on 14 or 15 April in India. It occurs around the same time as other Hindu or Sikh harvest festivals including Vaisakhi, Vishu (in Kerala) or Puthandu (in Tamil Nadu). In Bangladesh, Pahela Bhaishakh is non-sectarian – it is celebrated with equal enthusiasm by the Muslim majority and Hindu minority. The festival is marked by processions, fairs and lots of eating, singing and dancing. Boishakhi Mela is no less festive in London – in 2017, it was celebrated on 14 May in Weavers Fields and was supported by John Biggs, the Executive Mayor of Tower Hamlets.

10. Asian Dub Foundation and State of Bengal.

Asian Dub Foundation (ADF) is not a British Bengali or Bangladeshi band per se. Formed in 1993, it blends and subverts multiple genres, including punk, hip hop, electronica, reggae and bhangra. Its line-up has changed over the years but not its politics – explicitly anti-colonialist, anti-racist and critical of neoliberalism. ADF has also attracted more well-known fans along the way, including Radiohead, Sinead O'Connor and Primal Scream. According to Anirvan Chatterjee, the self-described 'progressive Desi' activist based in San Francisco, ADF's output 'is more obviously music of second generation South Asians than music for second generation South Asians'. Yet ADF has never shied away from embracing its Bengali roots either. Before its first album was even released, ADF recorded the anti-racist anthem 'Rebel Warrior', directly inspired by the classic Bengali poem 'Bidrohi' by the nationalist poet Kazi Nazrul Islam. This is why, as Chatterjee puts it, discovering ADF in his youth was 'electrifying': 'Hearing them incorporate Bengali poetry into anti-racist anthems reminded me that I'm allowed to pick, choose, and remix parts of my culture in ways that make sense to me.'

We close the list with this taste of how incisive ADF's political analysis can be. Here's an excerpt from their single 'Fortress Europe':

Keep banging on the walls of Fortress Europe
We got a right to know the situation

We're the children of globalisation
No borders only true connection
Light the fuse of the insurrection
This generation has no nation
Grassroots pressure the only solution
We're sitting tight
Because asylum is a right
Put an end to this confusion
This is a twenty-first century Exodus.

You'd be forgiven for thinking this was a response to the 2015 refugee crisis or post-Brexit fallout. But they released this prescient track in 2003. (Cue YouTube search now.)

(Thanks to Irum Shehreen Ali, Anato Chowdhury and Saif Osmani for their contributions to this list.)

CITATIONS

Introduction: Probing the Paradox by Shanon Shah

The quotation by Adnan Hossain is from his article, 'Beyond Emasculation: Being Muslim and Becoming Hijra in South Asia', *Asian Studies Review* 36 (4): 495–513.

For more up-to-date reports on the status of hijras and LGBT activists, see: Human Rights Watch. 2016. 'I Want to Live with My Head Held High.' December 23. https://www.hrw.org/report/2016/12/23/i-want-live-my-head-held-high/abuses-bangladeshs-legal-recognition-hijras; and Ta*. 2017. 'One Year after the Murders of Xulhaz Mannan and Mahbub Rabbi Tonoy'. Amnesty International. April 25. https://www.amnesty.org/en/latest/news/2017/04/one-year-after-the-murders-of-xulhaz-mannan-and-mahbub-rabbi -tonoy/.

For more on the Biharis, the Mukti Bahini and war criminals, see: Bhaumik, Subir. 2011. 'Book, Film Greeted with Fury among Bengalis'. *Al Jazeera*. April 29. http://www.aljazeera.com/indepth/features/2011/04/2011 429174141565122.html; Das, Bijoyeta, and Khaled Hasan. 2014. 'In Pictures: Plight of Biharis in Bangladesh - Al Jazeera English'. *Al Jazeera*. March 26. http://www.aljazeera.com/indepth/inpictures/2014/03/pictures-plight-biharis-bangla-2014325152839952229.html; Jamal, Ahmed Abdullah. 2008. 'Mukti Bahini and the Liberation War of Bangladesh: A Review of Conflicting Views'. *Asian Affairs* 30 (4): 5–17; Shankar, Sneha. 2014. 'British Journalist David Bergman Convicted in Bangladesh For Questioning 1971 War Death Toll'. *International Business Times*. December 2. http://www.ibtimes.com/british-journalist-david-bergman-convicted-bangladesh -questioning-1971-war-death-toll-1731760.

An account of the Shahbag protests can be found at: Anam, Tahmima. 2013. 'Shahbag Protesters versus the Butcher of Mirpur'. *The Guardian*, February 13. https://www.theguardian.com/world/2013/feb/13/shahbag-protest-bangladesh-quader-mollah.

Population figures for Bangladesh are from https://www.populationpyramid.net/en/bangladesh/2050/. On the specific threats the country faces from climate change, see Asian Development Bank. 2014. 'Bangladesh Could See Climate Change Losses Reach Over 9% Of GDP - Report'. August 19. https://www.adb.org/news/bangladesh-could-see-climate-change-losses-reach-over-9-gdp-report; 'Better Assessment Pivotal for Tackling Vulnerability'. 2015. *NGO Forum for Public Health*. http://www.ngof.org/nrc/page/latestnews511.php. The implications of geopolitical myopia on the Paris Agreement are summarised in Minx, Jan Christoph, and Christoph von Stechow. 2016. 'How Political Inertia Threatens the Paris Climate Accord'. *Huffington Post*. April 22. http://www.huffingtonpost.com/jan-christoph-minx/paris-climate-accord-politics_b_9749268.html. The text of the Agreement can be downloaded from http://unfccc.int/files/essential_background/convention/appl ication/pdf/english_paris_agreement.pdf

See also: Jennings, Hannah Maria, Janice L Thompson, Joy Merrell, Barry Bogin, and Michael Heinrich. 2014. 'Food, Home and Health: The Meanings of Food amongst Bengali Women in London'. *Journal of Ethnobiology and Ethnomedicine* 10 (44): 1–13; Mannur, Anita. 2010. *Culinary Fictions: Food in South Asian Diasporic Culture*. Philadelphia: Temple University Press; and the special issue, 'Imagining Bangladesh', by the *South Asia Multidisciplinary Academic Journal*, published in 2014.

Dhaka by Hassan Mahamdallie

Special thanks to Mahmudul Hasan for being my guide and companion during my visit and Muhammad Ahmedullah from the Brick Lane Circle for putting me in touch with his contacts in Dhaka and for advice. Thanks also to Naeem Mohaiemen, Saiful Islam, Nazmus Chowdhury, Farhad Mazhar and Zonayed Saki for their time and to Rupom, Jannati, Shohail and the students and lecturers at the University of Dhaka.

Drik can be found at http://drikimages.com/ and Shahidul Alam's blog is at www.shahidulnews.com. The muslin project can be found at http://bengalmuslin.com.

An article on the World Bank's report on youth unemployment in Bangladesh can be found at http://www.businesshabit.com/2016/09/educated-unemployed-youth-in-bangladesh.html

An article on the 2014 census on slum dwellers can be found at http://bdnews24.com/bangladesh/2015/06/29/number-of-slum-dwellers-in-bangladesh-increases-by-60.43-percent-in-17-years

Nazmus Saquib Chowdhury's report *Unlimited Dreams in Limited Spaces: Feasibility Study for establishing a community learning centre at Mohammadpur Geneva Camp in Dhaka* can be downloaded from his Academia.edu page at http://independent.academia.edu/NAZMUSSAQUIBCHOWDHURY

A report on the arson attack on the Bihari Khalshi camp is at http://archive.dhakatribune.com/crime/2014/jun/15/mirpur-clashes-kill-10-biharis.

'Left for What?', a political profile of Farhad Mazhar by Naeem Mohaiemen published in 1998 can be found at http://old.himalmag.com/component/content/article/2403-farhad-mazharleft-for-what.html

Information of the Baul tradition is at http://bauliana.blogspot.co.uk The site also includes an article by Farhad Mazhar on Lalon Shah. UBINIG, the alternative NGO set up by Mazhar is at http://ubinig.org

An article on Zonayed Saki by Dr Samia Huq: 'Zonayed Saki: What could a leftist leader offer Bangladesh today?' is at https://alalodulal.org/2015/04/08/saki-2/

For more background reading, see *Bangladesh: History, Politics, Economy, Society and Culture* edited by Mahmudul Huque (The University Press Limited Dhaka, 2016), *History of Bangladesh 1905-2005* by Milton Kumar Dev and Md. Abdus Samad (Bishwabidyalaya Prokasoni Dhaka, 2015) and *Dhaka: From Mughal Outpost to Metropolis* by Golam Rabbani (The University Press Limited, Dhaka 1997).

Real Bengali Muslims? By Zeeshan Khan

Works cited in this article are WM Thackston, Jr (translator), *The Baburnama — Memoirs of Babur, Prince and Emperor* (The Modern Library, New York, 2002); Richard M. Eaton, *The Rise of Islam and the Bengal Frontier, 1204-1760*, (University of California Press, Berkeley, 1993); Sk. Abdul Latif, *The Muslim Mystic Movement in Bengal: 1301-1550* (K.P. Bagchi, Kolkata, 1993); Dinesh Chandra Sen, *History of Bengali Language and*

Literature (Calcutta University Press, Kolkata, 1911); Peter Custers, 'Secularism and Religious Tolerance – the Historical Experience of Bangladesh', speech at The European Conference on Modern South Asian Studies, Leiden, 2006.

The Fraudulent Circle by A Qayyum Khan

The research for this article is fully documented in A Qayyum Khan's *BittersweetVictory:A Freedom Fighter's Tale* (University Press, Dhaka. 2013).

Garment Workers by Dina M Siddiqi

This essay draws upon the author's own extensive work on this subject, namely: Dina M Siddiqi. 2017. 'Before Rana Plaza: Toward a History of Labor Organizing in Bangladesh's Garment Industry.' *Labour in the Clothing Industry in the Asia Pacific*. Vicki Crinis and Adrian Vickers (eds.) New York: Routledge; 2015. 'The Unspoken and the Unspeakable.' *New Internationalist Magazine* 2 July 2015, available at: http://newint.org/features/web-exclusive/2015/07/02/the-unspoken-and-the-unspeakable/; 2004. *The Sexual Harassment of IndustrialWorkers: Strategies for Intervention in the Workplace and Beyond.* CPD-UNFPA Programme on Population and Sustainable Development, Occasional Paper 26. Dhaka: Centre for Policy Dialogue; 1998. 'Taslima Nasreen and Others: the Contest over Gender in Bangladesh.' *Women in Muslim Societies: Diversity within Unity.* Herbert Bodman and Nayereh Tohidi eds. Boulder: Lynne Rienner: 205-228.

Other works cited include: Shelley Feldman. 2009. 'Historicizing Garment Manufacturing in Bangladesh: Gender, Generation and New Regulatory Regimes.' *Journal of InternationalWomen's Studies* 11: 1(268-288); Maimuna Huq. 2009. 'Talking Jihad and Piety: Reformist Exertions among Islamist Women in Bangladesh,' *Journal of the Royal Anthropological Society*, 163-182; Samia Huq. 2009. 'Islam in Urban Bangladesh: Between Negotiation and Appropriation.' Pathways of Women's Empowerment, available at: http://www.pathwaysofempowerment.org/archive_resources/islam-in-urban-bangladesh-between-negotiation-and-appropriation; International Labor Rights Forum. 2015. 'Our Voices, Our Safety: Bangladeshi Garment Workers Speak Out'. *International Labor Rights Forum*, available at: http://www.laborrights.org/publications/our-voices-our-safety-bangladeshi-garment-workers-speak-out; Naila Kabeer. 2002. *The Power to Choose*: Bangladeshi Garment Workers in London and Dhaka. Verso: London; Seuty Sabur. 2013. 'Did "NGOization" deradicalize the women's movement?', available at: https://alalodulal.org/2013/05/28/ngoization/; Elora Shehabuddin. 2008. *Reshaping the Holy: Democracy, Development and Muslim Women in Bangladesh*. Columbia University Press: New York; Nazneen Shifa. *Feminist Anxiety over 'child marriage' in Bangladesh*. *The New Age*. 8 March 2017, available at: http://www.newagebd.net/article/10707/feminist-anxiety-over-child-marriage-in-bangladesh

I would like to thank Hasan Ashraf for his generosity in sharing fieldwork notes and insights.

Patriarchy and Patronage by Irum Shehreen Ali

This essay is based on my doctoral research: Irum Ali. *Understanding the Illiberal Democracy: The Nature of Democratic Ideals, Political Support and Participation in Bangladesh*. Unpublished doctoral thesis. Oxford: University of Oxford, 2014. I conducted field work in 2010, which also involved interviews with 108 women and 127 men. Other works cited include:

Salahuddin Aminuzzaman, Rizwan Khair, and Ipshita Basu (Eds). *Governance at Crossroads: Insights from Bangladesh*. Dhaka: University Press Limited and BRAC, 2013.

Inge Amundsen. 'Democratic Dynasties.' *Party Politics* 22, no. 1 (2016): 49-58. Accessed February 05, 2017. https://doi.org/10.1177/1354068813511378.

Najma Chowdhury. 'Lessons on Women's Political Leadership from Bangladesh.' *Signs: Journal of Women in Culture and Society* 34, no. 1 (2008): 8-15. Accessed February 05, 2017. http://www.journals.uchicago.edu/doi/pdfplus/10.1086/588584

Rounaq Jahan and Inge Amundsen. *The parliament of Bangladesh: representation and accountability*. No. 2. Centre for Policy Dialogue (CPD), 2012. Accessed February 05, 2017. http://www.cpd.org.bd/pub_attach/CPD_CMI_WP2.pdf

Adil Khan. 'Democracy and its Electoral Challenges: The Case of Bangladesh'. Department of Economic and Social Affairs, United Nations, New York (2016). Accessed Febraury 05, 2017. http://unpan1.un.org/intradoc/groups/public/documents/un/unpan028465.pdf

David Lewis and Abul Hossain. *Understanding the Local Power Structure in Bangladesh*. Stockholm: Swedish International Cooperation Agency, Sida Studies 22, 2008.

David Lewis. 'Organising and Representing the Poor in a Clientelistic Democracy: The Decline of Radical NGOs in Bangladesh.' *The Journal of Development Studies*, 2017, 1-23. Accessed February 05, 2017. http://dx.doi.org/10.1080/00220388.2017.1279732

Pranab Kumar Panday. 'Representation without Participation: Quotas for Women in Bangladesh.' *International Political Science Review* 29, no. 4 (2008): 489-512. Accessed February 10, 2017. https://www.jstor.org/stable/pdf/20445157.pdf.

Arild Engelsen Ruud. 'Democracy in Bangladesh: A Village View.' In *Trysts with Democracy: Political Practice in South Asia*, edited by Madsen Stig Toft, Nielsen Kenneth Bo, and Skoda Uwe, 45-70. London: Anthem Press, 2011. Accessed February 05, 2017. http://www.jstor.org/stable/j.ctt1gxp91k.10.

Word Bank. *Whispers to Voices: Gender and Social Transformation in Bangladesh*. Bangladesh Development Series: Paper No.22. South Asia Sustainable Development Department, South Asia Region. (2008) Washington D.C. Can be accessed at: worldbank.bd/bds.

An Uncomfortable Closet by Anato Chowdhury

For information on the Bandhu Social Welfare Society, see http://www.bandhu-bd.org/about-2/donors/ and http://www.bandhu-bd.org/hijra-pride-2014/.

Further details on Roopbaan can be found in the Bengali article by Niloy Neel (2014). 'On the subject of Bangladesh's first gay magazine Roopbaan'. Available from https://blog.mukto-mona.com/2014/01/22/39377/.

Background on the murder of Avijit Roy can be found at *BBC News* (2015). 'Obituary: US-Bangladesh writer Avijit Roy.' Available from http://www. bbc.co.uk/news/world-asia-31664262; *The Daily Star* (2016). 'Blogger Avijit murder prime suspect killed in "gunfight" with cops.' Available from http://www.thedailystar.net/city/criminal-killed-dhaka-gunfight-1242112; J. Shiffman (2015). 'Exclusive: Widow of slain U.S.-Bangladeshi blogger lashes out at Dhaka.' Available from http://www. reuters.com/article/us-usa-bangladesh-assassination-exclusiv-idUSKBN 0NW04S20150511.

More background on the government's treatment of secular or progressive bloggers is at: *The Daily Star* (2013). 'Blogger Asif Mohiuddin held.' Available from http://www.thedailystar.net/news/blogger-asif-mohiuddin-held.

On threats by various Islamist groups against sexual minorities, LGBT activists and pro-LGBT individuals, see: Nirapata (2015). 'Olama League's Press Advert 20th September 2015 (translated from Bengali).' Available from: http://www.nirpata.com/post/129481898862/olama20sept; C. Stewart (2016). 'Bangladeshi fundamentalists incite anti-gay violence.' Available from https://76crimes.com/2016/05/30/bangladeshi-fundamentalists-incite-anti-gay-violence/; Émirat Islamique (2016). 'Aqsi op.Benga.vs.Lgbt.man.' Available from https://www.youtube.com/watc h?v=mpBKyIZRhEg&feature=youtu.be which contains graphic content of the murder scene; S. Alam (2013) 'MuhammadYunus, Bangladesh's Nobel Prize Laureate, Targeted By Anti-Gay Clerics.' Available from http:// www.huffingtonpost.com/2013/10/24/muhammad-yunus-gay-protest-_n_4154089.html

On the Holey Artisan Bakery attacks, see C. Graham and A. Marszal (2016). '20 hostages killed in "Isil" attack on Dhaka restaurant popular with foreigners.' Available from http://www.telegraph.co.uk/news/2016/ 07/01/gunmen-attack-restaurant-in-diplomatic-quarter-of-bangladeshi-ca/

Some of the government's responses to the killings of Xulhaz, Tonoy and Avijit Roy are in: *The Daily Star* (2016). 'US Secretary of State Kerry calls Bangladesh PM Hasina, seeks justice for Xulhaz.' Available from http:// www.thedailystar.net/frontpage/kerry-calls-pm-seeks-justice-xulhaz-1216450; *Priyo.com* (2016). 'Home Minister: homosexuality is not compatible with our society (translated from Bengali)'; *bdnews24.com* (2016). 'Court indicts 35 including Nur Hossain, three ex-RAB officials for Narayanganj seven-murder.' Available from http://bdnews24.com/bangladesh/2016/02/08/court-indicts-35-including-nur-hossain-three-ex-rab-officials-for-narayanganj-seven-murder; *Reuters* (2016). 'Bangladesh police arrest Islamist over gay activists' killing.' Available from http://uk.reuters.com/article/uk-bangladesh-arrest-idUKKCN0Y60B3

Birangona Women by Onjali Q Raúf

Birangona: Women of War was shown at the New Wimbledon Theatre, London, on 16-17 May 2014. Written by Samina Lutfa and Leesa Gazi, it was directed by Filiz Özcan, and produced by the Komola Collective. For a more detailed account of the Birangona Women, see *Bangladesh: the first four years (from 16 December 1971 to 15 December 1975),* Nurul Momen, Dhaka, K.A.A. Kaumruddin for the Bangladesh Institute of Law & International Affairs, 1980; Debnath, A, 'The Bangladesh genocide: The plight of women' in S. Totten, editor, *Plight and fate of women and children during and following genocide* (pp. 47–66). Transaction, New Brunswick, 2009; and N Mookherjee, 'A lot of history: Sexual violence, public memories and the Bangladesh Liberation War of 1971', unpublished doctoral dissertation, SOAS, University of London, 2002.

See also *Testimonials of the Birangona Women*, Video archives, Komola Collective, 2014-2017.

American, Bangladeshi, Writer by Sharbari Z Ahmed

For the ACLU's position on Jeff Sessions's appointment as attorney general, see https://www.aclu.org/other/jeff-sessions-facts.

On the facts behind President Obama's use of drone strikes, see Conor Friedersdorf. 'The Obama Administration's Drone-Strike Dissembling'. *The Atlantic*, 14 March 2016. https://www.theatlantic.com/politics/archive/2016/03/the-obama-administrations-drone-strike-dissembling/473541/ and Jessica Purkiss and Jack Serle. 'Obama's Covert Drone War in Numbers: Ten Times More Strikes than Bush'. *The Bureau of Investigative Journalism*, 17 January 2017. https://www.thebureauinvestigates.com/

stories/2017-01-17/obamas-covert-drone-war-in-numbers-ten-times-more-strikes-than-bush.

On Islamophobia in Hollywood, see Lorraine Ali. 'Has Hollywood Lost Touch with American Values?' *Los Angeles Times*, 7 January 2017. http://www.latimes.com/entertainment/la-et-hollywood-values-updates-how-hollywood-s-muslim-portrayals-1483650479-htmlstory.html.

For background on the Dotbusters, see Michel Marriott. 'In Jersey City, Indians Protest Violence'. *The New York Times*, 12 October 1987, sec. N.Y. / Region. http://www.nytimes.com/1987/10/12/nyregion/in-jersey-city-indians-protest-violence.html.

New findings about the lynching of African Americans are summarised in Mark Berman. 'Even More Black People Were Lynched in the U.S. than Previously Thought, Study Finds'. *Washington Post*, 10 February 2015. https://www.washingtonpost.com/news/post-nation/wp/2015/02/10/even-more-black-people-were-lynched-in-the-u-s-than-previously-thought-study-finds/.

The *Saturday Night Live* skit on Election Night can be viewed at https://www.youtube.com/watch?v=SHG0ezLiVGc.

Brent Staples's seminal essay can be found online at http://www.myteacherpages.com/webpages/rspriggs/files/staples%20just%20walk%20on%20by%20text.pdf

Two Poems by Kaiser Haq

Award-winning Bangladesh poet Kaiser Haq, Director of the Dhaka Translation Centre, translated two songs by the revered mystic Lalon Shah and a poem by the late celebrated poet Shaheed Quaderi for this issue. On Lalan Shah, see Abadula Caudhri, *Lalana Shah 1774-1890* (Bamla Ekademi, Dhaka, 1992) and Abu Ishahaq Hossain, *Lalon Shah: The Great Poet* (Palai Prokashoni, Dhaka, 2009).

Haq has been a Royal Literary Fund Fellow and Café Poet at the Poetry Café, London, and a recipient of the Bangla Academy Award for Translation. See his books: *Published in the Streets of Dhaka: Collected Poems* (UPL); *Pariah and Other Poems* (Bengal Lights); *Selected Poems of Shamsur*

Rahman (trans.) (Pathak Samabesh); *The Wonders of Vilayet* (trans.) (Peepal Tree, Leeds; Writers Ink); *The Woman Who Flew* (trans.) (Penguin India); and *The Triumph of the Snake Goddess* (Harvard).

Religious Medleys by Giles Goddard

The quote on the Albigensian crusade is from Kurt Jonassohn, *Genocide and Gross Human Rights Violations: In Comparative Perspective*, Transaction Publishers, New Brunswick, 1998, p50.

Yuna, Herself by Laych Koh

Yuna performed Live at Scala, London, 20 September 2016. Quotes in this review were from: Halabian, L., 2016. *Live Nation TV*. [Online]

Available at:https://livenation.vice.com/en_us/article/how-yuna-became-r-and-b-brightest-new-star-chapters; Horowitz, S. J., 2016. *Billboard Magazine*. [Online]

Available at: http://www.billboard.com/articles/news/magazine-feature/7341537/yuna-interview-pharrell-williams-usher-muslim-faith-new-album; Koh, L. C., 2010. *The Nut Graph*. [Online]

Available at: http://www.thenutgraph.com/yuna-on-being-%E2%80%9Cmalay-malay%E2%80%9D/; McKinney, J., 2016. *Vibe*. [Online]

Available at: http://www.vibe.com/featured/yuna-interview-uber-music-chapters-interview/; Ng, S. A., 2016. *Time Out Kuala Lumpur*. [Online]

Available at: http://www.timeout.com/kuala-lumpur/music/yuna-interview-if-youre-not-in-it-to-be-great-dont-get-into-it; Payne, T., 2016. 'Interview: Yuna Discusses Cultural Influences & Being a Malaysian Musical Icon', *New York*: s.n.; Zarai, Y., 2016. Instagram. [Online]

Available at: https://www.instagram.com/p/BIFp9Vmhn3B/

Last Word on Nadiya Hussain by Samia Rahman

Reactions to Nadiya Hussain's post-Great British Bake-Off adventures quoted here can be found in Jenny Colgan. 2017. 'The Secret Lives of the Amir Sisters by Nadiya Hussain Review – What the Bake Off Winner Did next'. *The Guardian*, January 12, sec. Books. https://www.theguardian. com/books/2017/jan/12/the-secret-lives-of-the-amir-sisters-by-nadiya-hussain-review-what-the-bake-off-winner-did-next; Rebecca Hawkes. 18:35. 'The Chronicles of Nadiya, plus 10 Inspiring Things Nadiya Hussain Has Done since Winning Bake Off'. *The Telegraph*, sec. 2016. http://www. telegraph.co.uk/tv/2016/08/24/11-inspiring-things-that-nadiya-hussain-has-done-since-winning-t/; and Homa Khaleeli. 2015. 'Bake Off Winner Nadiya Hussain: "I Wasn't Thinking about Representing Muslims, I Was Thinking about My Bakes"'. *The Guardian*, October 12, sec. Life and style.https://www.theguardian.com/tv-and-radio/2015/oct/12/bake-off-winner-nadiya-hussain-muslims-britain.

The List: Ten Bangladeshi Revelations

Saif Osmani's website is at http://saifosmani.moonfruit.com. More information on the Sylheti revival can be found at http://www.sylheti. org.uk/.

A good quality YouTube clip of Akram Khan's segment in the 2012 Olympics opening ceremony is at https://www.youtube.com/ watch?v=0xLjGrRPMxs. The 'multicultural crap' tweet is covered in https://www.theguardian.com/politics/2012/jul/28/olympics-opening-ceremony-multicultural-crap-tory-mp. Khan's smackdown of NBC for sidelining his work is at http://www.bbc.co.uk/news/entertainment-arts-19037588.

The Bangla Stories website is http://www.banglastories.org/.

More information on the Bengal tiger can be found at https://www. worldwildlife.org/species/bengal-tiger, and the Sundarbans at http:// whc.unesco.org/en/list/798/. The controversial coal plants and protests against them are mentioned here: http://www.dhakatribune.com/ bangladesh/environment/2017/01/08/protests-held-globally-rampal -plant/.

To find out more about the Bauls, go to http://www.unesco.org/culture/ich/en/RL/baul-songs-00107 and https://www.thoughtco.com/the-bauls-of-bengal-1769990.

A short but colourful video on rickshaw art in Dhaka is at http://www.bbc.co.uk/news/av/magazine-30854038/painting-bangladeshs-colourful-rickshaws.

To see how the hilsa fish fits into a Bengali wedding, go to http://www.indiatimes.com/culture/who-we-are/12-things-that-happen-at-a-bengali-wedding-247614.html. On the crisis of hilsa overfishing, see http://economictimes.indiatimes.com/news/international/business/bangladesh-imposes-22-day-ban-on-hilsa-fishing/articleshow/54814289.cms.

The Dhaka Art Summit is at https://www.dhakaartsummit.org/, while the Dhaka Lit Fest is at http://dhakalitfest.com/. The Ekushey Book Fair has a Wikipedia entry.

The Wikipedia entry for Pohela Bhoishakh is quite extensive, but if you're in London, go to http://www.towerhamlets.gov.uk/mela/whatsOn.htm.

The Asian Dub Foundation maintain an active official website (http://asiandubfoundation.com/site/) and have an extensive Wikipedia page. Anirvan Chatterjee's writings and further thoughts on them (and other contemporary diasporic Bengali acts) are at http://www.diasporic.com/articles/suman_adf/ and https://www.reddit.com/r/ABCDesis/comments/2pla1b/im_anirvan_chatterjee_and_i_curate_the_berkeley/.

CONTRIBUTORS

Sharbari Z Ahmed is a writer of screenplays, stage and fiction ● **Ahsan Akbar** is a poet, writer, and director of the Dhaka Literary Festival ● **Irum Shehreen Ali** is a London-based writer, project manager and development practitioner ● **Anato Chowdhury** is an activist and engineer based in Scotland ● **Maria Chaudhuri** is the author of the acclaimed memoir *Beloved Strangers* ● **Canon Giles Goddard** is the Vicar of St John's Church in Waterloo, London ● **Kaiser Haq** is an award-winning poet, essayist, translator, Liberation War veteran, and professor of English at the University of Liberal Arts Bangladesh ● **A Qayyum Khan** is the author of *Bittersweet Victory: A Freedom Fighter's Tale* ● **Zeeshan Khan** is a Dhaka-based journalist and author ● **Laych Koh** is a Malaysian freelance journalist and writer now based in London ● **Hassan Mahamdallie** is a playwright, theatre director and director of the Muslim Institute ● **Shaheed Quaderi** (1940–2016) was one of the most important Bengali poets of his generation ● **Rajib Rahman** is working on his first novel ● **Samia Rahman** is Deputy Director of the Muslim Institute, London ● **Onjali Q Raúf** is the founder and CEO of Making Herstory, which works to end the abuse and trafficking of women and girls ● **Sadaf Saaz** is a poet, writer, entrepreneur, women's rights advocate and producer of the Dhaka Literary Festival ● **Tamim Sadikali** is the author of *Dear Infidel* (Hansib, 2014) he is currently working on a short story collection ● **Lalon Shah** (1772–1890), philosopher, social reformer and songwriter, is one of the most noted Baul saints and mystics of Bengal ● **Shanon Shah** is Deputy Editor of *Critical Muslim* ● **Dina M Siddiqi** is Professor of Anthropology at BRAC University in Dhaka